GOVERNMENT
LOANS
THE ROAD TO REAL ESTATE WEALTH

WAYNE PHILLIPS

SIMON AND SCHUSTER
New York

Published by Simon and Schuster
A Division of Simon & Schuster, Inc.
Simon & Schuster Building
Rockefeller Center
1230 Avenue of the Americas
New York, New York 10020
SIMON AND SCHUSTER and colophon are registered trademarks
of Simon & Schuster, Inc.
Designed by Irving Perkins Associates
Manufactured in the United States of America
1   2   3   4   5   6   7   8   9   10
Library of Congress Cataloging in Publication Data
Phillips, Wayne, date.
Government loans.

1. Real estate investment—United States.
2. Government lending—United States.   I. Title.
HD1382.5.P439   1986   332.63'24   86-15453
ISBN: 0-671-60352-3

To my daughter Nicole and future generations.

CONTENTS

INTRODUCTION

GREAT SPIRITS HAVE ALWAYS ENCOUNTERED
VIOLENT OPPOSITION FROM MEDIOCRE MINDS.

Albert Einstein

This is not another one of those "how to get rich quick" books. It will not show you how to make a million dollars in thirty days. But it does have something for you and for everyone. *Government Loans* will tell you how to make a small amount of money in a very short time. This will motivate you to do it again and again. Each time the process becomes a little bit easier, a little bit faster, and a lot more profitable. I call it "the power of momentum."

Before long, this power of momentum will help you change your life for the better. You won't make a million overnight, but you will dramatically increase your income. In the real world are billions of dollars that our government has available for people like you and me to invest in ourselves and our nation's housing. Use the secrets I've discovered that I reveal in this book, and you'll learn how to take advantage of this opportunity.

Would you like to increase your income by 20 to 25 percent in thirty to forty days? You can. Take a look at page 113, where I show you how to get loans at as low as 3 percent. How would you like to get a zero percent loan that is forgiven after five years? Turn to page 134, and find out where to go and whom to talk to. Maybe you're sick and tired of throwing your rent money down the drain and want to own your own home, with monthly payments less than your present rent. Flip over to page 56, and learn the secret of buying beautiful government-acquired homes for little or no money down that put cash in your pocket after you move in! Or how about moving into that dream house you've always wanted? Read chapter 7 and learn how by using America's best-kept secret. Wouldn't you like to receive $100 to $600, cash, per month on each property you acquire? Turn to page 116 to learn how. I put cash into my pockets each time I acquire property, and so can you. Want to find out how to sell special government tax benefits for cash or get a refund from your last three years' taxes, courtesy of the IRS? Look on page 191 to find out the way. By the way, the same chapter reveals how anyone, young, elderly, rich, poor, bankrupt, unemployed, American citizen or not, can buy one type of property, a historic property, and pocket $20,000.

Would you like to learn how to buy properties for pennies on the dollar, rent them out, and get 100-percent-guaranteed rents from the government mailed directly to you? How can you go wrong with 100-percent-guaranteed rents from our government? That's what I teach you, beginning on page 138.

Whatever your goals, our government has a program for you to use to help achieve them. I call this "the road to wealth." You see, we're all on the road to wealth. But for one reason or another, people run into obstacles and potholes on that road and get sidetracked from their destination. The pothole may be unemployment, too many bills, too much work, a bankruptcy, high taxes, divorce, lack of cash, or not enough time. The result is that people either stop or get stopped on the road to wealth before reaching their destination.

I've been there. I was a jazz drummer, living each day as it came, stretching every dollar as far as it could go. I hit just about every obstacle there was on the road to wealth. I fell in all the potholes. But by solving a problem, I discovered the many fantastic government loan programs available and learned how to profit from them. And folks, this is a very, very profitable method. Government loans and programs will get you to your destination—financial freedom.

Remember: The road to wealth doesn't stop; people stop or get stopped. That's where this book comes in. It's your road map to keep you on the road to wealth. Though I had many failures and made mistakes, they were honest ones, none unethical. Please, benefit not only from my many successes but also from my failures, so that you profit.

I never dreamed I'd pave the road to wealth for hundreds of thousands of Americans with government loans and programs. I didn't create these programs. People have been making money with government loans for years—they just kept this a secret. I'm the first one to write, teach, and give seminars about government loan opportunities.

This book, a follow-up to my 1983 best-selling *How to Get Government Loans*, is a powerful and profitable tool for anyone wanting to apply my proven and profitable methods to tap into this incredible money source. It tells you what you need to know and do to go out tomorrow and get started with government loans.

Since government programs, addresses, and phone numbers change from time to time, I've also given you a special bonus. In the back of this book you will find a coupon to mail in for a free government loans update to help you keep abreast of the latest money-making opportunities as they arrive. I also invite you to write to me about your government success story so I can share it with others and motivate them. You'll find my address on the jacket of this book.

I sincerely believe this book and method to be truly unique. Most authors only write or teach theory. I don't teach theory. I'm speaking from actual experience with the state of the art government loan information that you need to succeed.

You'll know where to go, what to ask for, whom to speak with, how to qualify, and what to do to reach your financial destination in the safest, fastest, and most profitable way. Because, when you profit, I profit; everyone profits. It's exciting, it's easy, it's profitable. I've done it, thousands are doing it, and so can you.

Wayne Phillips

1

TAP INTO THE GOVERNMENT WEALTH

PUT PEOPLE BEFORE PROFITS, AND THE GOOD LORD
WILL THROW IT BACK TO YOU A THOUSAND TIMES
OVER.

Anonymous

I have discovered the road to wealth in the eighties: an investment program that has created a new wave of great opportunities for everyone, from the first-time home buyer to the sophisticated investor and anyone else who ever dreamed of financial freedom. It is a method that has been embraced from coast to coast by people utilizing the spirit of our country to create their own wealth.

An Indian immigrant in Shreveport makes $300,000 cash through government foreclosures. A Phoenix businessman receives a 3 percent government loan to rehabilitate an apartment building that he sells for a $45,000 profit. A single woman in California receives $17,000 in five days with only a phone call to a governnment lender. A San Diego engineer gets a zero percent loan to add a room to his $200,000 home.

A Houston entrepreneur takes $21,000 in government-subsidized rents to the bank every month. What's going on?

These people are working with government programs, and they love it. They say they have never made so much money so quickly and easily. They have learned to work *with* the government, not just for it. They have discovered how to create wealth with government loans.

Let me share with you why I'm so excited about working with the government. I want to share with you how I've helped these people and others make a fortune. You may have heard theories, but I'm going to show you actually how to put cash in your pocket. I'm going to give you the phone numbers, addresses, everything you need to be financially free. In fact, before you finish reading this book you'll know how to put $17,500 in your pocket in ten days.

In writing this book I had three goals. First, I want to share my own story with you. I want to let you know how I've helped others and how I've made a fortune working with the government. And when I talk about being a millionaire, I'm talking about real dollars, jumbo CDs, not equity in a bunch of real estate—COLD, HARD CASH!

Second, I'm going to share with you information about some of the government loans available to you right now. The same government loans that I used. The same methods and techniques that made me a fortune in cash. You have them available to you right in your own home town, and I'm going to show you how to tap that source.

Third, my final goal in this book is to teach you to work with the government to help other people and help yourself, starting from scratch.

GOVERNMENT REWARDS WITH REAL ESTATE

Government and real estate go hand in hand. It's our right as Americans to own real estate. There are many investments available today: savings accounts, stocks, money market accounts. But I have found that real estate offers the best opportunity to be free financially. Let me explain why.

Five years ago I decided that I wanted $1,000 a month income. I didn't think about making a million; all I wanted—all I needed—was $1,000 a month. Once I had that $1,000 a month, I wouldn't have to play drums in a beer bar somewhere. I wouldn't have to work for a boss I didn't particularly care for. I would consider myself self-sufficient. Back then I figured the best way to get that $1,000 a month was to work as hard as I could, for as long as I could, and to stash away as much money as I could in a savings account. Then, once I got enough money into that savings account I figured I would get my $1,000 a month in interest and live happily ever after.

Do you know what? I could never seem to work hard enough or long enough to have any money left over after I paid my rent, my car payment, and my credit card bills. I never had enough discretionary income left over to put into a savings account so I could get my $1,000 a month interest income.

The chart below shows us that the average wage an American earns every year is $18,350 a year, or about $8.00 an hour. If you are one of these people, working for $8.00 an hour, then you know you have to find a better way to live than working and trying to save. As a matter of fact, just a short while ago I learned that only one out of two Americans manages to save $5,000 by the time they are sixty-five years of age. There must be a better way.

1984 AVERAGE ANNUAL PAY
(ANNUAL PAYROLL DIVIDED BY AVERAGE EMPLOYMENT)

State	Average Annual Pay
United States average	$18,350
Alabama	16,203
Alaska	28,806
Arizona	17,349
Arkansas	14,973
California	19,873
Colorado	18,774
Connecticut	19,980
Delaware	18,505
District of Columbia	25,120
Florida	16,176
Georgia	16,951
Hawaii	16,671
Idaho	15,793
Illinois	19,733
Indiana	17,832
Iowa	15,668
Kansas	16,665
Kentucky	16,627

1984 AVERAGE ANNUAL PAY
(ANNUAL PAYROLL DIVIDED BY AVERAGE EMPLOYMENT)

State	Average Annual Pay
Louisiana	17,769
Maine	14,850
Maryland	18,151
Massachusetts	18,428
Michigan	20,940
Minnesota	18,038
Mississippi	14,398
Missouri	17,599
Montana	15,521
Nebraska	15,197
Nevada	17,565
New Hampshire	16,163
New Jersey	19,889
New Mexico	16,426
New York	20,754
North Carolina	15,422
North Dakota	15,289
Ohio	18,783
Oklahoma	17,625
Oregon	17,474
Pennsylvania	17,931
Rhode Island	16,150
South Carolina	15,305
South Dakota	13,532
Tennessee	16,216
Texas	18,864
Utah	17,201
Vermont	15,263
Virginia	17,271
Washington	18,371
West Virginia	17,482
Wisconsin	17,021
Wyoming	18,322

U.S. Department of Labor, Bureau of Labor Statistics

Once I realized I was never going to get anywhere with savings accounts, I decided to take my money out of savings and get into the stock market. Not only did I believe I was going to get $1,000 a month in stock dividends, I actually believed I was going to become a millionaire by investing in the stock market. I even bought one of those books — you know, *How to Make a Million Dollars in the Stock Market in Twelve Months*.

To show you how smart I really was, I took all of my money and invested in a wonderful airline stock. In a few short months the airline went bankrupt. Even though the airline is flying again, they lost $80 million. I'll never get my money back. As a matter of fact, my stock broker made more money than I did. He didn't care about Wayne Phillips. Do you know what he cared about? Getting paid a commission, that's all. The average person, like myself, should be careful about investing in the stock market.

Another popular investment I tried was a money market account. Money market accounts are much like savings accounts, except you can earn a higher rate of interest — usually 3 to 5 percent higher than a regular savings account. If you have $1,000 or more, I would recommend that you put it into a money market account, because you get a higher interest rate. However, it will never make you rich. Just think of money market accounts as temporary parking places for your funds until you find an investment that earns a higher rate of return.

The investments mentioned so far are great if you already have a lot of money. But, if you are as broke as I was and tired of your situation, and if you want to make money, real estate is your best choice. Not just any kind of real estate. Real estate that will make you money. I'm not talking about buying foreclosures or paying 12 to 14 percent interest on a loan to buy a home. I don't mean the kind of real estate you look for in a newspaper, trying to find a motivated seller. Even Robert Allen says you have about a 4 percent chance of finding a motivated seller through the newspaper ads.

I'm talking about the kind of real estate that you can get right now from our government for 30 cents on the dollar. The kind of loans you can get from the government at zero, 1, and 3 percent interest. That's the kind of real estate that will make you big money. That's the kind of real estate you need to learn to buy. And that's why I'm so excited about writing this book. To teach you about these government programs so you can go out Monday morning and get started yourself.

Let's take a look at the chart on page 18 comparing some of the investments we've discussed. Real estate stands up pretty well against some of the other investments. Look at the first item, *cash flow*. This is one of the main reasons that I love working with real estate government programs.

Cash flow is the little green stuff we are supposed to have left over as real estate investors after we receive our rent money, make our loan payment, and pay taxes, insurance, expenses, and management fees. We're supposed to have $50 or a $100 each month to put into our back pocket—the Hip National Bank. But unfortunately, given the high price of real estate and high interest rates, it's nearly impossible to buy real estate for no money down and still have a positive cash flow each month.

A COMPARISON OF INVESTMENTS

	REAL ESTATE	MONEY MARKETS	STOCKS	SAVINGS ACCOUNT
Cash Flow	√	√	√	√
Depreciation	√			
Loan Amortization	√			
Appreciation	√			

When you learn to work with the government, get ready for cash flow, because two things you are going to love about the government are:

1. The government won't lend you money unless you make money. Now that appeals to me, because I've never met any sellers before who cared anything about Wayne Phillips when I bought their property. The only things they cared about were how much I was going to pay for their property and what kind of down payment I could make. They didn't care if I went bankrupt the day after I bought it.

But our government cares. They won't lend you money unless you make money.

2. You can buy your first home and have house payments cheaper than your rent. Or, as an investor, you can put some serious positive cash flow in your pocket.

Are you beginning to see why I'm so excited about the government programs available to us? Our government wants us to own real estate. Why? Because the more people own real estate, the more jobs will be created, and the larger our tax base will be. For every dollar that is loaned by a government agency at zero or 3 percent, several more dollars are returned to the community in the form of overall benefits. In fact, these programs work to reduce our federal deficit by removing abandoned and repossessed real estate from our government inventories and placing them back on the tax roles.

In almost every major city across the nation, there are special loan programs to buy or rehabilitate real estate at zero, 1, 3, and 8 percent interest. It's hard to have cash flow when you're paying top market rate interest on your loans. But when you are paying zero to 8 percent interest, you can afford a house. You can have positive cash flow. That's the first reason I love working with the government, because I receive cash flow on every property I own, and you can too. It's exciting, and the opportunities are for all of us.

The second reason I like working with our government is because of something called *depreciation*. By that I mean tax benefits. You may be saying, "Hey, Wayne, I don't need any tax benefits, I need money to pay my bills." A few years ago I was in that same situation. I needed tax benefits like I needed a hole in the head. Then I discovered by accident that you and I can sell those tax benefits to people in the 50 percent tax bracket for cash in our hands.

What kind of real estate does it take to do this? Historic properties, for one. Buy one single-family historic property, and you can put $20,000 in your pocket. Anyone can do this—young, old, rich, poor, bankrupt, unemployed—even if they are not an American citizen.

You see, I've discovered that folks like you and me receive over $5.3 billion a year selling tax benefits to people in the 50 percent tax bracket. All you have to do is learn to locate people who make their living selling tax benefits. I show you how to do this in chapter 14, "Selling Tax Benefits for Cash." That's the second reason I love working with the government. I can sell the tax benefits for cash in my hands. It's safe, it's easy, and it takes about thirty days.

The third item on our chart is *loan amortization*. This is one you'll love too. What does *amortize* mean? *Amortize* to us means to borrow money and pay it back in equal payments. Almost every property you buy will have a loan on it. Many times it will be amortized. How it's amortized, and at what interest rate, depends on the property and how you buy it.

A lot of people go around the nation nowadays telling you to find motivated sellers, buy real estate for no money down, and rent the properties out and in five years you'll be a millionaire. What they don't tell you are the bad things about real estate. They often fail to mention that the properties you buy for super low prices may have loans on them that are not amortized. They have balloon payments due in three years (this means the loan must be paid off) and high interest rates. They don't tell you that it is hard to find motivated sellers who sell real estate for no money down. And frequently, the people who are extremely motivated to sell are in some kind of distressful situation. They have lost their jobs, had a death in the family, or maybe are going through a divorce.

But do you know what? All of that leaves a sour taste in my mouth. I don't need to take advantage of anyone to make money in real estate. And neither do you. What those people also don't tell you is that it's hard to get good tenants and that some tenants can't pay rent on time, through no fault of their own. Sometimes tenants have to be evicted, and that's a nasty thing to do. Sometimes these tenants get mad at you for evicting them and tear up your rental property. That's a lousy way to make money.

I don't teach you these things. Instead, I teach you how I made my fortune in cash, working with government programs. I have taught thousands of people how to do this in the last two years, and you can learn too. I don't teach you to take advantage of people. I teach you how to work with the government and buy property for 30 cents on the dollar. I teach you to get amortized loans at zero, 1, 3, and 8 percent. Then I teach you how to rent those properties to our elderly population and have the government mail you the rent each month, guaranteed. That's what you'll learn in this book.

Half a Million Dollars in Rents

Do you have a rental property with a negative cash flow? If so, Uncle Sam has the answer for you. Let me tell you about one property owner in San Francisco who made a deal with our government. He agreed to rent his two-bedroom apartments to elderly people for fifteen years and, in return, the government agreed to mail his rent, guaranteed, for fifteen years. Each month he receives $1,688 per apartment. Every year the rent goes up 7 percent automatically, even in rent-controlled areas. After fifteen years the total rent this property owner could receive for one two-bedroom apartment under this special program is $509,013.36.

Multiply this by the forty-seven units this property owner has in his entire building, and you come up with $23,923,627 in total guaranteed rents for the next fifteen years. Even if he runs short of cash, he can borrow against next year's rental income. Why? Because Uncle Sam is paying the rent. Even if an elderly tenant moves, the government must pay up to 80 percent of the rent owed for one year or until a new tenant is found.

You may not own forty-seven apartment units. But you might own a one- or two-bedroom rental house or duplex. If so, you can rent your property to elderly people and have your rents mailed to you, guaranteed. I get my rents mailed to me, and I use those guaranteed rents to make my loan payments on time and put the leftover cash in my pocket. This program is exciting because it's profitable and you help people get decent and affordable housing.

The last item on the chart is *appreciation*. You may have been told it's all right to buy an investment property with a $200 negative cash flow each month, because five years from now it will appreciate (go up in value), and you'll make a lot of money. In the meantime you shell out $200 each month to make up the difference between the rental income and mortgage payment. Please don't buy real estate this way. You are not investing, you're gambling. You're speculating that the real estate will increase enough in value for you to recoup your negative outlays each month. We all hope real estate will continue to increase in value, but don't depend on it. If it doesn't increase enough, you could be wiped out financially.

Don't depend on inflation to create appreciation. Use government rehab loans to make improvements that raise property values. You can borrow money from the government at zero to 8 percent interest and have loan payments so low that you're putting cash in your pocket each month.

RPP (Rapid Principle Payoff)

Furthermore, when you learn to borrow money from the government at low rates your loans will get paid off extremely rapidly. Let me explain how this works. If you borrow $100,000 from your bank or savings and loan at market interest rates—say 14 percent—at the end of five years you will still owe almost $98,000. This is because only a small fraction of your payment goes toward paying off the principal portion of the loan. The majority of the payment goes toward your interest charges.

However, when you borrow that same $100,000 from your rich and generous Uncle Sam at only 3 percent, the story changes. At the end of that same five years, you will only owe about $75,000, not $98,000. Since the amount of interest you pay is less, a much larger portion of your payment goes toward principal reduction. As a result, the equity (the difference between the amount you owe and the value of your house) in your house grows much more quickly.

At first, I didn't understand the potential behind this concept. Then, as I became more involved with the many government programs available to everyone, I realized that I could really make these programs work for me. I could use these government programs to get better cash flow and build huge equities in my real estate.

The point I'm making is this. If you are happy with your life and your job, fantastic! But if you feel your job is a dead end, do something about it. Don't go to your grave wishing you had done something different. Life is too short not to go for the opportunities. If you want to be a top-rate musician, become one. If you want to make a million dollars, you can. You can be anything you desire. The only ingredient it takes is action! Don't be one of the people who say to me, "Mr. Phillips, I can't do what you do. I'm too young (old, white, black)." There is no excuse. Colonel Sanders was sixty-seven years old when he started Kentucky Fried Chicken. He succeeded and so can you. But you have to take action.

That's why I'm writing this book: to let you know about these opportunities and get you involved. These programs are designed by the people for the people. They are for everyone.

FROM RAGTIME TO RICHES

Before I started in real estate, I was a professional drummer for a well-known jazz trio. The music was great, but the pay was poor. When not on tour, I rented an apartment and practiced my music. But after twenty years, playing drums had turned into a job and was no longer fun. I had to find a way to do more than work for a living. I had to take action to improve my life.

A House from a Rich Uncle

That's when I found out about a little-known and less used Veterans Administration program. I discovered that the Veterans Administration (VA) offered repossessed houses, for sale to anyone—veteran or not, American or not, regardless of their circumstances.

If I could demonstrate to the government that I could make the small down payment and make the monthly payments, a house was mine. I knew I could make the mortgage payments, but the down payment would be tough. Then, with a little more footwork, I learned that the only down payment required was the amount necessary to cover the real estate brokerage fees. With that in mind, I proceeded to find a real estate broker who would exchange his commission for my manual labor. After much rejection I found a broker who agreed to let me paint his rental house in exchange for his commission. The first obstacle was overcome.

I still had to come up with the monthly payments of $208.00 for the house I wanted. To solve that problem, I got a roommate to sign an agreement to share the house with me for $190.00 a month. That met the government financial requirements, and I qualified for my first home—a VA-repossessed house.

This program really appealed to me. I began buying properties from the government like hotcakes. I pocketed $50 to $100 per house per month. It didn't matter whether the houses increased in value. I had cash coming in every month. Turn to chapter 3 to find out more about the program and the addresses of every Veterans Administration office in the nation.

A Problem That Created Wealth

Over the next few years, my wife, my brother, and I bought all kinds of real estate. Before long we came across a thirty-one unit apartment building that was a super bargain. A man had inherited the property and wanted nothing to do with real estate. What a deal! The purchase price was only $200,000. We put $2,000 down, and the seller financed $198,000 at 8 percent interest for thirty years. We thought we had gotten a real bargain from the man—until we discovered that each month during the winter we had to pump $10,000 worth of heating oil into the building's furnace to provide heat for the tenants. We had a serious problem.

I figured if we could get hold of $75,000, we could install thirty-one separate gas furnaces and water heaters. This way all the tenants would have their own thermostats and be responsible for their own heating bills.

That's when I decided to go to the bank for a loan to renovate the heating system. Have you ever tried to borrow money from a bank when you really needed it? Will they lend you the money when you need it most? No. They're not going to lend you or me a peanut butter and jelly sandwich. Even if they did, the interest rate would be astronomical.

I went back to the government to solve my problem. And it worked. The city where the building was located granted me a twenty-year loan for $119,800 at 8 percent interest to modernize the heating system and make other necessary improvements. In the end, I replaced the heating system, saved $10,000 a month in heating bills, and pocketed $30,000. If you can't wait to find out how I managed to turn a $10,000 problem into a $30,000 profit, read chapter 9. I explain it in detail.

The Multi-unit King

Since then, I have worked with federal, state, and local government programs nationwide to build and renovate our country's housing. In January 1982 I received a 3 percent interest rate loan to rehabilitate an apartment building the city of Baltimore sold to me for $100.00. The government program I used was the Community Development Block Grant program.

Do you remember what the prime interest rate was in January of 1982? It was 21½ percent! I was only paying 3 percent interest to the government. When they gave me my first loan draw, I ran down to Merrill Lynch and stuck the money in my money market account, where it could earn 15 to 16 percent interest, or about 1 percent profit each month over the amount I paid the government. I was earning thousands of dollars a month in interest alone! My wife and I had all kinds of fun with that money. In the meantime, we used the loan funds to rehabilitate the apartment building for the city. It was a tough project, but we did it.

YOU MAY BE SITTING ON A GOLD MINE

That's how I got started. Now I want to tell you how to get $17,500 mailed to you by next week. I call it the Gold Mine loan program. The real name is the FHA Title I Home Improvement Loan.

By making one phone call you can borrow up to $17,500 on each of your properties, regardless of the amount of equity you may have. The only condition is that you must use the money to repair or improve your property. This of course improves the value of your real estate, but, furthermore, you may find that you can get most of the work done for far less than the $17,500 you receive from the government. The rest goes into your pocket to save for future improvements. The best part of this program is that the bank will give you all the money up front before any of the work is done.

You will learn in chapter 10 how to create your own gold mine program.

SUPER GOVERNMENT BARGAINS

As long as the government is willing to lend me money and also allow me to earn a fair profit, there is no limit to the amount of money I can make. To this day I buy properties far under market value, fix them up with low interest rate government loans, and earn a healthy profit each time. Today I own hundreds of apartments nationwide, all with positive cash flows. I provide decent, affordable housing, create jobs, and help reduce our federal deficit, while I profit.

That's not all. The elderly tenants living in our properties think I'm the greatest person since Franklin Roosevelt. They love me, because I got the government to pay 100 percent of their rents directly to me. One tenant, Mrs. Galloway, started crying when she found out she didn't have to spend half of her social security check on rent and the other half on utility bills trying to keep warm with the kitchen stove. Isn't that what it's all about?

The neighborhood associations also like me. When I start making improvements on the local run down properties, three or four neighbors start painting their houses and cleaning their yards. Before long, entire neighborhoods are sprucing themselves up.

Let me tell you the most beautiful thing about all this. While we were working on one property, an elderly lady in the neighborhood asked how she could get money from the city to fix her house. She had heard we were using low interest rate government loans for the rehabilitation and wanted to do the same. I introduced her to a few officials in the local housing department and told her how to get started.

A few months later she visited me again to thank me for the help. She had not only received a loan to repair her house, but it was a zero percent deferred payment loan. Meaning that after a number of years the loan is forgiven, and the nice old lady does not have to repay the amount she borrowed. It's a good feeling to know I'm responsible for that. (See chapter 10 for additional information.)

The programs I have mentioned are only some of the many opportunities available from the government. The book you hold in your hands will put you on the same road that has made me and many others millionaires.

This Is Your Book

All of the government programs described in this book are available to you. As an American you are entitled to these programs and their benefits. With this book you will learn to use them to help others and yourself. I have done the research and footwork for you. I have used and made money with these programs. In this book, I take you by the hand and walk you through the process. If you read this book and follow the easy-to-understand steps I provide, it will also work for you.

This book is like no other. It is not to be read once and then put away. It is a reference book, filled with government forms, instructions, names of programs, and addresses to assist you whenever you need guidance.

It will tell you:

1. Where to go for government money.
2. Whom to speak with.
3. What to ask for.
4. How to qualify.
5. How to help others.
6. How to profit.

KEEP THESE POINTS IN MIND
1. When you use government loans and programs you stimulate the economy and reduce the federal deficit.
2. Right now government loans are available at interest rates as low as zero to 3 percent.
3. Combine real estate with low interest government loans, and you have a vehicle that will earn you big money.
4. You can buy your first home, and your house payments can be cheaper than your rent.
5. Government loans are available to anyone. You don't have to be rich, poor, or brilliant to use them.
6. The government wants you to profit with government loans and programs.

The information in this book is the same as is used by my office staff to locate, analyze, and put together our proposals and projects to help us achieve our goals in business. Use this book as a tool to build your fortune. If you do, you will awaken to the economic gifts our country has for us to use. If you use them as they are intended, you will indeed be on your road to wealth.

2

GOVERNMENT MONEY: UNVEILING THE SECRETS

EVEN IF YOU'RE ON THE RIGHT TRACK, YOU'LL GET
RUN OVER IF YOU JUST SIT THERE.

Will Rogers

Tomorrow, while you work diligently at your job, the U.S. government
will give away thousands of dollars to Americans all around the nation.
This year alone government housing agencies will allocate over $56
billion in funds to people like you and me. At the same time, other
government agencies will unload thousands of excellent-quality houses
to investors and homeowners at prices far below market value. They
will sell even more homes with thirty-year loans at interest rates un-
heard of in the conventional lending market since the early 1970s.

Why does the government choose to give this money away or lend
it at interest rates far below market? For the most part, to stimulate
the economy and provide decent, affordable housing to all Americans.
Last year Elizabeth Loney of Bethesda, Maryland, used government

programs to provide housing for individuals who could not get loans from conventional lending sources. In the process, she made over $80,000 and provided houses to hundreds at rates far below market level.

John Arcidiacono of Philadelphia received a $30,000 loan to renovate a building he bought for a fraction of its value. With this money he will fix up the property, provide jobs in the community, and make a large profit upon resale. The terms of the loan? Eight percent payable over thirty years!

This year, for the first time in their lives, Karen and George Smith were able to own their own home. Through a first-time home buyer government program in San Francisco, they bought a beautiful home with only 5 percent down. Since the interest rate on the home's thirty-year loan was only 7 percent, their monthly mortgage payments were less than their previous rent! Not too bad for a couple who was turned down by every conventional lender in town.

The Government Wants to Lend Money to You

You see, it has always been a primary goal of government to provide citizens with economic incentives to purchase their own homes. By its doing so, people are given a place to live, jobs are created through new construction and real estate sales, and the city tax coffers bulge with increased tax revenue. And it's hoped that the more people own real estate, the more participation they will have in our political process—an ideal situation for a healthy economy.

Homeowners are not the only ones to benefit. Investors benefit too. Construction programs, rent subsidies, and low interest loans are also provided to encourage investors to build and renovate rental housing for those who cannot afford to own their own homes. To get an idea of the total picture, take a look at what I call the "Government Money Machine."

These programs are not new. The government has been giving away money to homeowners and investors for half a century. Thousands have profited with government programs. Why is it, then, that until now these programs were seldom used? For one thing, many people do not know of their existence or know how to use them to their advantage. But also, people simply fear working with government bureaucracies.

WAYNE PHILLIPS'
GOVERNMENT MONEY MACHINE

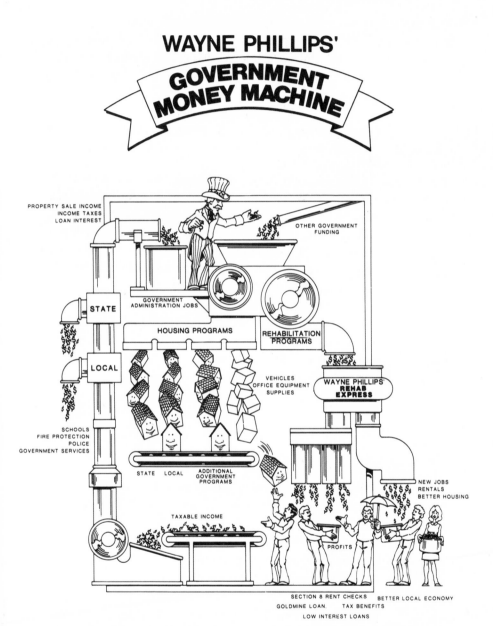

Recently, before I appeared in a televised interview, a gentleman stopped me backstage to remark that governmental loan programs were for a limited few and involved too much bureaucratic red tape. I responded by asking, "How do you know it's difficult to get the loans or that there is so much red tape? Have you ever tried to get a government loan?" "No," he replied.

Unfortunately, many misconceptions sabotage our desires for wealth and success. Let's take a look at a few.

MISCONCEPTION 1: GOVERNMENT LOANS INVOLVE TOO MUCH RED TAPE

It is commonly held in our society that anything having to do with the government is complex. We conjure up visions of lengthy applications, government runarounds, long waiting periods, and cold rejections. The fact of the matter is that getting government loans for purchasing or improving real estate is a straightforward process. If you know how to fill out the paperwork properly and follow the correct steps, the programs involve little red tape.

Ben Franklin once said, "The road to wealth is as plain as the road to the mill." The key, however, is to find the proper road. Government loan programs are not complex once you know the methods the experts use. Find the path through the red tape, and you can utilize them to create your own wealth.

MISCONCEPTION 2: THE ONLY PROPERTIES AVAILABLE ARE UNDESIRABLE TO MOST PEOPLE

Contrary to what many think, there are a vast number of beautiful houses ready for the taking. Many are luxury homes with swimming pools and large yards. Several are in areas of town any of us would be willing to live in. Most would make excellent rental properties. The key is learning to locate these properties.

MISCONCEPTION 3: GOVERNMENT LOANS ARE ONLY AVAILABLE TO LOW-INCOME AMERICANS

Sometimes government loans and grants are only available to individuals whose incomes are below the median income in their area. However, I have one former student who earned $45,000 a year and still qualified for these moderate income programs. How? The median income for her area was $54,000 per year. By government standards, she was considered "moderate income."

Even so, why would someone rich and successful want to borrow money from the government? Because there are two secrets about making money.

First, if you really want to be rich, you have to be able to borrow big bucks. You will never become financially successful without borrowing to invest. Government loans and grants are the only way for the average person to borrow the big money.

Second, if you want to make money in real estate, you need what I call "staying power." By that I mean the ability to stick with your plan through the tough times as well as the good in order to achieve your desired goals. You need cash flow. When you borrow money from the government at 3 percent annual interest, you're able to use your cash flow for other things besides high interest expense.

That's why these government programs work. They can be used by anyone who is tired of high interest rates, negative cash flow, high acquisition costs, or balloon payments. By providing low-cost funds for people to acquire or improve housing throughout the country, the government provides affordable and decent housing while it catapults us toward success and financial independence. The funds are available for anyone willing to work with these programs. Belief in the next misconception is the reason many people do not realize the opportunities that exist with government programs.

MISCONCEPTION 4: GOVERNMENT CUTBACKS HAVE LIMITED THE PROGRAMS AND FUNDS AVAILABLE

I don't know the number of times I've been told in government offices that due to the cutbacks in the current administration there were no funds available for the programs I wanted. But when I visited the office at a later date, I found that a new issue of funds had been recently appropriated.

As of this writing, the funds available for HUD programs have had few cutbacks. Annual budget *increases* have been reduced. However, there has been little reduction in funds, and no programs have been eliminated.

What I am excited about is that the government has put more money into the rehabilitation of existing housing and less into new construction. Millions of dollars are being shifted away from the new construction programs and into the programs I like the best: rehabilitation programs.

EQUAL DOLLAR COST

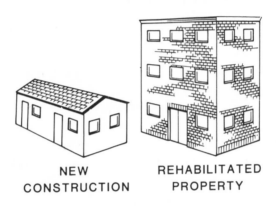

NEW
CONSTRUCTION

REHABILITATED
PROPERTY

Knowledge and Perseverance Get Results

I have years of experience at dealing successfully with government programs at all levels—federal, state, and local. Believe me, you can do it too! The programs are not as difficult to work with as you've been lead to believe. It does take knowledge and perseverance, plus a desire to get ahead. Once you know the steps to follow, the process becomes routine. There is a program for everyone and an opportunity to profit for anyone who knows the system.

To see what I mean, take a look at the chart opposite. Although it by no means represents all of the programs available, it clarifies some of the major areas.

A SUMMARY OF MAJOR GOVERNMENT PROGRAMS

	Federal	State	Local
HOMEOWNER PROGRAMS			
FHA/VA			
New loans (insured)	X		
Foreclosures	X	X	
First-time homebuyer loans		X	X
FmHA	X		
Urban homestead	X		X
3 to 5% Fix-up loans			X
Gold mine loan	X		X
Weatherization			X
INVESTOR PROGRAMS			
FHA/VA			
Foreclosures	X	X	
203k Purchase/fix-up loan	X		
Rehabilitation Programs			
Commercial revitalization			X
Section 312 rehab loans			X
3 to 8% rehab loans			X
FmHA	X		
SBA business loans	X		
IRS-owned properties	X		
SPECIAL INTEREST PROGRAMS			
Historic property renovation		X	
Farm loans/grants (FmHA)	X		
Disabled housing projects		X	X
Indian housing	X		
Military housing	X		
Rent guarantees		X	X
0% Deferred payment loans			X

These programs involve three levels of government: federal, state, and local. The benefits can come directly from the government in the form of insured loans, direct loans, or government grants. Most programs are for homeowners, investors, developers, and persons in special situations (e.g. elderly, low/moderate income, disabled). Some programs originate at the federal level but are administered at the state or local level.

TWELVE STEPS TO GET YOU STARTED

For those of you who want to learn what programs are available, whom to talk to, and how to successfully apply for them, this book is for you. I am confident that the knowledge you will gain about these government programs will prove to be invaluable. If you're ready to go, here are my twelve steps to get you started on the road to wealth with government loans.

1. *Define your goals, make a plan, and stick to it.* What would you like to have right now? A home? Increased income or cash flow? Perhaps you need to shelter income from taxation or to purchase appreciation and profit. Where do you want to be five or ten years from now? Retired? Vacationing in Tahiti? Heading a real estate empire? Whatever your desires are, you must make a game plan and stick with it.

2. *Review the programs and instructions provided in this book.* I have provided step-by-step instructions to make government programs work for you. Use the table of contents to find the type of program you need to achieve your goal. Then turn to the appropriate chapter to learn how to use the program to achieve your objective.

3. *Find a property that fits into your objective.* If you are looking for a place to live, take a drive through various parts of town to see which neighborhoods suit you. Then read the classified sections of the newspaper or visit a government-approved Realtor to get an idea of what is curently on the market. If your objective is to increase your wealth or shelter your income, find a government-owned residential or commercial rental property to use as an investment.

4. *Find a government program that fits your objective.* This is the easiest part. Find a government program that fits into your game plan. It may include a loan to purchase a property, a loan to rehabilitate a property, or both.

5. *Do the legwork to see if your property will qualify for a loan and/ or rehabilitation.* Find out the exact requirements for the loan or grant. Gather the necessary forms and applications. Be sure to learn what fees are involved in application and approval. Some projects can involve numerous fees. In chapter 12 we discuss how to avoid most of them.

6. *Develop a working relationship with key people.* Personalize your approach. Visit the seller of the property, the lender, the loan pro-

cessor, the government official, and the loan administrator. Remember that government officials are there to help you. Be friendly, open, and courteous. Don't just call them on the phone. Establish yourself as a "regular." You'll be treated much better than if you were just a faceless number.

7. *Control the property without actually buying before you apply for government assistance.* Many times with government applications it will take 60 to 90 days before you get your money. In most cases, you will not be able to get government assistance without a copy of the purchase contract. So make the offer subject to your getting the government money. Whether the loan is for purchase or rehabilitation, tie up the property while the loan is being processed.

8. *Submit the loan application and proposal.* In essence, your application and proposal should explain what your project is, what you plan to do, and how much it will cost. In chapter 12 you will find an example of a successful application to assist you with yours.

9. *Settle on the property and close the loan.* You own the property and have the funds from the government. Now the fun begins. You're ready to get started.

10. *Get the rehabilitation work done according to schedule.* When you are involved in projects that require rehabilitation, it is important that you get the property into shape according to the schedule set forth in your agreement with the government agency. Many times the agency will pay you according to the work you have completed. By getting the rehabilitation done on schedule, you keep the checks coming in.

11. *When the project is almost complete, start locating another property.* Don't wait to finish your current project. By the time you're finished with the first project, the money on your next project will be available.

12. *Repeat the process.* Try a larger project this time, using the same techniques with different programs. Review the mistakes you may have made along the way and make corrections. Now that you have a feel for the system, streamline the process and go for it!

These steps are a guide. You should read this entire book before making your next (or first) government application. Prepare for any project you are about to undertake by going through the chapter that deals with it. Later you can use it as a reference to give you new ideas, answer questions, or solve any problems you might run into. To help you, the chapters contain information about specific government programs, and addresses. An application package checklist is also included to ensure that your applications are complete.

All set? Ready to go? Then keep reading and find out how to get the best buys in government housing!

KEEP THESE POINTS IN MIND
1. Government loans and programs are available at all three levels of government; federal, state, and local.
2. The government wants to lend you money in order to stimulate the economy.
3. Don't let misconceptions sabotage your desire for wealth and success.
4. Use the twelve steps above to get involved in fantastic government loan opportunities.

3

NO MONEY DOWN: SOMETHING FOR EVERYONE

MANY RECEIVE ADVICE; ONLY THE WISE PROFIT FROM IT.

Syrus

Don't you hate the word *rent*? It calls up visions of dollars swirling down a drain. Yet buying a house in today's real estate market can be viciously competitive. For every bargain, there are a hundred properties with high prices, impossible down payments, and horrendous interest rates. The one time you hear about a good deal will be at a cocktail party, from the lucky person who grabbed it.

The American dream is to own your own home. But when conventional mortgage rates hover at over 13 percent, 75 percent of us can't afford to buy a house. Even at today's interest rates and prices, most people can't qualify for conventional loans, much less scrape up the cash necessary to make a down payment. So much for the American dream.

Or is there still hope?

A Program to Save You Thousands

In December 1982, four months after getting a new job in Houston, Donna Shomen was making $900 a month. When Donna took the job, she had rented an apartment for six months with the intention of buying her own home in the near future.

Since her lease would expire in two months, Donna was looking for a place to buy. But with conventional mortgage rates skyrocketing at 15 to 17 percent and her current income what it was, Donna faced nothing but rejection from conventional lenders.

A short time later, during an office party, a real estate agent mentioned to Donna that she probably qualified for a home through a little-known government program called the Veterans Administration (VA) sales listing program. Under this program she could easily purchase a home from among a large inventory of VA-repossessed houses, some with prices far below market value. What's more, with her income, not only could she buy her own home, but most likely she could get it for no money down!

The real estate agent explained how Donna would be able to afford a home. She had two choices. She could buy a house at full market value with a below-market interest rate loan. Her loan balance would be larger, but the low interest rate would create a monthly payment she could live with. Or, she could buy a house at a bargain price and get a loan at market interest rates. She could probably handle these payments as well, because the balance of the loan would be less. To simplify the matter, the agent drew the following diagram:

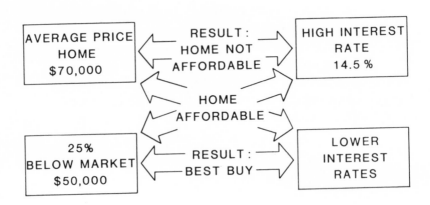

Then, with the chart below, the agent demonstrated the price Donna could afford to pay for her new home.

MONTHLY PAYMENT OF MORTGAGE AND INTEREST

Price of House	Interest Rate								
	7.5%	8.5%	9.5%	10.5%	11.5%	12.5%	13.5%	14.5%	15.5%
$40,000	279.69	307.57	336.35	365.90	396.12	426.91	458.17	489.83	521.81
50,000	349.61	384.46	420.43	457.37	495.15	533.63	572.71	612.28	652.26
60,000	419.53	461.35	504.52	548.85	594.18	640.36	687.25	734.74	782.72
70,000	489.46	538.24	588.60	640.32	693.21	747.09	801.79	857.19	913.17
80,000	559.38	615.14	672.69	731.80	792.24	853.81	916.33	979.65	1043.62
100,000	699.22	768.92	840.86	914.74	990.30	1067.26	1145.40	1224.56	1304.52

To see how this chart works, let's assume that Donna has decided that she can afford monthly mortgage payments of approximately $595.00. How can we relate this to the price and interest rate she should pay for her home? The method is simple. If the house Donna was interested in had a $70,000 price tag on it, we follow the $70,000 column horizontally to the right to find the payment she can afford— in this case $588.60. The loan would have to be at about 9.5 percent to make her payments affordable. Now let's say Donna finds a great buy in the same neighborhood for $50,000, but it has a 13.5 percent loan. This would still work, because the payments would be $572.71— still within her budget. Of course, this chart assumes the loan amount equals the purchase price.

Anyone is Eligible

The real estate agent then explained to Donna that the VA program was available to anyone, veteran or non-veteran. He suggested that she look at several homes that would fit her budget.

On Monday, Donna reviewed the list of local VA-acquired properties with her agent and found a perfect three-bedroom home close to work. She submitted her application and bid to the VA, and in less than two weeks learned that she had been awarded the property and qualified for a loan. She put no cash down, purchased the home she had always dreamed of for 22 percent below market value, and received a 12½ percent thirty-year mortgage from the VA. Donna's monthly payments were $533.63, which she shared with two rommmates. Today, Donna has over $27,000 in equity. She and her fiance plan to use the equity to buy their first home together—a VA-acquired home with a 9.5 percent loan.

How This Program Works

If you have ever wanted to buy your own home or investment property, the Veterans Administration sales program is a little-known and less-used government program that can help you. Whether or not you are an American citizen, or are struggling financially, bankrupt, or a millionaire, you can buy your first home, your first investment property, or, for that matter, your hundredth investment property.

I bought my first home through this program and so can you. It is one of the most beneficial programs today, and is available to everyone. In the words of our government, "These properties are available to anyone veteran or non veteran with stable employment and the ability to repay the government loan without regard to race, color, sex or national origin."

Here's a typical scenario. The Veterans Administration is authorized to guarantee loans made by private lenders to eligible veterans for the purpose of purchasing, constructing, improving, or repairing a home. Typically, the veteran purchases a home and, using his or her eligibility, receives a loan from the local bank or savings and loan, with the VA guaranteeing repayment. The veteran is given the opportunity to own a home with 100 percent financing, but, like anyone, is responsible for payments to the bank.

The vet moves into the property, and, after a period of time, for one reason or another, stops making payments. There might be an unexpected job layoff, enormous medical bills, a big jump in property taxes, divorce, or a death in the family. The government will work with the vet to save the property, but before long the grace periods pass, the mortgage goes unpaid, and the amount owed soars. The borrower can't meet the financial responsibility and stops trying. If several opportunities to make up the back payments pass, the bank forecloses on the property.

At this time the bank notifies the VA that the veteran has defaulted on the loan. The VA takes the property back and pays the lender for the loan as guaranteed. Once the VA does this, Uncle Sam owns the real estate. This is where you step in.

How to Do It

Now let's get down to the meat of the matter and find out how you can go out tomorrow and buy your first home or investment property through this program. To get started, you need to take a look at the list of available properties the VA publishes. How do you get hold of this list? Basically, there are two ways.

1. *Contact your local VA property management division.*Tell them you are interested in buying some properties, and ask if they would send you a copy of the sales listing sheet for your area. They will probably discourage you. If so, visit your local VA office property management division, and get to know the people directly. Explain what you would like to do, and get the listing sheet that way.
2. *Find a VA-approved real estate broker.* If the previous method doesn't work, then do as Donna did in our example. Find a local real estate broker who is registered with the VA sales listing program. (Not every real estate broker knows about this great program.) Visit the broker personally and set up a rapport.

I have found that personal contact makes a lot of difference and will improve your success. Be sure the real estate agent or broker is flexible and will work for you. Five questions I ask every real estate agent give me a good idea of how much the agent knows about VA repos. They are:

1. *How does the VA repo program work?* A qualified agent should be able to explain the entire process to you without hesitation. He (or she) will be registered with the VA and will have a master key so he can show you the interiors of all the VA properties. Be sure he knows about the application, bidding, processing, and other VA procedures.
2. *How do you get paid your commission?* Where is his money going to come from? Is he willing to trade his commission for work you could do? Or is he expecting cash when the deal closes? Settle these

questions now. It will save you a few headaches in the future. And you may walk away with a beautiful home *and* cash in your pocket.

3. *How many VA repos have you sold?* This will give you an idea of the agent's experience. If he tells you that he has sold fifteen houses, ask for the addresses so you can go look at them.

4. *Can I buy VA repos for no money down?* My favorite question. This lets you know how creative the agent is willing to be in order to help you make your fortune. If he says "yes," ask him how. This will not only be reassuring, but it may give you an idea or two. If the agent answers "no" to this question, head for the door.

5. *How much can I expect to pay?* This question is a bit harder. The VA has three categories of properties for you to choose from. They are usually labeled "A", "B", or "C." The price and terms you get will depend upon from which list you choose. The "A" category lists properties having full-market price minimum bids. The "B" properties are the ones I prefer. These are properties on which you can bid less than the minimum price. The final category, "C," contains the bonus properties. These are the properties that the VA has possessed for the longest period of time and is willing to negotiate on to get them sold. In category "A," owner occupant bids will be preferred over investor bids. *Note:* Your best buys will come from list "B." The best real estate agents will know this.

If you are a real estate broker and not registered with this free service, I suggest you get involved. You will receive the VA list at no charge and be paid a commission for any property you sell. Think of all the people you can help with this fantastic program!

Now let's look at your next steps.

Find a Property You Like.

You can make money anywhere in the United States with this fantastic program. To see what I mean, let's take a typical purchase situation. To make it difficult, we'll pick a house from the "A" sheet of a VA listing in the San Francisco area—one of the most expensive areas in the country. Looking over the list we find the following item: a nice four-bedroom house in Sacramento.

Address	City	Bed–Bath	Down payment	Mo. Pymt.	Price
7006 Gatlin Way	Sacramento	4–2.5	$4,500	$1,174	$110,000

The listing reveals that the price is $110,000 and the down payment is $4,500. But, you say, these government properties were supposed to require little or no money down. They do. Be patient. I'll tell you how to buy these properties with little cash down and end up with money in your pocket. Let's go on. Next to the down payment is the monthly payment amount and the list price. The house is in a great part of town with lots of appreciation in the area, so you're not going to be buying a dump. You're not going to be buying a mansion in Beverly Hills either. Many VA houses are in nice areas of town, and this is one of them. So far, so good.

Place a Bid on the Property.

Since this property is on the "A" sheet, the price listed is the minimum bid. Don't go to the VA and offer them a contract to buy a property. You have to bid on these properties. To do this, you have to bid at least the minimum price listed on the sheet. Obviously, you can bid more than the minimum price, but not less. Now, from the time these lists are issued to the VA-approved brokers, you have about five working days to visit the property and submit your bid. So the first thing you do is have your broker show you the house.

Hot Tip #1. While you are in the house with the broker, go into the kitchen and look on the kitchen counter. There will be a list of brokers who have already shown the house to other buyers. To the VA, this list is a register of all persons visiting the property. To you, this list is an activity record. If it contains several names, there's a pretty good chance that you're not going to get the house for the minimum bid. On the other hand, the list may have no names. In this case you may have stumbled onto a gold mine!

The secret to buying VA repos is to bid correctly without over-bidding. If you want to buy a repo for a price that is higher than the minimum bid, you must bid a minimum of 3 percent higher than the listed price. Therefore, if the listed price for our house is $110,000, take that price and add 3 percent to get the next bid price ($110,000 X 1.03 = $113,300). Any bid between $110,000 and $113,300 would not be accepted.

Before I bought my first home, I submitted minimum bids on eleven

VA repos and was turned down on every one. I finally realized that there were others bidding on these properties, and I would have to do something different. Then I discovered a formula that worked.

Hot Tip #2. My VA bidding formula for repos goes like this:

minimum bid x 1.03 + Wayne's insurance ($65.00) = your bid

The first time I did this, *zap!* I was awarded my first home. Where did the $65.00 come from? Plucked from the air. It worked then, and it still works for thousands of my seminar graduates nationwide. Those who use it say it works, and you can't knock success.

I mentioned earlier that the houses could be bought for no money down. In our example they're asking $4,500 down plus an additional $3,365 in cash ($110,000 × 3 percent + $65.00 = $3,365), for a total payment of $7,865. You're probably thinking that you can hardly afford to pay your rent, let alone come up with almost eight grand. But there is a way.

Shoot from the Hip

First, let me ask if you ever heard of this VA repo program before. Now, let me ask if you have ever bought a repo. Of all the hundreds of thousands of people that I have spoken to, many have heard of this program, but only a handful have tried to use it to purchase a property.

So what? How does that help you with your down payment? It's simple. Here's what I do, and this hint is worth many times the cost of the book you're reading right now.

I go into the VA office on the last day of the bidding period, about fifteen minutes before the bidding closes. Very casually, I start chit-chatting with the person behind the counter. Within a few moments I'll ask, "By the way, has anyone submitted bids on that property in Sacramento—you know, the one at 7006 Gatlin Way?" Chances are, the person will check and return saying, "As a matter of fact, Mr. Phillips, we've had three bids on that property." Now if I really want to buy that property on Gatlin Way, I'll reach into my back *right* pocket and pull out a completed application for $113,365, using my formula of minimum bid plus 3 percent plus Wayne's insurance of $65.00.

But you know what? Because very few people know about these VA treasures and even fewer have tried to buy them, the person I ask many times will return and say, "As a matter of fact, Mr. Phillips, no one has bid on that property." What do you think I do when that happens? I reach into my back *left* pocket and pull out a bid of—how much? You got it—$110,000, the minimum bid amount.

Now, you understand how this works, but what about the $4,500 down payment? Remember that the real estate broker makes a commission. In fact, he earns 5 percent of the sale price. Five percent of $110,000 is a lot of money. It's $5,500. How much is the down payment? $4,500.

When I bought my first property, I had no money or credit. But I was sick and tired of paying rent and throwing my money down the drain. I had no money, but I did have gray matter stuck between my ears. I figured that if I asked a lot of real estate brokers, I could find one willing to barter the real estate commission for a talent that I had.

Hot Tip #3. A real estate broker does not make a dime until you buy real estate. This is one of the most important concepts for you to grasp. Once you allow this concept to take hold in your mind, it can make you fabulously wealthy and you can become a real estate tycoon. You must allow it to work for you.

I asked a number of brokers if they would trade the sales commission the VA pays them for something I could do. Paint their house, play drums for their daughter's wedding, anything. Many threw me out of their offices. But there was one agent in Encino, California, named Bob Cranford, who agreed to let me paint his house in exchange for his commission. You might not want to paint, but you may be a dentist, auto mechanic, or carpenter who could offer a service. You may be willing to babysit or clean houses. You may be someone with a talent, who would love to own your own home but have no cash to buy it. The point I'm making is this. Ask and ye shall receive. Do something to change your life now! Because if you don't do something to change your life now, where are you going to be in five more years besides older?

In our example, let's say the real estate broker agrees to pay you $5,500 for a coin collection you inherited. You use a portion of the money to make the $4,500 down payment and close on the VA repo.

The broker reimburses himself the $5,500 for your coin collection when he receives his commission from the VA. He ends up with a nice coin collection. You walk away with $1,000 in your pocket and a beautiful home.

Eliminate Monthly Payments

That's great, Wayne, you say, but what about the monthly payment of $1,174? Let's look at that. You're thinking, "I can hardly pay the $500 rent on my apartment. How am I going to pay $1,174 every month?" Remember what I told you earlier? I was broke, playing drums for $50.00 per weekend in Ventura, California, driving back and forth in my Volkswagen. You may have seen me broken down on the road with my drums in the back seat. Here's how I made my mortgage payments and still qualified for a VA repo.

My first house was a VA-repossessed two-bedroom starter home. That was the good news. The bad news was that I had a $208.00 payment to make each month, and I was only making $200.00 per month. How was I ever going to make my payment, let alone qualify for the loan?

One of the nice things about this government program is that you don't have to go to a bank to get your loan. The VA will make you a direct thirty-year loan. And the government's credit policy is very lenient. After all, if they will sell a property to an unemployed drummer with long hair and no credit, just about anyone can qualify.

To make my payments, I placed a notice at the musicians' union headquarters in Hollywood that read, "DRUMMER WANTED. Practice your drums any time of the day or night with me." I received hundreds of calls from drummers and, in only a few days, rented a room in my house for $190 per month. You have to give in order to get what you want out of life. Sure, I had to give up a bedroom and have a room-mate, but I owned my own home. And only had to pay $18.00 per month!

What if you are married, and don't want a full-time roommate living with you and your spouse? Try renting a room out in a bed and breakfast program. Many tourists are willing to pay up to $75.00 per day for a room to stay in while visiting your town. The American Bed and Breakfast Association can help you get involved. To inquire about this program, write to the American Bed and Breakfast Association, P.O. Box 23294, Washington, D.C. 20026.

Another way to handle the payment is to get investors to invest in the house with you. Give them half-ownership in the property and most of the tax benefits on the condition that they make all or part of the monthly payments for you. You'll end up with a nice place to live, and they will have half-interest in a property with 99 percent of the write-offs. Not too bad.

To do this, run an ad in the newspaper. Better yet, check with several certified public accountants or financial planners. Tell them you have a dynamite property at 7006 Gatlin Way, and that if one of their clients will put up the monthly payment he or she can have half of the ownership in the property and receive 99 percent of the tax benefits.

Be prepared to get a lot of responses! There are many professional people in the world who would love to own a beautiful home with no problem tenant to worry about and that would enable them to shelter some of their income from taxation. Once you do the first deal, you'll have the CPAs and investors asking you for more properties. Then you can start renting out the properties, building equity, and eventually collecting huge profits on the resale of the buildings. (For more information on how to put tax benefits to work in real estate, take a look at chapter 14. We'll cover this in detail there.)

If you use the proven ideas in this chapter, they will work for you. You won't get properties for 50 cents on the dollar through the VA. But these houses can be bought for 10 to 25 percent below market value. They have thirty-year fixed rate loans (at below-market interest) that are fully assumable. They are easy to qualify for and easy to sell. Furthermore, if you arrange your own financing, you get an automatic 10 percent price discount. Those of you who don't own your home can buy a VA repo for little or no money down, move into your home three to five weeks from the time your bid is accepted, and perhaps pocket cash as a bonus.

New VA Pricing Policy for Investors and Home Owners in Many Cities

The VA now has a new pricing policy, so even an investor can buy these houses with no money down. As I mentioned earlier in the chapter, it's been a long-standing VA policy to consider only purchase offers (bids) for the full list price on "A" properties. If you wanted a house with a list price of $97,000 and you offered the VA a bid of $96,995, they would reject your offer. Also, if you were an investor, you had to have a 10 percent down payment.

But now, in an effort to broaden the program to everyone's advantage, the Veterans Administration has announced a new major policy change which allows below-list-price offers to be considered for acceptance on some "A" properties and lowers the 10 percent down payment requirement for investors.

You see, in many cases the VA has so many properties in its inventory that it is willing to do anything to liquidate them. Think about it. When the government has thousands of properties each year to sell, it can't give them away! So the VA changed its policy. Now if you are an investor, the down payment can be as low as 0%. Also, if you want to bid, you can bid *below* the list price on many properties. You get a property at a great price and great terms, and the government gets the building back on the active tax rolls.

The key is to get started. Begin first thing in the morning. Take a look at some of the properties on the VA list, then go out and do something to change your life. Buy your starter home now. Don't wait for the perfect dream home to come around. Find a house that is in decent shape in a good neighborhood. Then, using the methods I've described in this chapter, buy the place. In time, your dreams will come true.

WASHINGTON'S WEALTHY LADY

One student of mine in Washington, D.C. (I'll call her Ms. Lui) decided to put this program to work for her. On the Monday following the class on VA repos, she contacted an aggressive VA-approved broker and started looking at properties. Ms. Lui bought several of the finest homes from the list of VA-repossessed properties with no money down and got thirty-year VA loans at 12½ percent (the current VA rate at the time).

But that's not all. She then took these gorgeous homes and resold them to successful professional persons in the city for no money down and with thirty-year loans at interest 2 percent higher than she owed. Her houses sold quickly because: 1) They were sold for no money down. 2) The buyers didn't have to qualify for the loan. 3) Every house had a thirty-year, fixed interest rate mortgage. Compared to other houses on the market, her houses were a very good buy.

In little over a year this young lady was earning over $100,000 income every year and didn't even own any real estate! How did Ms. Lui earn the 2-percent spread? Look at the following example:

	Buy with VA loan @ 12½%	Sell with wraparound @ 14½%
Ms. Lui buys at:	$110,000.00	$110,000.00
Loan amount:	$110,000.00	$110,000.00
Monthly payment:	$ 1,174.80	$ 1,347.50

You see, Ms. Lui sold her VA repo on a "wraparound" mortgage, sometimes called an all-inclusive trust deed (AITD). This means that her new buyers were not assuming the VA loan that had been created when Ms. Lui bought the home, but received a loan from Ms. Lui that "wrapped around" or included the existing VA loan.

WAYNE'S FIVE STEPS FOR BUYING VA REPOS
1. Locate the part of town in which you want to live.
2. Find a flexible real estate agent to show you the list of VA-acquired properties and let you see interiors.
3. Do your homework. Shop around the neighborhood to find out what nearby houses are selling for and how much down. Be sure to compare three-bedroom houses with three-bedroom houses (compare apples with apples, oranges with oranges). If one house is more expensive than another, find out if it has any special improvements that justify the price difference.
4. Check the inspection sign-up sheet in the kitchen. Use the two-pocket bidding method to submit the best bid.
5. Close on the government property. Repeat the process.

Each month the new owners pay Ms. Lui $1,347.50 through a lawyer or title company. The lawyer or title company in turn pays the VA payment of $1,174.80, and sends Ms. Lui the remaining $172.70.

Payment received:	$1,347.50
less VA payment:	$1,174.80
Ms. Lui's profit:	$ 172.70 per house each month

Ms. Lui has bought and sold over fifty houses using this method. She will continue to earn $100,000 per year for the next thirty years. She has no problems with property management and is free to travel and enjoy her new wealth. Not bad.

Remember, "Ask and ye shall receive." Try it. It really works.

KEEP THESE POINTS IN MIND
1.   VA-acquired properties are easy to buy and are available to anyone.
2.   VA-acquired properties are easy to qualify for. You don't need great credit. The loans are at below-market rates.
3.   You don't have to go to the bank to get a loan.
4.   Work with a real estate agent willing to work for you.
5.   Go to the VA fifteen minutes before the bidding closes with two bids.
6.   Use roommates or investors to put cash in your pocket.
7.   It takes little or no cash to buy these properties. With a little time, you can do it!

SPECIAL RESOURCE: VETERANS ADMINISTRATION
LOAN GUARANTY SERVICE REGIONAL OFFICES

Veterans Administration Washington, DC 20420

Alabama
VA Regional Office
474 South Court Street
Montgomery, AL 36104

Alaska
VA Regional Office
235 East 8th Avenue
Anchorage, AK 99501

Arizona
VA Regional Office
3225 North Central
Avenue
Phoenix, AZ 85012

Arkansas
VA Regional Office
1200 West 3d Street
Little Rock, AR 72201

California
VA Regional Office
Federal Building
11000 Wilshire
  Boulevard
Los Angeles, CA 90024

VA Regional Office
211 Main Street
San Francisco, CA 94105

Colorado
VA Regional Office
Denver Federal Center,
  Building 20
Denver, CO 80225

Connecticut
VA Regional Office
450 Main Street
Hartford, CT 06103

Delaware
VA Medical and Regional
  Office Center
1601 Kirkwood Highway
Wilmington, DE 19805

*NOTE: Loan Guaranty
  consolidated with
  Philadelphia.*

District of Columbia
VA Regional Office
941 North Capitol Street,
  NE
Washington, D.C. 20421

Florida
VA Regional Office
P.O. Box 1437
144 First Avenue, South
St. Petersburg, FL 33731

Georgia
VA Regional Office

730 Peachtree Street, NE
Atlanta, GA 30365

Hawaii
VA Regional Office
P.O. Box 50188, 96850
PJKK Federal Building
300 Ala Moana
  Boulevard
Honolulu, HI 96813

Idaho
VA Regional Office
Federal Building and
  U.S. Courthouse
550 West Fort Street
Box 044
Boise, ID 83724

Illinois
VA Regional Office
536 S. Clark Street
P.O. Box 8136
Chicago, IL 60680

Indiana
VA Regional Office
575 North Pennsylvania
  Street
Indianapolis, IN 46204

Iowa
VA Regional Office
210 Walnut Street
Des Moines, IA 50309

Kansas
VA Medical and Regional
  Office Center
901 George Washington
  Boulevard
Wichita, KS 67211

Kentucky
VA Regional Office
600 Federal Place
Louisville, KY 40202

Louisiana
VA Regional Office

701 Loyola Avenue
New Orleans, LA 70113

Maine
VA Medical and Regional
  Office Center
Togus, ME 04330

Maryland
VA Regional Office
Federal Building
31 Hopkins Plaza
Baltimore, MD 21201

*NOTE: Montgomery and
  Prince Georges
  counties are under the
  jurisdiction of VARO,
  Washington, D.C.*

Massachusetts
VA Regional Office
John F. Kennedy
  Building
Government Center
Boston, MA 02203

Michigan
VA Regional Office
Federal Building
477 Michigan Avenue
Detroit, MI, 48226

Minnesota
VA Regional Office and
  Insurance Center
Federal Building
Fort Snelling
St. Paul, MN 55111

Mississippi
VA Regional Office
100 W. Capitol St.
Jackson, MS 39269

Missouri
VA Regional Office
Federal Building, Room
  4705
1520 Market Street
St. Louis, MO 63103

Montana
VA Medical and Regional
    Office Center
Fort Harrison, MT 59636

Nebraska
VA Regional Office
Federal Building
100 Centennial Mall
    North
Lincoln, NE 68508

Nevada
VA Regional Office
245 East Liberty Street
Reno, NV 89520

*NOTE: Loan Guaranty
    consolidated with San
    Francisco. Loan
    Guaranty activities for
    Clark and Lincoln
    counties, Nevada
    consolidated with Los
    Angeles.*

New Hampshire
VA Regional Office
Norris Cotton Federal
    Building
275 Chestnut Street
Manchester, NH 03101

New Jersey
VA Regional Office
20 Washington Place
Newark, NJ 07102

New Mexico
VA Regional Office
Dennis Chavez Federal
    Building,
U.S. Courthouse
500 Gold Avenue, SW
Albuquerque, NM 87102

New York
VA Regional Office
Federal Building
111 West Huron Street
Buffalo, NY 14202

VA Regional Office
252 Seventh Avenue (at
    24th St.)
New York, NY 10001

North Carolina
VA Regional Office
Federal Building
251 North Main Street
Winston-Salem, NC
    27155

North Dakota
VA Medical and Regional
    Center
655 First Avenue North
Fargo, ND 58102

*NOTE: Loan Guaranty
    consolidated with St.
    Paul.*

Ohio
VA Regional Office
Anthony J. Celebrezze
    Federal Bldg.
1240 East Ninth Street
Cleveland, OH 44199

Oklahoma
VA Regional Office
125 S. Main Street
Muskogee, Ok 74401

Oregon
VA Regional Office
Federal Building
1220 Southwest 3rd
    Avenue
Portland, OR 97204

Pennsylvania
VA Regional Office and
    Insurance Center
P.O. Box 8079
5000 Wissahickon
    Avenue
Philadelphia, PA 19101

VA Regional Office
1000 Liberty Avenue
Pittsburgh, PA 15222

Puerto Rico
VA Medical and Regional
    Office Center
GPO Box 4867
San Juan, PR 00936

Rhode Island
VA Regional Office
380 Westminster Mall
Providence, RI 02903

*NOTE: Loan Guaranty
    consolidated with
    Boston.*

South Carolina
VA Regional Office
1801 Assembly Street
Columbia, SC 29201

South Dakota
VA Medical and Regional
    Office Center
P.O. Box 5046
2501 West 22nd Street
Sioux Falls, SD 57117

*NOTE: Loan Guaranty
    consolidated with St.
    Paul.*

Tennessee
VA Regional Office
110 Ninth Avenue, South
Nashville, TN 37203

Texas
VA Regional Office
2515 Murworth Drive
Houston, TX 77054

VA Regional Office
1400 North Valley Mills
    Drive
Waco, TX 76799

Utah
VA Regional Office
P.O. Box 11500
125 South State Street
Salt Lake City, UT 84147

Vermont
VA Medical and Regional
   Office Center
White River Junction,
   VT 05001

Virginia
VA Regional Office
210 Franklin Road, SW
Roanoke, VA 24011

NOTE: Arlington,
Fairfax, Loudoun,
Prince William,
Spotsylvania, and
Stafford counties and
the cities of
Alexandria, Fairfax,
Falls Church, and
Fredericksburg are
under the jurisdiction

of VARO, Washington,
D.C.

Washington
VA Regional Office
915 Second Avenue
Seattle, WA 98174

NOTE: Clark, Klickitat,
and Skamania
counties are under the
jurisdiction of VARO,
Portland, Oregon.

West Virginia
VA Regional Office
640 4th Avenue
Huntington, WV 25701

NOTE: Brooke, Hancock,
Marshall, and Ohio

counties are under the
jurisdiction of VARO,
Pittsburgh, PA.

Wisconsin
VA Regional Office
VA Center
P.O. Box 6
Wood, WI 53193

Wyoming
VA Medical and Regional
   Office Center
2360 East Pershing
   Boulevard
Cheyenne, WY 82001

NOTE: Loan Guaranty
consolidated with
Denver.

4

REAL ESTATE AT BARGAIN PRICES: *The Big Government Programs*

THE WORST BANKRUPT PERSON IN THE WORLD IS THE
PERSON WHO HAS LOST HIS ENTHUSIASM.

H. W. Arnold

Now let's look at another government program. In the last chapter we covered the Veterans Administration foreclosure program. Now we are going to look at a similar program offered by HUD that has many different benefits from the VA program.

I call these properties "HUD repos." They are actually FHA (Federal Housing Administration) loan foreclosures. Properties that had FHA loans on them that HUD foreclosed on and now holds in inventory— repossessed properties. HUD sells these properties to remove them from their inventory and get them back on the tax rolls. Both home-owners and investors are encouraged to participate in the program. Every time a HUD repo is sold, the sale reduces the monetary burden on our government and helps lower the deficit.

Recently, I appeared on a nationally known television talk show with the former Undersecretary of Housing, Mr. Phil Abrams. On this program Mr. Abrams said that there were over 20,000 HUD-acquired single-family homes out there for folks like you and me. Think about it—20,000 homes for us to buy. All at bargain prices. A nice opportunity.

There are basically three ways to buy these HUD repos. Although all three can be used by both homeowners and investors, sometimes one program will favor homeowners over investors. It is to your benefit to know when. With that in mind, let's take a look at them.

USING AN FHA-INSURED LOAN

The first way to pick up one of these HUD repos is to buy the property and get an FHA (Federal Housing Administration) insured loan to pay for it. If you submit a bid to purchase that is accepted, HUD will have you fill out a loan application. Fortunately, they do all of the remaining paperwork for you.

If you qualify as a good risk prospect with the FHA, your paperwork is sent to an FHA-approved lender—a bank, savings and loan, or whatever. That lender agrees to make the loan, as long as the FHA insures it. If you don't pay the lender, the lender will get paid back by the FHA. This program is available for purchase of single-family homes and apartments of up to four units.

Below are a few listings typical of those you might see in a Public Information Release sale listing sheet issued by the U.S. Department of Housing and Urban Development (HUD). This listing sheet is used to advertise the HUD-acquired properties available for sale. This example happens to be from Philadelphia.

SECTION 1

NEW LISTINGS—FINANCED SALES

Case Number	Street Address	City	Bdrms	Price
441-263254-203	2908 S. 63rd St.	Philadelphia	3	$28,000
071-047359-503	717 Darley Rd.	Claymont	4	$52,000
441-283949-235	6423 Fairfax Circle	E. Petersburg	3	$47,500

SECTION 2

EXTENDED LISTINGS—FIRST COME FIRST SERVE

Case Number	Street Address	City	Bdrms	Price
441-276112-256	6 Bentley Court	Reading	2	$32,500
441-220016-216	4944 N. Smedley St.	Philadelphia	3	$29,000

Whenever the listing reads "Financed Sales," these are properties you can buy with an FHA loan. The listing gives the address, basic information about the type of property, and the price. The price is the minimum bid, meaning that with these listings you have to bid at least the listed amount. This is the main reason I don't like to buy HUD-acquired properties with FHA insured loans. The minimum amount is usually full market value.

Another reason I don't buy these properties is that investors are required to put at least 15 percent down. If the minimum price is $50,000, 15 percent down is $7,500. Too much for me.

Now let's move down the list to Section 2; "Extended Listings—First Come First Serve." These are properties that received no acceptable bids when listed in the "New Listings" category. In essence, this means that the first acceptable offer received in the HUD property disposition office that provides the greatest net return to the department will be accepted. In many states properties listed in this category require no investor down payment. They are still eligible for the FHA-insured loans and require minimum bids, but the down payment is waived.

That's the first way to acquire these properties. The next is a little easier.

USING A PURCHASE MONEY MORTGAGE

The second way is to get a purchase money mortgage direct from HUD. What is a purchase money mortgage? It is simply a loan that sellers give you when you purchase their property. Let me give you an example. If you bought a duplex from Harry Smith for $100,000 with $5,000 down, and he let you pay back the remaining $95,000 over ten years, that's a purchase money mortgage. If you were to buy that same property from Harry for $100,000 with $5,000 down but went over to Security National Bank to get a loan to pay Harry the $95,000 in cash, that's not a purchase money mortgage. That is a new loan. A purchase money mortgage from HUD is simply seller financing with HUD as the seller.

What makes the purchase money mortgage so great? A lot. In the past, HUD would carry back the loan for seven years at an interest rate of 8 percent plus ½ percent service charge.

When the market rate of interest was anywhere from 15 to 21 percent, you could get a loan from HUD at 8 percent interest! Let me tell you something. When you get below-market-rate interest on a loan to buy a house, mortgage payments can be cheaper than rent. On your rental properties, this means you get positive cash flow. That's the money that jingles in your pocket after you pay the mortgage payments and all the expenses. It's the money you're *supposed* to have left over at the end of each month. Now that interest rates have lowered, HUD uses purchase money mortgages only on large foreclosed housing projects. But I suspect that in the event interest rates climb to the high rates experienced a few years ago, we will see the return of the purchase money mortgage as a way to finance the purchase of HUD repos.

The third and final way to buy these HUD-acquired properties is to use all cash. This is my favorite way. Why do I like to pay all cash? It's very simple. If you pay cash for these properties, you are allowed to bid a great deal less than the minimum required bid.

BUY WITH CASH

The Public Information Release also contains properties that are available for cash. Let's look again at a few more of the available properties from the Philadelphia PIR.

SECTION 1-a

NEW LISTINGS—ALL CASH PROPERTIES

Case Number	Street Address	City	Bdrms	Price
441-195752-221	6701 N. 21st St.	Philadelphia	2	$29,500
441-278833-203	158 E. Parkway Ave.	Chester	4	$32,500

SECTION 2-a

EXTENDED LISTINGS—FIRST COME FIRST SERVE—ALL CASH PROPERTIES

Case Number	Street Address	City	Bdrms	Price
441-309040-203	2207 Kensington St.	Harrisburg	3	$21,000
441-279296-203	416 Rose Inn Ave.	Nazareth	3	$59,500
441-268267-221	931 Keystone Road	Chester	3	$13,000

Again the list is divided into two sections; "New Listings" and "First Come First Serve." As before, the list provides us with the addresses, property information, and asking prices. On the actual list, prices can range from about $5,000 to $60,000. Many are around $30,000. But that's a lot of money. Who has that much cash? You're probably saying, "Wayne, $30,000 is a lot of money. I don't have $30,000 in cash. It might as well be $30 million."

Well, you know what? Here's the beauty of the all-cash deals from the government. First, the government has drastically discounted the price of these properties well below market value. Obviously, if HUD was going to sell these properties and give you a mortgage, they could probably ask a higher price. The government realizes this and is willing to discount the price to those of us who can come up with the cash to buy them.

A property that is listed for $30,000 in many cities is probably worth about $50,000. But because HUD wants cash and wants to sell the property with no guarantees, they discount the price, letting you pick it up for $20,000 below market value. But there's more.

Best Deals from HUD

Your best buys come from the "First come First Serve-All Cash Properties." On these properties, HUD has the discretion to accept offers lower than the listing price, but only the highest acceptable offer will be considered.

Do you know what that means? It means that a property that the government has priced at $21,000 may be purchased for much less than $21,000. Of course, the highest bidder will get the property.

However, do you remember my two-pocket bidding technique from the last chapter? It will work for HUD properties as well. Go to the HUD office downtown in the last few minutes before the bidding has stopped and bid any price you wish. What I would do is bid $12,000 to $15,000 cash on a $21,000 property.

That's fine if you're rich, but you may not even have fifty bucks. You don't have enough cash to even come close. How can you get this property?

Coming Up with the Cash

Although you have to pay cash for these properties, it doesn't have to be your cash. The first time I bought an "all-cash" property from HUD, my brother, my wife, and I marched down to the bank and tried to borrow $20,000 to buy a HUD property listed for $28,000. Of course the bank threw us out and wouldn't let us borrow anything. What did we do then?

We gave half interest in the property to an investor willing to cosign the loan. In other words, to enable us to get the loan, the investor agreed to sign the loan with us so we could get the cash from the bank. We bought a property worth $28,000 for $19,000, cash. It's one of the very first duplexes we bought back in Baltimore. We paid all cash with the help of the investor.

Here are the details of what we did. We borrowed the money on a ninety-day note from a commercial bank and paid cash for the property. By doing so, we accomplished two things.

1. We now owned a house free and clear.
2. We owed the bank $20,000, payable in ninety days, with no security or collateral, just our signatures on a promissory note.

We immediately started fixing up the property. In the meantime, we arranged permanent financing on the duplex through a local mortgage lender. As we expected, our fixed-up duplex was appraised at $30,000, and the bank loaned us $25,500 for thirty years. We paid the first bank their $20,000 and pocketed the rest. We now had an income-producing property with a positive cash flow and a very happy cosigner.

The loan amount could have been $50,000 or $90,000, whatever it cost to buy the property. If this same house had been in San Francisco, it probably would have cost $100,000. The principles are the same, regardless of the dollar amount of the loan from the bank.

To repeat, the idea is to go to the bank, get a promissory note, and use the money to pay cash for the HUD-acquired property. If you don't have the ability to get the loan on your own, get an investor or relative to cosign for you. This may take a little time and work, because you will have to go out and find an investor. Tell him about the benefits and rewards he will receive. Explain that he will not lay out a nickel by cosigning the loan for you. No payment or interest on the loan is due for ninety days (at which time you'll be expected to pay off the amount you owe plus any accrued interest).

Once you buy the property, start making the necessary improvements so that you can refinance it with a permanent loan. This is the best way to pay off the ninety-day note. I have many techniques that I use to refinance properties. We will discuss them later.

One word of warning: Do not go out and buy a property from the government using a ninety-day note, sit on it a few days, spend a lot of time and money fixing it up, and then go out and try to get a permanent loan. It doesn't work that way.

Do you want to see ninety days go by fast? Just borrow $90,000, and have no permanent loan to pay it back with. That will be the fastest ninety days you've ever seen in your life. I know, because I've been there, and it's a very scary situation. Fortunately, because of our financial position we were able to bail ourselves out.

To prevent this from happening to you, have your paperwork on the permanent financing completed and your lender selected before finalizing the all-cash purchase from HUD.

Fix Up to Increase Value

As I mentioned before, to get a decent appraisal you'll need to make a few cosmetic improvements. Below are the things I want you to do to the house once you take possession. It's important that you do them to increase the value of the property, so you will get a higher appraisal for your permanent loan. They may sound a little corny, but they work. Each suggestion is a proven way to increase the value of your investment.

The first thing you do is clean all the windows in the house. Use ammonia and newspaper to get them spotless. This makes the house look 100 percent better. If the windows are cracked, replace them, and caulk around the ones that are all right.

Paint the inside of the house antique white or off-white. Paint the kitchen and bathroom yellow, however. Don't paint them blue or white. pale yellow works the best. Every time we painted the bathroom and kitchen blue or any other color, it didn't work. So stick with a winner— yellow.

The next thing to do is pick up some used real wood cabinets from a salvage company. They may be chipped or slightly scratched, but you can get enough for an entire kitchen for $100 to $150. Touch up the scratches and chips with wood stain and have them installed. While you're in the kitchen, replace that ancient porcelain sink with a nice clean chrome one. A plumber will put one of them in for $75 to $100.

Then I want you to put no-wax vinyl flooring in the kitchen and bathroom. After you do all of this, cut the grass, pick up all of the trash around the house, trim the bushes and trees, and water the lawn.

Once you're through with the cosmetic improvements, have an electrician upgrade the electrical wiring in the house. If the house has fuses, have the electrician remove the fuse box and install circuit breakers. Also have him install 200-amp service. Electrical upgrading may cost you $1,000 to $1,500, but it will make a big difference in your appraisal.

Does the house have hardwood floors? For $40 per day you can rent a floor sander, and sand the dining room and hallway floors. If the house is carpeted, find some carpet remnants for $20 per yard, negotiate to buy the carpet for $7 per yard, and have it installed. If you know how, install it yourself.

Last but not least, get rid of those dumb little square or round ceiling light fixtures in all of the rooms. Go to K-mart or some other discount store, and get some modern-looking light fixtures to install.

Hire an FHA Appraiser

OK. The house is freshly painted, the new fixtures are in, and the lawn looks well groomed. Now you are ready to have the house appraised. I want you to hire an FHA-approved appraiser. The bank is not going to hire him. You are.

Before you meet the appraiser at the property, contact your local real estate broker to determine what properties are selling for in the neighborhood. The broker should be able to provide you with a list of houses that have sold in the past six months.

Now, if you bought this house as I instructed, you should own a $65,000 home, say, bought for $35,000 to $40,000 cash. My first rule of buying is to *buy the worst properties in the best areas.* That way you buy a house at a great cash discount and then do the necessary cosmetic work to bring it up to the neighborhood standard.

Once you have your list of comparable sales in the neighborhood, you are ready to meet the appraiser. When he arrives at the property, be friendly and courteous and let him know you'll help him in any way. Introduce yourself as Mr. or Ms. Investor, and then say, "Did you know that the house right down the street sold on September 15 of this year for $67,500? And they only had one and a half bathrooms in their house. This one has two." Most likely he will make a note of this and ask you for the address.

Once you are inside the house, let him know about the new electrical upgrade, the $20-per-yard carpet, and other small improvements. If you don't let him know about these things, he won't notice. You have to give him all the reasons that your appraisal should be high. When he is on his way out, hand the appraiser your list of houses sold in the neighborhood.

STEPS TO USE WHEN REFINANCING AN ALL-CASH DEAL
1. Go through the HUD-acquired property list to find an "all-cash" property.
2. Find an investor to put the cash for the property into the bank or cosign a ninety-day promissory note for the money.
3. Submit an all-cash bid on the property. Prepare the paper work for a permanent loan before your bid acceptance.
4. Buy the property with the investor's cash and close the deal with HUD.
5. Clean and fix up the property using Wayne's methods.
6. Hire an FHA appraiser to appraise the property. Be sure to provide a list of price comparisons in the neighborhood.
7. Go to your lender and refinance the property, based on the appraised value.
8. Use proceeds from the permanent loan to pay the ninety-day note. Split any cash remaining with your investor.
9. Put house up for sale or lease.
10. Repeat the process.

In a week to ten days the appraisal will be completed. If you have done everything as I have told you to, your $35,000 purchase should be appraised at around $65,000. Obviously, this is only an example. But if you have this kind of appraisal you have gold. You can go to any lender and refinance the home with permanent financing, then pay off the ninety-day note. Since many lenders will lend up to 85 percent of the appraised value, you may even pocket a few bucks. I show you how to do this in the supplement to this chapter.

Buying "all cash" is an excellent way to get a property for 40 to 50 percent under market value. You can fix up the property, refinance it with a permanent loan and maybe put extra cash, tax free, into your pocket. With a nice thirty-year mortgage that is fully assumable, the property should be desirable to most prospective investors.

OTHER DETAILS YOU NEED TO KNOW

Let's take a look at some of the other details involved with HUD-acquired properties.

Sealed Bid Procedures

All properties are made available for a single ten-day period, during which sealed bid purchase offers will be accepted. They must be in the HUD office by 4:45 P.M. on the last day of the period. The bids are opened in the HUD office at 11:00 A.M. on the following business day.

Sealed bids may be submitted by prospective owner-occupants or investor buyers on all properties. However, owner-occupants will be given priority only on the FHA-insured sales. In other words, if you're going to be an investor, don't get involved with FHA-insured loan properties, because owner-occupant bids will be accepted over yours. All-cash and purchase money mortgage buyers are treated equally, so these make better investment properties.

Sales Commissions

HUD will pay commissions of 5 percent of the sales price for houses and rental properties and 10 percent of the price for vacant lots. As a purchaser of one of these properties, you must go through a HUD-approved real estate broker. On the rare occasions when you cannot find a broker in your area, HUD will let you submit the bid yourself. I encourage you to go through a broker. They know the market and the bidding procedures.

Earnest Money Requirements

On all the properties eligible for FHA insured loans and purchase money mortgages, a $500 deposit is required from both owner-occupants and investors. The all-cash properties require a deposit of 5 percent of the sales price or $2,000, whichever is less. The deposit must be in the form of a certified personal check, bank money order, or cashier's check. Don't use anything else. I had one real estate broker submit my offer with a business check from her company's trust account, and I lost out on a good deal because it wasn't certified. Keep that in mind.

Closing Costs

The closing costs on a HUD-acquired property are next to nothing. HUD usually pays for everything. Points, fees, commissions—everything is included in your bid price.

BUYING LARGER PROPERTIES THROUGH HUD

Up to this point, we have been talking about single-family homes and one- to four-unit income properties. Now let's mention bigger properties, an area that I especially like because you can create a much better cash flow and the tax benefits are bigger. Furthermore, since most people are busy with the smaller properties, very few people venture into these larger deals.

Why do I like the big properties? Face it. Let's say you can buy a 100-unit property and bring in cash flow on those 100 units. How many houses would you have to buy to bring in the same cash flow? A lot. And the houses would be in many different locations.

To get these properties you have to write to your local HUD office and ask to be put on the multi-family project sales mailing list. The invitations to bid mailed to you will describe the properties in detail and tell you their location. I always check to see who pays the heating and cooling for an apartment building. Make sure the tenants pay their own utilities. It will save you a lot of money in the long run.

On a typical $1 million property, you would have to put down 5 percent, or $50,000. This may be out of your range right now. But it's good to know these larger HUD-acquired properties are available for when the day comes that you can get involved with them.

Special Resource:
How to Use FHA Loans to Buy HUD Repos

When you buy any property using an FHA 203b or 203k loan (not only a HUD repo), the FHA uses a simple formula to calculate how much of a down payment you'll have to make. The formula differs for owners and investors (it depends on whether you live in the property yourself or rent it to others).

The down payment for an *owner-occupant* is:

3 percent of the first $25,000 of the property's price
plus
5 percent of any remaining amount over $25,000

For example, if you bid $75,000 successfully for a HUD repo and used an FHA loan to refinance the purchase, you would be required to make the down payment as calculated.

3 Percent of the first $25,000	$ 750
5 percent of amount over $25,000	
($75,000–$25,000 × .05)	$2,500
Total down payment required	$3,250

Therefore the maximum you, the owner-occupant, could borrow on this $75,000 property would be $71,750:

Purchase price	$75,000
less Down payment	$3,250
Maximum owner-occupant loan amount	$71,750

Recently, the FHA has permitted *investors* to borrow up to 85 percent of the property's list price. Therefore, the most an investor could borrow on a $75,000 home would be $63,750:

Price on HUD repo list	$75,000
Investor maximum loan (85%)	× .85
Maximum investor loan amount	$63,750

This means that an investor would have to come up with $11,250 down.

This is still better than the old down payment rule for investors, when the FHA really socked it to us. As investors, we were allowed to borrow only 85 percent of the amount an owner-occupant could borrow. To buy the same house as in the above example, an investor could only get a loan for $60,988:

Purchase price	$75,000
Maximum owner-occupant loan amount	$71,750
Investor maximum loan (85%)	×.85
Maximum investor loan amount	$60,988

Investors are better off under the new rule, because they can get a larger loan ($63,750 as opposed to $60,988). Even so, as an investor you would still have to make a $11,250 down payment to buy a $75,000 HUD repo. That doesn't sound too good, does it?

With this in mind, let's go back to the FHA all-cash deals. Let's assume that you bid $40,000, cash, on a repo that is listed for $50,000. Because HUD is asking all cash for the property, they discount the price for a buyer able to pay cash. The property is in a great neighborhood, where other properties sell in the $60,000 to $80,000 range. However, your property is the worst property in this good neighborhood.

It needs a lot of work: a fresh coat of paint, landscaping, new interiors. Although the neighbors volunteer to help you get the eyesore fixed up, you figure it will cost $3,500 to get it in good shape.

You bid successfully for the house. You borrow $45,000 from the bank in the form of a note for ninety days. Because interest rates are around 15 to 18 percent, you may need a partner to cosign (if your credit is not strong enough to get a $45,000 loan).

Once HUD is paid its $40,000 cash, you own the property free and clear. You owe the bank $45,000, but your note or IOU is unsecured, or at least not secured by the property you have just purchased from HUD. With closing costs of $1,000 you have now spent $41,000 of the $45,000 you borrowed.

With the $4,000 remaining you get the property fixed up and, as expected, it is appraised for $70,000. Using the investor formula typical for most conventional lenders, you estimate that the amount of money you can borrow on a permanent loan is $59,500. (Investors are not allowed to use an FHA loan to refinance a property and pull out cash in excess of what is owed against it. Therefore, conventional lenders are the best source for refinance loans.) Here's a summary of the refinance results.

Borrow from bank	$45,000
All-cash price for HUD Repo	40,000
Closing costs	1,000
Fix-up costs for property	3,500
Appraised value after fix-up	70,000
Maximum investor loan	$59,500

The loan is 85 percent of the appraised value.

You now proceed to pay yourself back. Your results might look like this.

Refinanced loan proceeds		$59,500
less Principal amount owed to bank	45,000	
Interest due bank	2,025	
Closing costs for refinancing	1,650	
Points paid for refinancing	2,050	50,725
Cash paid back to you		$8,775

That's not too bad, is it? What about the monthly payments? We discussed several ways to handle negative payments in the last chapter.

If you choose to live in or rent the property, try one of these methods. Otherwise, you may want to use the method of Ms. Lui in Washington, D.C., and sell the property for no money down to professional people wanting a nice home.

KEEP THESE POINTS IN MIND

1. HUD-acquired properties offer excellent opportunities for home buyers and investors. Thousands are available.
2. There are three basic methods for buying HUD-acquired properties.
   a) Use an FHA loan to finance the property. (Good up to five units.)
   b) Use a HUD purchase money mortgage to finance the property.
   c) Pay all cash for the property.
3. The best buys for investors are all-cash properties.
4. Buy all-cash properties at significant discounts using a ninety-day loan from a bank. Have an investor cosign the loan if necessary.
5. Use Wayne's fix-up tips to increase the value of the property and the appraisal amount.
6. Buy the worst properties in the best areas.
7. Move up to multi-unit HUD offerings to make really big bucks.

SPECIAL RESOURCE: U.S. DEPARTMENT OF HOUSING AND URBAN DEVELOPMENT REGIONAL OFFICES

Region I (Boston)

Boston Regional Office
Room 800, John F. Kennedy Federal Building
Boston, Massachusetts 02203-0801
and
Bulfinch Building, 15 New Chardon Street
Boston, Massachusetts 02114-2598

Field Offices

Hartford Office
One Hartford Square West
Hartford, Connecticut 06104-2943

Manchester Office
Norris Cotton Federal Building
275 Chestnut Street
Manchester, New Hampshire 03101-2487

Bangor Office
U.S. Federal and Post Office Building
202 Harlow Street
Bangor, Maine 04401-1357

Burlington Office
110 Main Street
Fairchild Square
Burlington, Vermont 05402-0989

Providence Office
330 John O. Pastore
  Federal Building
  and U.S. Post
  Office—
  Kennedy Plaza
Providence, Rhode Island
02903-1745

Region II (New York)

New York Regional Office
26 Federal Plaza
New York, New York
10278-0068

Field Offices

Albany Office
Leo W. O'Brien Federal
  Building
North Pearl Street and
  Clinton Avenue
Albany, New York
12207-2395

Buffalo Office
Mezzanine, Statler
  Building
107 Delaware Avenue
Buffalo, New York
14202-2986

Camden Office
The Parkade Building
519 Federal Street
Camden, New Jersey
08103-9998

Caribbean Office
Federico Degetau Federal
  Building

U.S. Courthouse, Room
  428
Carlos E. Chardon
  Avenue
Hato Rey, Puerto Rico
00918-2276

Newark Office
Military Park Building
60 Park Place
Newark, New Jersey
07102-5504

**Region III
(Philadelphia)**

Philadelphia Regional Office
Curtis Building, 6th and
  Walnut Streets
Philadelphia,
  Pennsylvania 19106-
  3392

Field Offices

Wilmington Office
IBM Building
800 Delaware Avenue
Room 511
Wilmington, Delaware
19801-1387

Baltimore Office
The Equitable Building
3rd Floor, 10 North
  Calvert Street
Baltimore, Maryland
21202-1865

Charleston Office
Kanawha Valley Building
Capitol and Lee Streets
Charleston, West Virginia
25301-1794

Pittsburgh Office
Fort Pitt Commons
445 Fort Pitt Boulevard
Pittsburgh, Pennsylvania
15219-1361

Richmond Office
701 East Franklin Street
Richmond, Virginia
23219-2591

**Washington, D.C.
Office**
Universal North Building
1875 Connecticut
  Avenue, NW
Washington, D.C. 20009-
  5768

Region IV (Atlanta)

Atlanta Regional Office
Richard B. Russell
  Federal Building
75 Spring Street, SW
Atlanta, Georgia 30303-
  3388

Field Offices

Birmingham Office
Daniel Building
15 South 20th Street
Birmingham, Alabama
35233-2096

Columbia Office
Strom Thurmond Federal
  Building
835-45 Assembly Street
Columbia, South
  Carolina 29201-2480

Coral Gables Office
3001 Ponce de Leon
    Boulevard
Coral Gables, Florida
33146-2911

Greensboro Office
415 North Edgeworth
    Street
Greensboro, North
    Carolina 27401-2107

Jackson Office
Federal Building, Suite
    1016
100 West Capital Street
Jackson, Mississippi
39269-1016

Jacksonville Office
325 West Adams Street
Jacksonville, Florida
32202-4303

Knoxville Office
One Northshore Building
1111 Northshore Drive
Knoxville, Tennessee
37919-4090

Louisville Office
539 Fourth Avenue
Post Office Box 1044
Louisville, Kentucky
40201-1044

Memphis Office
100 North Main Street
28th Floor
Memphis, Tennessee
38103-5080

Nashville Office
1 Commerce Place, Suite
    1600
Nashville, Tennessee
37239-1600

Orlando Office
Federal Office Building
80 North Hughey
Orlando, Florida 32801-
    2226

Tampa Office
700 Twiggs Street
Post Office Box 2097
Tampa, Florida 33601-
    4017

Region V (Chicago)

Chicago Regional Office
300 South Wacker Drive
Chicago, Illinois 60606-
    6765
and
547 West Jackson Blvd.
Chicago, Illinois 60606-
    5760

Field Offices

Springfield Office
524 South Second Street
Room 600
Springfield, Illinois
62701-1774

Cincinnati Office
Federal Office Building
Room 9002
550 Main Street
Cincinnati, Ohio 45202-
    3253

Cleveland Office
777 Rockwell Avenue
2nd Floor
Cleveland, Ohio 44114-
    1670

Columbus Office
200 North High Street
Columbus, Ohio 43215-
    2499

Detroit Office
Patrick V. McNamara
    Federal Building
477 Michigan Avenue
Detroit, Michigan 48226-
    2592

Flint Office
Genesee Bank Building
352 South Saginaw
    Street, Room 200
Flint, Michigan 48502-
    1953

Grand Rapids Office
2922 Fuller Avenue, NE
Grand Rapids, Michigan
49505-3409

Indianapolis Office
151 North Delaware
    Street
Indianapolis, Indiana
46204-2526

Milwaukee Office
Henry S. Reuss Federal
    Plaza
310 West Wisconsin
    Avenue
Suite 1380

Milwaukee, Wisconsin
53203-2289-2290

Minneapolis-St. Paul Office
220 Second Street, South
Minneapolis, Minnesota
55401-2195

Region VI (Fort Worth)

Fort Worth Regional Office
221 W. Lancaster
Post Office Box 2905
Fort Worth, Texas 76113-2905

Field Offices

Albuquerque Office
625 Truman Street, NE
Albuquerque, New
    Mexico 87110-6443

Dallas Office
1403 Slocum Street
Post Office Box 10050
Dallas, Texas 75207-5007

Houston Office
2 Greenway Plaza East
Suite 200
Houston, Texas 77046-0294

Little Rock Office
Savers Building
320 West Capitol
Suite 700
Little Rock, Arkansas
72201-3523

Lubbock Office
Federal Office Building

1205 Texas Avenue
Lubbock, Texas 79401-4001

New Orleans Office
1661 Canal Street
New Orleans, Louisiana
70112-2887

Oklahoma City Office
Murrah Federal Building
200 N.W. 5th Street
Oklahoma City,
    Oklahoma 73102-3202

San Antonio Office
Washington Square
800 Dolorosa
Post Office Box 9163
San Antonio, Texas
78285-3301

Shreveport Office
New Federal Building
500 Fannin Street
Shreveport, Louisiana
71101-3077

Tulsa Office
Robert S. Kerr Building
440 South Houston
    Avenue, Room 200
Tulsa, Oklahoma 74127-8923

**Region VII
(Kansas City)**

Kansas City Regional Office
Professional Building
1103 Grand Avenue
Kansas City, Missouri
64106-2496

Field Offices

Topeka Office
444 S.E. Quincy Street
Room 297
Topeka, Kansas 6668-3588

Des Moines Office
Federal Building
210 Walnut Street
Room 259
Des Moines, Iowa
50309-2155

Omaha Office
Braiker/Brandeis Building
210 South 16th Street
Omaha, Nebraska 68102-1622

St. Louis Office
210 North Tucker
    Boulevard
St. Louis, Missouri
63101-1997

Region VIII (Denver)

Denver Regional Office
Executive Tower Building
1405 Curtis Street
Denver, Colorado 80202-2349

Field Offices

Casper Office
4225 Federal Office
    Building
P.O. Box 580
100 East B Street
Casper, Wyoming 82602-1918

Fargo Office
Federal Building
P.O. Box 2483
653 2nd Avenue North
Fargo, North Dakota
58102-4701

Sioux Falls Office
119 Federal Building
U.S. Courthouse
400 South Phillips
Avenue
Sioux Falls, South
Dakota 57102-0983

Helena Office
Federal Office Building
Drawer 10095
301 S. Park, Room 340
Helena, Montana 59626-0095

Salt Lake City Office
125 South State Street
Salt Lake City, Utah
84138-1102

**Region IX
(San Francisco)**

**San Francisco Regional
Office**
Phillip Burton Federal
Building and U.S.
Courthouse
450 Golden Gate Avenue
Post Office Box 36003
San Francisco, California
94102-3448

Field Offices

**Indian Programs Office,
Region IX**
Arizona Bank Building

101 North First Avenue
Suite 1800
Post Office Box 13468
Phoenix, Arizona 85002-3468

Fresno Office
1315 Van Ness Street
Suite 200
Fresno, California 93721-1775

Honolulu Office
300 Ala Moana
Boulevard
P.O. Box 50007
Honolulu, Hawaii 96850-4991

Las Vegas Office
720 S. 7th Street
Suite 221
Las Vegas, Nevada
89101-6930

Los Angeles Office
2500 Wilshire Boulevard
Los Angeles, California
90057-4361

Phoenix Office
Arizona Bank Building
101 North First Avenue
Suite 1800
Post Office Box 13468
Phoenix, Arizona 85002-3468

Reno Office
1050 Bible Way
Post Office Box 4700
Reno, Nevada 89505-4700

Sacramento Office
545 Downtown Plaza
Suite 250
Post Office Box 1978
Sacramento, California
95809-1978

San Diego Office
Federal Office Building
880 Front Street
San Diego, California
92188-0100

Santa Ana Office
34 Civic Center Plaza
Box 12850
Santa Ana, California
92712-2850

Tucson Office
Arizona Bank Building
33 North Stone Avenue
Suite 1450
Tucson, Arizona 85701-1467

Region X (Seattle)

Seattle Regional Office
Arcade Plaza Building
1321 Second Avenue
Seattle, Washington
98101-2054

Field Offices

Anchorage Office
701 "C" Street, Box 64
Anchorage, Alaska
99513-0001

Boise Office
Federal Building—U.S.
   Courthouse
P.O. Box 042
550 West Fort Street
Boise, Idaho
83724-0420

Portland Office
520 Southwest Sixth
   Avenue
Portland, Oregon 97204-
   1596

Spokane Office
West 920 Riverside
   Avenue
Spokane, Washington
99201-1075

CHAPTER

MORE REAL ESTATE AT SUPER BARGAIN PRICES: Smaller Government Programs

THE SECRET OF SUCCESS IN LIFE IS FOR A MAN TO BE
READY FOR HIS OPPORTUNITY WHEN IT COMES.

Benjamin Disraeli

Ready for some more? So far, we have concentrated on the big government programs you can use to get special buys on real estate. There are also some exciting smaller programs that offer even bigger profit potential. You should know about these as well and learn how to use them to your benefit.

A $100 INVESTMENT TURNS INTO $10,000

The General Services Administration (GSA) is a little-known and less-used area of the federal government that offers some great deals too good to pass up. Under the U.S. Surplus Property Sales Program, various items are sold directly from the GSA. Typically, the GSA is known for its bargain prices on Jeeps, trucks, office supplies, and military surplus. However, sometimes surplus government real estate can be purchased from the GSA at super bargains.

As with the HUD-acquired properties, General Services Administration properties require sealed bids from prospective buyers. What do you do? When I see an interesting property, I submit a ridiculous bid for one tenth of the bid price, then wait to see what happens. Sometimes no one bids on the property, and I end up with a super bargain.

Most of the time I'm outbid. But I did acquire a former garbage dump. And I bought a few strips of land for peanuts. I even bought some land-locked land once for pennies on the dollar.

What is land-locked land? It's land that you can't get to without going across someone else's land. I picked this land up for $100, and then tried to figure out how to make a few bucks. I bought the lots next to this property, and then sold them as a package deal. In the end I made about $10,000 profit. Not bad.

All Kinds of Property for Sale

In North Dakota, a father and son bought a deserted Air Force base through the GSA, paying $100,000 for it. Using low interest government rehabilitation money, they turned the base into housing for the elderly. Eighteen months later they sold the project for $3 million cash. That's the way to put the government to work for you. There's one other benefit. GSA properties are all over. Each time I place my ridiculous bids on these properties, I'm sent a list of all the bidders and informed who the successful bidder was. Over the years I've developed good business relations with some of these other bidders and even done a few projects with them.

Who Can Bid on GSA Properties?

Let's discuss who *cannot* bid on these properties. You can't bid if you are under eighteen years of age. You also can't bid if you are an employee of an agency of the federal government, either as a civilian or as a member of the Armed Forces of the United States. Agents and immediate family members of the households of government employees are also barred from bidding. Anyone else is allowed to bid and purchase as much property as they can afford.

Methods for Bidding on GSA Properties

- Sealed Bids
- Public Auction
- Brokers
- Negotiation

1. **Sealed Bids**

   When surplus property is to be offered for sealed bids, an "Invitation to Bid" form containing terms and conditions of sale, description of the property, and complete instructions for bidding is mailed to prospective buyers.

   Bids are submitted, along with the required deposit and in line with the terms and conditions of the "Invitation" to the appropriate GSA regional office.

   Bids are opened and read publicly on a specified bid-closing date. If the highest bid is acceptable, an award is made, usually within 60 days, and the successful bidder is notified. Deposits are returned promptly to all unsuccessful bidders when they are notified of the rejection of their bids.

2. **Public Auction**

   The sale of surplus property also is conducted by qualified auctioneers. The highest bidder must execute an earnest money deposit in a fixed amount predetermined and publicly announced.

3. **Brokers**

   Services of realty brokers are secured by contract to supplement other GSA sales efforts. Their services are used principally in the sale of complex industrial properties and other special-purpose properties which require the organizational capabilities, diversified clientele, professional affiliations, and other services of real estate brokers. Brokers are selected and registered with the GSA.

4. **Negotiation**

   Surplus real property sales for private use may be negotiated under the following conditions:

   (A) When the estimated fair market value of the property does not exceed $1,000.00;

   (B) Where, after advertising, bid prices (either as to all or some part of the property) are not reasonable or have not been independently arrived at in open competition;

   (C) Where the condition of the property or unusual circumstances make it impractical to advertise publicly for competitive bids and the fair market value of the property and other satisfactory terms of the sale negotiated.

I like the negotiated sale method best, because you can sit down with the government bureaucrats and try to work out a good deal in person. With all of the methods you must include a 20 percent deposit with your bid in the form of a certified check. If your bid is not successful, the check is returned uncashed. If the bid is accepted, the deposit is applied toward the purchase price. If you are interested in GSA properties you should contact the GSA office in your area and request a free brochure. We've listed a few GSA addresses throughout the United States.

SPECIAL RESOURCE:

GSA Personal Property Disposal Divisions

Region	States Covered	Address
1	CT, ME, MA, NH, RI, VT	John McCormick Post Office & Court House Boston, MA 02109
2	NJ, NY, Puerto Rico, Virgin Islands	2600 Federal Plaza New York, NY 10278
3	DE, MD, PA, VA, WV	9th & Market Street Philadelphia, PA 19107
4	AL, FL, KY, GA, MS, NC, SC, TN	175 Spring Street, SW Atlanta, GA 30303
5	IL, IN, MI, OH, WI, MN	230 S. Dearborne Street Chicago, IL 60604
6	IA, KS, MO, NE	1500 E. Bannister Rd. Kansas City, MO 64131
7	AR, LA, NM, OK, TX	819 Taylor Street Fort Worth, TX 76102
8	CO, MT, ND, SD, UT, WY	Denver Federal Center Building 41 Denver, CO 80225
9	AZ, CA, NV, HI, Guam, American Samoa	525 Market Street San Francisco, CA 94105
10	AK, ID, OR, WA	GSA Center Auburn, WA 98002
11	U.S. Capital Region	7th & D Streets, SW Washington, D.C. 20407

State Surplus Agencies Also Have Property

Every state has programs that enable people to buy surplus government property. How does the state get these properties, especially real estate? They usually get property through foreclosures. Occasionally states will provide low interest loans to home buyers and investors wishing to buy and rehabilitate local real estate.

But if a citizen uses this below-market interest rate loan program to buy a home and then for some reason or other stops making payments on the loan, the property goes through foreclosure. The state repossesses the property and turns it over to their state surplus property agency. The name, address, and phone number of every state surplus agency in America is listed for you on pages 82-85. In addition to real estate, you can buy airports, trucks, cars, boats, and much more from these agencies.

Be sure to look at states other than your own. You never know where an opportunity may arise. I used this program to buy some land in another state for ten bucks. A year later another government agency bought it back from me for $1,500. So use this information. If you can't buy the property, perhaps a relative in another state can benefit. The property is there for the taking.

If you need additional information about acquiring personal or real property from state surplus agencies, contact the director of the Personal Property Disposal Division of the GSA office nearest you.

Making Money with State-Owned Properties

Every year state governments practically give away millions of dollars worth of properties. Not too long ago, a student of mine sent me an offering from the state of California for the sale or lease with option to purchase of the Richard M. Nixon school site. It is quite common for states to request bids to lease or buy properties. Included in the offering were the bid date and information about the property.

Now, I want to make something perfectly clear at this time. *Don't buy these properties at auctions.* People who go to auctions end up paying cash for the properties. They may get them for 50 cents on the dollar, but many times they overpay. Although cash worked great with the HUD repos, there's a better way to buy state-owned properties.

I like to submit proposals to buy these state-owned properties. There is usually no competition for properties like the Nixon schoolhouse, so the bid will close with no offers. The best thing to do is to wait for the bid deadline to pass and then contact the school district or whoever is in charge of the bidding to see if any bids were accepted. If there were none, submit your proposal. In the proposal, let them know you would really like to buy the property but would need an option for about twelve months to "get your ducks in line," secure financing, and see whether the project is economically feasible.

What do I mean by this? We'll use this school site to explain. Let's say the school district is asking $1.8 million for the place. The bid date comes and goes. Probably because the district is asking too much for the school, no one bids. At this point, I would submit a proposal that states that I am interested in acquiring the school for $1.8 million, subject to the project being economically feasible. By telling them this you are letting them know that you'll pay their price, but you have to make sure that the project will pay for itself.

In the next paragraph of my proposal, I would add that I am planning to rehabilitate the school site. In the interest of the community, the school will be converted into housing for the elderly (or whatever its current need is). I like doing housing projects for the elderly, because the average age in the United States is increasing and the demand for their housing is soaring.

At this point I send my letter of interest (not a bid) to see if they are interested in the kind of project I have in mind. Then I visit the proper officials to let them know that I want to buy the school, get it back on the tax rolls, and provide jobs for the community. I make it a point to tell them I'll need their help while I do a feasibility study. This way I can tie the property up with an option and have time to do my study.

The key is finding out what the specific agency wants for its community and giving it to them. It doesn't have to be a million-dollar project, although big projects make you more money. In 1983, a gentleman bought an old school in California, paying $300,000. He put $50,000 down, and the school district gave him a $250,000 purchase money mortgage. But do you know what? He didn't have to make payments on the mortgage for five years!

What was the school worth? The real estate broker who sold the property appraised it for $3 million. This guy paid $300,000 for a school and got something worth $3 million. Just think what that school would be worth if it were rehabilitated as a home for the elderly, a small shopping center, or a technical school. The man could also just as easily sell the deal to a developer without making improvements and pick up a few million. That's the way to make money.

Thousands of Schools Available Nationwide

There are thousands of schools being closed across the nation, and they're not all expensive deals. I know of a grade school in a small northern Arizona town that was purchased for $15,000. Its end use? Since it lies at the base of a popular but secluded ski slope, the buyer plans to turn it into a dormitory for overnight skiers. Not only will he put the building back on the tax rolls, but he will provide extra revenue for the community since the skiers have up till now had to stay thirty miles away in a larger city. Below is a list of state surplus property agencies across the nation.

STATE SURPLUS PROPERTY AGENCIES

ALABAMA: Alabama State Agency for Surplus Property Assistance, P.O. Box 210487, Montgomery, Alabama 36121-0487.

ALASKA: Alaska Surplus Property Service, 2400 Viking Drive, Anchorage, Alaska 99501.

ARIZONA: Arizona Department of Administration Surplus Property Division, 312 South 15th Avenue, Phoenix, Arizona 85007.

ARKANSAS: The Arkansas State Agency for Surplus Property, 8700 Remont Road, North Little Rock, Arkansas 72118.

CALIFORNIA: State Agency for Surplus Property, Department of Education, 721 Capitol Mall, Sacramento, California 95814.

COLORADO: The Colorado Surplus Property Agency, 4700 Leetsdale Drive, Denver, Colorado 80222.

CONNECTICUT: Connecticut State Agency for Federal Surplus Property, P.O. Box 298, Wethersfield, Connecticut 06109.

DELAWARE: The Delaware Division of Purchasing, P.O. Box 299, Delaware City, Delaware 19706.

DISTRICT OF COLUMBIA: The General Services Administration, Bureau of Material Management Surplus Acquisition Section, 5 D.C. Village Lane, Southwest, Washington, D.C. 20032.

FLORIDA: Florida Division of Surplus Property, Department of General Services, Larson Building, Tallahassee, Florida 32301.

GEORGIA: Georgia State Agency for Surplus Property, 1050 Murphy Avenue, S.W., Building 1A, Savannah, Georgia 30310.

GUAM: Guam Agency for Surplus Property, The Department of Administration, P.O. Box 884, Agana, Guam 96910.

HAWAII: The Hawaii Department of Accounting and General Services, Surplus Property Branch, 729 Kakoi Street, Honolulu, Hawaii 96819.

IDAHO: Idaho Bureau of Surplus Property, P.O. Box 7414, Boise, Idaho 83707.

ILLINOIS: Illinois Federal Surplus Property Section, Department of Administrative Services, Industrial Park, P.O. Box 1236, Springfield, Illinois 62705.

INDIANA: Indiana State Agency for Federal Surplus Property, 601 Kentucky Avenue, Indianapolis, Indiana 46225.

IOWA: Iowa Surplus Property Section, Department of General Services, The Hoover State Office Building, Level A, Des Moines, Iowa 50319.

KANSAS: Kansas Department of Administration Surplus Property Section, R.R. 4, Box 36A, Topeka, Kansas 66603.

KENTUCKY: Kentucky Department of Educational Division of Surplus Properties, 514 Barrett Avenue, Frankfort, Kentucky 40601.

LOUISIANA: Louisiana Surplus Property Agency, Box 44351 Capitol Station, Baton Rouge, Louisianna 70804.

MAINE: The State Agency of Surplus Property, Division of Community Services, State House Station 95, Augusta, Maine 04333.

MARYLAND: State Agency for Surplus Property, P.O. Box M, College Park, Maryland 20740.

MASSACHUSETTS: Massachusetts State Agency for Surplus Property, 1 Ashburton Avenue, Room 1010, Boston, Massachusetts 02108.

MICHIGAN: Department of Management and Budget, Office of Federal Property Assistance, 3369 North Logan Street, P.O. Box 30026, Lansing, Michigan 48909.

MINNESOTA: Department of Administration Material Management Division, Federal Surplus Property Section, 5420 Highway 8, New Brighton, Minnesota 55112.

MISSISSIPPI: The Mississippi Bureau of Surplus Property Commission, P.O. Box 5778, Jackson, Mississippi 39208.

MISSOURI: State Agency for Surplus Property, 117 North Riverside Drive, P. O. Drawer 1310, Jefferson City, Missouri 65101.

MONTANA: Department of Administration Surplus Property Bureau, Capitol Station, Helena, Montana 59620.

NEBRASKA: Federal Property Assistance Section, Department of Correctional Services, 3321 North 35th Street, Lincoln, Nebraska 68504.

NEVADA: Surplus Property Division, Nevada State Purchasing Bureau, 209 E. Musser, Room 104, Carson City, Nevada 89701.

NEW HAMPSHIRE: New Hampshire Surplus Distribution Section at 12 Hills Avenue, Concord, New Hampshire 03301.

NEW JERSEY: State Agency for Surplus Property, Division of State Police, P.O. Box 7068, West Trenton, New Jersey 08625.

NEW MEXICO: State Agency for Surplus Property, P.O. Box 4757, Coronado Station, Santa Fe, New Mexico 87502.

NEW YORK: The Bureau of Federal Property Assistance, Building 18, Campus Site, Albany, New York 12226.

NORTH CAROLINA: Federal Property Agency, P.O. Box 26567, Raleigh, North Carolina, 27611.

NORTH DAKOTA: Division of Surplus Property, 1812 Lee Avenue, Bismarck, North Dakota 58507.

OHIO: Ohio State Agency for Surplus Property Utilization, 226 N. Fifth Street, Columbus, Ohio 43215.

OKLAHOMA: Oklahoma State Agency for Surplus Property, P.O. Box 11355, Oklahoma City, Oklahoma 73111.

OREGON: Oregon Department of General Services, Federal Surplus Property Section, 1655 Salem Industrial Drive, N.E. Salem, Oregon 97310.

PENNSYLVANIA: Pennsylvania Bureau of Surplus Property, 2221 Forestor Street, P.O. Box 1365, Harrisburg, Pennsylvania 17105.

PUERTO RICO: State Agency for Surplus Property, General Services Administration, Purchase Services and Real Estate Property Supply Area, GPO Box 4112, San Juan, Puerto Rico 00905.

RHODE ISLAND: State Agency for Surplus Property, Division of Purchases, State Warehouse, 301 Promenade Street, Cranston, Rhode Island 02908.

SOUTH CAROLINA: Surplus Property Procurement Division of General Services, Boston Avenue, West Columbia, South Carolina 29169.

SOUTH DAKOTA: Federal Property Agency, 20 Colorado Avenue, Southwest, Huron, South Dakota 57350.

TENNESSEE: Tennessee Department of General Services, The Federal Property Utilization Division, 6500 Sentinel Boulevard, Nashville, Tennessee 37209.

TEXAS: Surplus Property Agency, 2103 Ackerman Road, P.O. Box 8120, San Antonio, Texas 78208.

UTAH: Utah State Agency for Surplus Property, 522 S. 700 West Street, Salt Lake City, Utah 84104.

VERMONT: Central Surplus Property Agency, 87½ Barre Street, Montpelier, Vermont 05602.

VIRGIN ISLANDS: State Agency for Surplus Property, Department of Property and Procurement, Division of Property, P.O. Box 1437, St. Thomas, Virgin Islands 00801.

VIRGINIA: Federal Property Agency, Department of Purchases and Supply, 1910 Daroypown, P.O. Box 1199, Richmond, Virginia 23209.

WASHINGTON: Washington Surplus Property Section, 6858 South 190 Street, Kent, Washington 98031.

WEST VIRGINIA: State Agency for Surplus Property, 2700 Charles Avenue, Dunbar, West Virginia 25064.

WISCONSIN: Federal Property Program, 201 South Dickinson Street, P.O. Box 1585, Madison, Wisconsin 53701.

WYOMING: Federal Surplus Property Agency, 2045 Westland Road, Cheyenne, Wyoming 82002.

What About Vacant Land?

Every state has land it acquired for new freeways, roads, or housing developments, but the projects never went through. Instead of holding onto the land, the state will often sell it to individuals willing to put it to good use. This is a great program for developers. If you are not in that position, try to get an option to purchase the land and then sell the option for big bucks to a developer.

LOCAL PROGRAMS

Now let's talk about some of the local programs available. If you want to make a lot of money, I would start at the local level. The easiest way to acquire property is to use the federal VA foreclosures program. But if you are on a tight budget and tired of throwing your rent money down the drain, you may want to contact your local development commission (also known as the urban renewal division or Department of Community Development) and ask about the urban homestead program.

Urban Homestead Program

Most cities have what is called an urban homestead program. This lists properties that have been foreclosed on or abandoned and turned over to city agencies. They sell for as low as $1.00 to qualified residents. Many times these houses are offered through a lottery drawing, so that all purchasers are treated equally. Sometimes the cities have so many houses in their inventories that they sell the houses directly without the use of a lottery. Your best bet is to check with the redevelopment agency in your city to find out their policy.

Some people buy these homes to live in. Others use a rental rehabilitation production program to get government loans at 5 percent to repair these houses and then use them for rentals or resale. Believe me, this program works. I've made a lot of money using 3, 5, 7, and 8 percent government money to fix up a property for rental that I bought for next to nothing. (See chapter 9 for details.)

How do you find these agencies in your city? You can look in the city government section of the white pages for your town or consult my "housing directory" (available by writing to me at the address shown on the jacket of this book), where I have listed all of these agencies nationwide for you (there are close to 4,000 of them). Once you find out where it is located, visit the office personally and inquire about the program by which you can pick up a property from the government for $1.00. (This is a federal program administered through a local community development housing agency.)

Vacant House Program

In addition to the urban homestead program, local cities may also have properties offered through a vacant house program. Almost every city has a vacant house program. Basically, these are properties your city has taken back through tax sales. Tax sales are simply government foreclosures for the non-payment of property taxes.

Here is a hot tip to help you get these properties. What I like to do is to go to my local city tax assessment bureau to see who owns properties. (This is usually in the same building as the community development agency.) As you look through the properties, every once in a while you'll see some with "MCC" after the name of the owner. What does "MCC" mean? It means that the property is city owned. MCC stands for *Mayor and City Council* in many cities. Any time you see a property with MCC or something equivalent next to it, it means your mayor or city council owns that property. Check to see how your city lists these properties and then see how many city-owned houses you can find.

Once you find a few properties that the city owns, drive by and check them out. Then go back to the redevelopment division of your local development commission. Let them know that the city owns a certain house and that you would like to buy the house to get it back on the tax rolls. Offer them only a fraction of its value. This way you beat the city to the punch, before the house goes to the tax sale auction and you have to bid against hundreds of others for this and other houses.

Suppose you find an old burned-out house that's owned by the city and not bringing a dime in to the government. Go to the local redevelopment agency and tell them you would like to buy the property for anywhere from a dollar to $10,000—just as long as it is a fraction of the value. You may be able to pick up a property worth $50,000 for $1,000. Even though the building is in terrible shape, the land may be worth thousands.

Tell the commission you plan to rehabilitate the property and put it back on the tax rolls. After all, the government doesn't make a dime on vacant property while they own it. Often city officials don't even know how many properties they own. You are doing them a big favor by removing this burden from their books. What's nice is that most development commissions realize this and are willing to help you.

Remember, I'm definitely profit-motivated and you should be too, as long as you are helping people. I'm telling you that this program will make you big bucks if you follow it through. By buying these properties cheap you can make money regardless of their condition. Sometimes the government will also guarantee the rents for tenants for up to fifteen years, eliminating a lot of management hassle. (See chapter 11 on rental guarantees.)

By now you may be thinking that these properties are located only in the rough areas of towns or the ghettos. This is not the case at all. The chances are good that there is a property in pretty bad condition in a good area within fifteen minutes of where you live right now. It can be purchased through this government program.

I buy problem properties in good areas of town. This is a secret of my success. What do I mean? Well, in many cities houses are available in middle-income areas for $30,000 to $70,000. People will pay $400 to $600 a month rent for these houses. I would try to buy a HUD-acquired property, VA repo, city-owned vacant house, or maybe even a tax sale property that is in bad shape—but in a good neighborhood.

If it is a city-owned property, I'd try to negotiate with the city to buy it for a few thousand dollars. Then I would obtain a low interest rate loan to rehabilitate the property. With the money I could then either hire someone to fix the place up or I could make what I call my "spread." This means that I become a contractor, borrow $40,000 to $50,000 at 5 percent interest, get the work done for $30,000, and pocket the difference. Remember, buy the worst properties in the best neighborhoods and you will do all right.

THE HOUSING RECYCLE PROGRAM

This is another program that provides for the purchase, rehabilitation, and resale to moderate-income people of vacant, substandard, or abandoned housing. Although it is very similar to the vacant house program, a housing recycle program requires a 5 percent down payment. Of course, 5 percent of $100.00 is $5.00, so don't worry about that too much. These homes are rehabilitated by you with the use of a second mortgage. The amount of the loan will vary according to the amount of work needed. The interest rate on the loan is usually 5 to 7 percent.

Every major city will have a housing program similar to the ones I have described. The specific terms and requirements may be different, but all in all the opportunities are there. Investors and homeowners can both take part in these programs. You do not have to be a first-time homeowner in all cases; this is an investor program as well.

KEEP THESE POINTS IN MIND
1. Many times surplus government real estate can be bought through the General Services Administration (GSA) at bargain prices.
2. Most GSA properties are sold using sealed bids.
3. Don't buy state-owned surplus property only at auctions. Wait for the bid deadline to pass and submit a purchase proposal to the selling agency.
4. Vacant homes can be purchased from the city for a fraction of their value.
5. Buy the worst properties in the best neighborhoods.

6

TRADITIONAL LOANS FOR TRADITIONAL HOMES

COME THEE FROM AMONGST THEM AND BE SEPARATE.

II Corinthians 6:17

There are a multitude of loans available for the purchase and rehabilitation of your home and of properties that include four units or fewer. HUD and the Farmers Home Administration (FmHA) are the major federal agencies associated with these programs. Let's take a look at some of the programs available for homeowners.

Under Section 203 of the National Housing Act of 1934, HUD operates a number of single-family home programs. There are many other loan programs involved in the Act, but some of the most important are the different loans available under Section 203, which we discuss here.

NEED TO BUY A HOME: TRY A 203B

The other day during a luncheon I asked a loan officer what kind of loans his company made. "Mainly FHA loans," he replied. When I asked him, "Which FHA loans?" he asked, "Is there more than one?"

The basic FHA 203b is the loan most people are referring to when they are getting "an FHA loan" on their property. This loan program for one- to four-unit housing is authorized by Section 203b of the National Housing Act. This is the program that was primarily responsible for making this a nation of homeowners.

In recent years, however, its use has fallen off sharply for a variety of reasons. Terms on conventional loans have been liberalized, making them comparable with FHA financing in regard to loan period and loan-to-value ratio. Additional requirements have been loaded onto government-backed financing, adding to processing time and paperwork—the familiar government red tape. Finally, FHA mortgage limits lagged behind the increase in housing costs, putting a large share of the housing market out of the FHA price range.

This last problem was alleviated with a large increase in loan limits in 1977 and another smaller increase in 1979. In 1980, certain parts of the country were allowed to set even higher loan limits. Today the maximum loan amounts vary around the country. The range is as follows:

1 unit	$67,500–$90,000
2 units	$76,000–$101,300
3 units	$92,000–$122,650
4 units	$107,000–$142,650

Under Section 203b, the FHA can insure mortgages for new or existing one- to four-unit properties. To obtain the most favorable terms on new construction, you must submit an application to the FHA before the project starts, since this is the only way the FHA can be sure that the construction meets its standards. Loans on existing properties are also subject to FHA approval, meaning that they must pass an inspection by an FHA appraiser.

There are no geographical restrictions on the 203b program. Loans are available in any community where the housing standards meet the requirements of the FHA. Though the 203b is primarily a home-purchase program, it can be used for rental properties of up to four units. If none of the units is to be occupied by the owner, the maximum loan-to-value ratio is reduced.

LOANS FOR DISASTER VICTIMS: FHA 203H

The next time you read about an area of the country that has been declared a disaster, you will know that the homeowners will be eligible for low interest purchase loans, sometimes at as low as 1 percent. These thirty- to thirty-five-year loans can be equal to 100 percent of the appraised value of a property, plus all closing costs related to the loan. The result is no down payment for the home buyer.

The purpose of this type of mortgage is to help those persons struck by major disasters in their community to finance home purchases.

LIVE OUTSIDE THE CITY? FHA 203I MIGHT HELP

The Section 203i program makes loans to single-family home purchasers in outlying areas, where it is not practical to impose some of the requirements applied to FHA-financed properties in cities. For example, the FHA may insure loans under Section 203i for properties that lack a water or waste-disposal system that meets the standards required under Section 203b. Section 203i may also be used to finance the mortgage on a farm home located on two and a half acres or more, as long as it is adjacent to a maintained highway.

This program fell into disuse in 1969, because the mortgage limits were set at $16,200. This changed in 1977, when the limit was raised to 75 percent of the Section 203b ceiling. Since the latter has been increased to $67,500 for a single-family home, a person wanting a Section 203i loan could be eligible for a loan of $50,625. Moreover, the limit will rise automatically in the future as the 203b ceiling is increased.

Vacation Home Loans: FHA 203m

This program is designed to finance the purchase of vacation or seasonal homes that are not necessarily occupied year-round. The maximum loan is 75 percent of the appraised value of the property or $18,000, whichever is less. The Secretary of HUD is authorized to suspend this program if it is determined that:

1. There is a shortage of funds.
2. The continued use of the program will adversely affect the financing of residential construction.
3. A cut-off of vacation mortgage funds will not hurt the balanced economic development of the area.

Urban Renewal Home Purchase Loans: FHA 221(d)2

The FHA Section 221(d)2 loan is available at rates sometimes as low as 7 to 9 percent for low- and moderate-income families, especially those displaced by urban renewal. The mortgage limits are much lower than under the 203b loan program, but there are concessions that make it easier for low-income families to make the initial cash down payment. The mortgage limits are:

1 unit	$31,000 ($36,000 for a family of five or more)
2 units	$35,000
3 units	$48,600
4 units	$59,400

Two- to four-unit properties are eligible only if one of the units will be occupied by the owner.

For a buyer who does not qualify as a displaced person, the minimum down payment on a single-family home is 3 percent of the acquisition cost. Settlement costs, initial payments for taxes and insurance, and other prepaid items may be included in this 3 percent, but the remaining mortgage amount cannot exceed 100 percent of the value of the house.

For example, if you found a house valued at $30,000 and total closing costs were $1,000, the total acquisition cost would be $31,000. Three percent of this amount is $930. But you would still have to pay $1,000 down so that the mortgage did not exceed the $30,000 value of the home. If, instead, you financed that same house with a 203b loan, your initial cash investment would be $2,000 ($1,000 for closing costs, plus 3 percent of the first $25,000 of the sales price and 5 percent of the remaining $5,000).

For two- to four-unit properties financed with a Section 221(d)2 loan, the minimum down payment is 3 percent of the first $25,000 of value and 5 percent of anything over that amount. These properties must be approved for loan insurance before their construction or after they are one year old. For other properties, the minimum down payment is 10 percent. Again, the buyer may include the closing costs in the minimum investment.

If you are displaced by an urban renewal project in your city, loan terms are more lenient. Loan terms are increased to forty years, meaning lower monthly payments than under shorter amortization schedules. Down payments can be as low as $200 and interest rates as low as 7 percent in some areas.

Clearly, there is considerable overlap between the 221(d)2 and the 203b loan programs at the lower end of the price scale. There was an attempt in 1977 to eliminate the 221(d)2 program, but Congress felt the benefits it provided to low-income families justified its existence, and the program was extended.

MILITARY SERVICE PAYS OFF: FHA 222

Under this program a member of the armed services buying a house with one of the FHA insured loans, such as the 203b, can have the mortgage insurance premium paid by the Department of Defense (for members of the Army, Navy, Marines, or Air Force), Department of Transportation (for Coast Guard members), or the Department of Commerce (for members of the National Oceanic and Atmospheric Administration). However, servicemen financing their homes under 203b cannot choose the lower down payment available to servicemen under that program and still have their insurance premiums paid by the government under Section 222. They must choose one or the other.

HUD has another program for veterans to assist them in the purchase of homes. The FHA 203V program provides loan insurance to eligible veterans wanting to buy a home. However, I would recommend that the veteran first go through the Veterans Administration program because it easier to get a loan through this agency. The VA program is discussed in Chapter 3.

HOUSING IN DECLINING NEIGHBORHOODS: FHA 223E

A high-risk loan insurance program, Section 223e, was added to the National Housing Act in 1968. Prior to the adoption of this loan program, many inner-city properties were determined to be ineligible for FHA mortgages because they were located in marginal neighborhoods. After the urban riots of 1967 and 1968, Congress decided that something had to be done to stop the decline of these neighborhoods and to provide a source of residential mortgage financing.

Today, Section 223e authorizes the FHA to insure mortgages in older, declining urban areas that would be eligible under the agency's regular programs except for the neighborhood conditions. If the area is "reasonably viable" and there is a need for low- and moderate-income housing, the normal standards of economic soundness can be waived. Therefore, people wishing to live in these neighborhoods can get a loan if their prospective property is an "acceptable risk."

Though it is doubtful that Congress intended the FHA to insure unsound loans, that's what happened. Loans that would not qualify under other FHA plans were insured under the 223e program. When the loan program is used correctly for applicants in sincere need, Section 223e can serve a useful purpose by helping to stop neighborhood disinvestment in its early stages. Ideally, this show of support from the federal government can encourage conventional lenders to return to these neighborhoods.

Unfortunately, there is a thin line between a neighborhood that is in the early, reversible stages of decline and one that cannot be saved through the mild medicine of mortgage insurance. When used on a large scale in the latter type of neighborhood, Section 223e was a disaster. It contributed to some of the most spectacular failures in FHA history, notably the massive foreclosures that made HUD Detroit's biggest landlord in the late 1960s and early 1970s.

LITTLE INCOME? BAD CREDIT? HERE'S SOME HELP: FHA 235 AND 237

The Section 235 mortgage plan helps families buy new homes, paying rates as low as 4 percent. HUD insures the mortgages on properties that are built to HUD standards and makes monthly payments to lenders so the interest rate is reduced for the homeowner. The homeowner must contribute 20 percent of adjusted gross income to monthly payments.

Section 237 is another program for special risk situations. In this case, families who do not qualify for other regular FHA loans because of a bad credit record can receive a loan after getting HUD-approved counseling. This program has often been combined with Section 235 loans, since many low-income buyers have had credit problems in the past.

Almost every major city today is participating in urban renewal programs. In many of these cities the urban areas were never really bad. As a result, you see lawyers, executives, and young professionals taking advantage of these urban renewal loans to buy and rehabilitate residences. Just because the program involves the "inner city" or urban renewal, don't ignore it. Find out what areas are eligible before you decide not to get involved. In one major city, the urban renewal target area is across the street from the city's most prestigious country club.

THE FHA 203K PROGRAM IS A REAL SLEEPER

This is a revision of another loan program that was discontinued because it involved too much paperwork. The purpose of the Section 203k program is to assist in the financing of one- to four-unit residential properties. A 203k mortgage can finance a purchase/rehabilitation transaction, a refinance/rehabilitation transaction, or a rehabilitation project.

Section 203k provides an FHA mortgage. This means that HUD provides mortgage insurance to FHA-approved lenders that fund the loan. Check with your own lender. A lender that is eligible to make

FHA single-family loans (such as 203b, 245, or 234c) is automatically eligible to loan money under the 203k program.

A 203k mortgage is different from most mortgages in that most lenders will not usually close a loan and give you money unless the property is in good condition and has adequate equity. When rehabilitation is necessary, most loans require the improvements to be finished before a long-term mortgage is made. If you wanted to buy a home in need of repair or modernization, you would have to obtain financing, first to purchase the property, then to start the rehab, and once again when the work was completed to pay off the interim loans with a permanent mortgage. This can be very costly.

With a 203k loan you can get just one mortgage loan, at a fixed rate, to finance both the acquisition and the rehab. If you already own the property, the 203k program can be used for refinance and rehabilitation. You can have marginal credit and income and still qualify for the loan.

All repairs and replacements to property are eligible for financing. Some typical examples are repairs to windows, stairs, walls, floors, roof, plumbing, electrical system, heating and cooling; solar equipment; new room additions; and remodeling. Swimming pools and additions or alterations for commercial use are not eligible. You can also use the loan to convert non-residential buildings into one- to four-unit housing or to convert a one-family house into a two-, three-, or four-family dwelling.

Profits for Owner-Contractors

As the owner of a property, it's to your benefit to be the owner-contractor for the rehabilitation. No license is required to be an owner-contractor, but it is required that you hire licensed subcontractors to do the work. The best thing about being an owner-contractor is that you can pay yourself $10.00 an hour as compensation when you rehabilitate your own property!

The maximum loan amounts are very similar to those of the FHA home buyers loan (Section 203b), although the dollar limitation may vary from area to area around the country. To find out the limits for your area, contact your lender or the local HUD office.

Investors are also eligible to use Section 203k financing. However, an investor who intends to hold the property after the rehab is completed is eligible for a loan amount of only up to 85 percent of the amount available to an owner-occupant.

Putting the 203k to Work

A short time ago a friend of mine named Jim found a burned-down house in a very nice area, where homes were in the $115,000 to $125,000 price range. When Jim found that he could buy the house for $10,000, cash, he went to the bank and borrowed the money on an IOU. For many people the house would have been a total loss.

But not for Jim. Under the 203k loan program, Jim borrowed $55,000 on a construction loan for nine months to rehabilitate the property. There was an additional $5,000 in architect, engineering, and interest fees. By the time he was finished, Jim had a total of $70,000 in the project: $55,000 for the rehabilitation, $10,000 for the purchase, and about $5,000 for "soft costs."

After the rehabilitation was completed, the property was appraised for over $130,000. Jim received a $90,000 permanent loan under the FHA 203k program. He used this money to pay off the $10,000 IOU, the $55,000 construction loan, and the $5,000 of other fees. Jim ended up with about $20,000 in his pocket, and still had about $40,000 in equity in the house ($130,000 value—$90,000 loan).

What did Jim do then? He put the house up for sale. Since it had a beautiful new interior and exterior, it sold promptly for $130,000. Jim took $5,000 down and carried back a second mortgage for $25,000 at a very favorable interest rate.

I want you to remember this program, because if you come across a single-family house or a two- to four-unit apartment building that needs at least $1,000 worth of repairs, this is a loan you can use immediately.

LIVE IN A SMALL TOWN? TRY FMHA

What do you do if you live in a small town away from the big city? There may not be a lot of HUD programs available. However, the Farmers Home Administration (FmHA) has many programs to help persons with low and moderate incomes to purchase and rehabilitate real estate.

Keep in mind that the terms *low and moderate income* are relative to the average income in the area. For example, in many parts of California a person can earn $23,000 a year and still be considered low-income. So we're not talking severe poverty in all cases. The income that qualifies you for low income in your area will depend what your neighbors make.

FmHA loans are administered through federal, state, and local government offices. At the local level are county FmHA offices that regulate small farm and home programs. Each county office reports to a district office, which generally oversees the operations of four to eight county offices. It is at this district level that major loans are approved for residential and income property rehabilitation. District offices report to a state office in each state. At the federal level is the national office in Washington, D.C., which is administered through the United States Department of Agriculture.

The best office to contact for housing rehabilitation and purchase loans is the district office. Unfortunately, often the county officers are unaware of every program offered by the FmHA. The district office may refer you to a county office to process the loan, but it is best to make your initial contact at the district level.

One Percent Mortgages: FmHA 502

Home ownership loans made through the FmHA 502 program may be used to buy, build, improve, repair, or rehabilitate rural homes. They are made to families with low and moderate incomes who:

- are without decent, safe, and sanitary housing
- are unable to obtain loans from private lenders at reasonable rates
- have sufficient income to meet loan payments
- have decent credit. (Cosigners may be used.)

Interest rates on these loans are based on the cost of money to the government. (In 1984 the rate was 11.87 percent.) Families with low incomes may qualify for interest credits to reduce the interest rate to as low as 1 percent in order to make the house payments affordable for them. Maximum time for repayment is thirty-three years. Since there is no down payment requirement, houses can be purchased with this loan for no money down.

This is the most active FmHA program. It has been the source of housing for many elderly and low-income rural persons who would not have a home otherwise.

One Percent Repair Loans: FmHA 504

The FmHA 504 program is designed to provide loans for the repair of homes in rural areas. The objective of this program is to bring properties up to present building code requirements. Therefore, loans are available to low-income rural families at 1 percent interest. The maximum amount is $7,500 and the term is twenty years.

For low-income individuals who are sixty-two or older, a one time $5,000 grant is available through this program. This is a straight gift, with no monthly payments or mortgage attached.

Apartment Loans: FmHA 515

Loans for rental or cooperative housing in rural areas are made through the FmHA 515 program to provide living units for persons with low and moderate incomes and for those sixty-two and older.

The money from these loans may used to build apartments, including duplexes and garden apartments. It may also be used to purchase and rehabilitate existing rental housing. Borrowers must agree to provide rental units that eligible tenants can afford.

The terms of these loans are what make them attractive. The loans are offered at lower than market interest rates and are repayable over fifty years. Apartment developers who build "low profit" complexes (with very low rents) can receive a 1 percent loan to make the low rents possible.

The FmHA 515 is an active program. Currently I am negotiating to buy two apartment buildings (one in the midwest, the other in Arizona) that have FmHA 1 percent 50-year loans. What's really great about these properties is that they both have 15-year guaranteed rents!

How to Get FmHA Loans

These programs are excellent sources of low interest rate loans, which can be used to buy and rehabilitate homes and apartment units in rural areas. Contact your local FmHA district office to get the details about program requirements in your area. Below is a list of addresses of the FmHA offices in each state.

KEEP THESE POINTS IN MIND

1. The Federal Housing Administration is the "loan division" of the U.S. Department of Housing and Urban Development. The Farmers Home Administration is the "loan division" of the U.S. Department of Agriculture.
2. FHA loans are designed to make us a nation of property owners, not renters.
3. FHA loan credit requirements are less stringent than those for conventional uninsured loans.
4. Use the FHA 203k purchase/rehab loan to buy a property that may need fix-up and wouldn't qualify for any other loan.
5. Live in a small town? Try FmHA loans.
6. HUD and FHA do not make loans; they insure loans.

SPECIAL RESOURCE; FARMERS HOME ADMINISTRATION STATE OFFICES

U.S. Department of Agriculture, Washington, DC 20250

Alabama
Room 717, Aronov
 Building
474 South Court Street
Montgomery, Alabama
36104

Alaska
Post Office Box 1289
Palmer, Alaska 99645

Arizona
201 E. Indianola
Suite 275
Phoenix, Arizona 85012

Arkansas
Rm. 5529, Federal
 Building
700 West Capitol
P.O. Box 2778
Little Rock, Arkansas
72203

California
459 Cleveland Street
Woodland, California
95695

Colorado
Room 231, #1 Diamond
 Plaza
2490 West 26th Avenue
Denver, Colorado 80211

**Delaware, District of
Columbia, Maryland**
2319 South DuPont
 Highway
Dover, Delaware 19901

Florida
Room 214, Federal
 Building
401 S.E. 1st Avenue
P.O. Box 1088
Gainesville, Florida
32602

Georgia
Stephens Federal
 Building
355 East Hancock
 Avenue
Athens, Georgia 30601

Hawaii
Room 311, Federal
 Building
Waianeunue Avenue
Hilo, Hawaii 96720

Idaho
Room 429, Federal
 Building
304 N. Eighth Street
Boise, Idaho 83702

Illinois
2106 W. Springfield
 Avenue
Champaign, Illinois
61821

Indiana
Suite 1700
5610 Crawfordsville
Road
Indianapolis, Indiana
46224

Iowa
Room 873, Federal
Building
210 Walnut Street
Des Moines, Iowa 50309

Kansas
Rm. 176, Federal
Building
444 SE. Quincy Street
Topeka, Kansas 66683

Kentucky
333 Waller Avenue
Lexington, Kentucky
40504

Louisiana
3727 Government Street
Alexandria, Louisiana
71302

Maine
USDA Office Building
Orono, Maine 04473

**Massachusetts,
Connecticut, Rhode
Island**
451 West Street
Amherst, Massachusetts
01002

Michigan
Room 209, Manly Miles
Building
1405 South Harrison
Road
East Lansing, Michigan
48823

Minnesota
252 Federal Office
Building &
U.S. Courthouse.

316 North Robert Street
St. Paul, Minnesota
55101

Mississippi
Room 831, Federal
Building
Jackson, Mississippi
39269

Missouri
555 Vandiver Drive
Columbia, Missouri
65202

Montana
Rm. 234, Federal
Building
Bozeman, Montana
59715

Nebraska
Room 308, Federal
Building
100 Centennial Mall
North
Lincoln, Nebraska 68508

New Jersey
Suite 100, 100 High
Street
Mt. Holly, New Jersey
08060

New Mexico
Room 3414, Federal
Building
517 Gold Avenue, SW.
Albuquerque, New
Mexico 87102

**New York, Virgin
Islands**
Room 871
James M. Hanley Federal
Building
100 South Clinton Street
Syracuse, New York
13260

North Carolina
Room 525

310 New Bern Avenue
Raleigh, North Carolina
27601

North Dakota
Room 208, Federal
Building
Third and Rosser
P.O. Box 1737
Bismarck, North Dakota
58502

Ohio
Federal Building
Room 507
200 North High Street
Columbus, Ohio 43215

Oklahoma
USDA Agricultural
Center Bldg.
Stillwater, Oklahoma
74074

Oregon
Rm. 1590 Federal
Building
1220 SW. 3rd Avenue
Portland, Oregon 97204

Pennsylvania
Federal Building
Room 728
P.O. Box 905
Harrisburg, Pennsylvania
17108

Puerto Rico
Rm. 623, Federal
Building
Carlos Chardon St.
Hato Rey, Puerto Rico
00918

South Carolina
Rm. 1007, Strom
Thurmond
Federal Building
1835 Assembly Street
Columbia, South
Carolina 29201

South Dakota
Huron Federal Building
Room 308
200 4th Street, SW.
Huron, South Dakota
57350

Tennessee
538 Federal Building and
    U.S. Court House
801 Broadway
Nashville, Tennessee
37203

Texas
Suite 102, Federal
    Building
101 South Main
Temple, Texas 76501

Utah, Nevada
Room 5438, Federal
    Building

125 South State Street
Salt Lake City, Utah
84138

**Vermont, New
Hampshire**
141 Main street
Post Office Box 588
Montpelier, Vermont
05602

Virginia
Room 8217, Federal
    Building
400 North Eighth Street,
P.O. Box 10106
Richmond, Virginia
23240

Washington
Room 319, Federal
    Office Bldg.

P.O. Box 2427
Wenatchee, Washington
98801

West Virginia
Room 320, Federal
    Building
P.O. Box 678
Morgantown, West
    Virginia 26505

Wisconsin
Suite 209, 1st Financial
    Plaza
1257 Main Street
Stevens Point, Wisconsin
54481

Wyoming
Room 1005, Federal
    Building
P.O. Box 820
Casper, Wyoming 82602

7

AMERICA'S BEST KEPT SECRET: Bonanza for First-Time Home Buyers

DREAM WHAT YOU DARE TO DREAM. GO WHERE YOU
WANT TO GO. BE WHAT YOU WANT TO BE.

Anonymous

One of the most amazing things about real estate investment counselors who write syndicated newspaper columns is what they recommend as the best real estate deals. They tell you the best ways to finance your home purchase, covering every kind of creative financing under the sun, from graduated payment mortgages to interest rate buydowns to fifteen-year mortgages. Then they go on to tell you how much money you can save with their recommendations. Yet none of them mentions one of America's best kept secrets: the first-time homebuyer plan offered through our state housing finance agencies. In this chapter, you will learn where to find out about this program and how to use it for your benefit. Also, you'll learn how to save $60,000 on a typical first-time home buyer loan.

LOANS AS LOW AS 6.5 PERCENT

There are loans available, often at as low as 6.5 percent, which enable people to buy their first homes. If you are a first-time home buyer (or have not owned a home in the last three years), you can apply for low interest government loans. They are not only for low-income persons. They are meant to benefit a broad spectrum of people who may not be able to make payments on conventional loans at market interest rates, but would qualify for loans at lower interest rates. These are the people who are building America and support our economy. Their home purchases through this program create jobs and increase the tax base of the community. Everyone benefits.

You see, local city and county governments raise money for their programs by selling tax-exempt bonds to investors. Because of the tax benefits these investors receive, the bonds are offered at extremely low rates. In turn, the state housing finance agencies use the bond proceeds to provide lower-than-normal interest rate loans for first-time home buyers. Loans are usually distributed through local lenders or developers, or directly from the government. (See chapter 9 for other low interest loan programs from housing finance agencies.)

Sometimes the homes available to the first-time home buyer are located in parts of a city or county designated as target areas. The target areas are not areas that are bad to live in. These are simply areas that are a little distressed economically. In such areas, the housing finance agencies may offer even lower interest rate loans to first-time home buyers, or they may waive the first-time home buyer requirement to encourage investors and current homeowners. For the most part, if you are a first-time home buyer, you can buy or build any house you want, anywhere you wish, as long as the purchase price doesn't exceed the specified limit for the area you choose.

In Arizona, for example, you can buy houses for up to $110,000 in value anywhere in the state, as long as you can demonstrate that you can make the payments. Simply put 5 percent down, and you'll receive a 9 percent thirty-year fixed rate loan for the balance—an absolutely fantastic opportunity for the first-time home buyer.

Each agency will have certain income and house price restrictions, which vary from state to state. In Connecticut, 44 percent of the people who recently bought homes through this program made from $20,000 to $30,000 a year. In Arkansas and Mississippi, the average borrower income was $20,000 to $29,000. In Arizona it was $33,000; not exactly low income.

Marin County, California, is one of the wealthiest counties in the nation. Yet, by means of a recent first-time home buyer bond offering, a single person can earn up to $56,000 a year and still buy a lovely home with a 9 percent fixed rate loan.

How to Find Out about the Details

Of course, finding out about these programs is not always easy. One of my research assistants recently called a housing finance agency in a western state only to be told the program didn't exist. This is a state that issued first-time homeowner bonds worth over $200,000,000 in 1985. After going through a few channels, my assistant finally reached the head of the department, who was more than helpful. Not only did this department head spend time explaining the program in detail, but sent our office loads of information.

Similarly, during an interview at radio station WJR in Detroit, I mentioned that the Michigan State Housing Development Authority had 8 percent loans available for the purchase of property. While on the air, I received a call from the woman in charge of this Michigan housing finance agency, informing us that there were no low interest rate loans. Having done my homework, I asked her to read the fourth paragraph of her program manual. Right over the radio she read, "Tax exempt bond issues starting at eight percent for the acquisition of rental properties are available through the Michigan State Housing Development Authority." As far as I am concerned, 8 percent interest is low interest. She then mentioned that there were several million dollars available in Michigan alone. (My research found the amounts to be $130,000,000 in 1984 and $150,000,000 in 1985.)

These first-time home buyer programs exist in all 50 states. Don't call the agencies and get discouraged by a receptionist. Instead, write or visit your state agency to get more information. Address your inquiry to the head of the department. You'll get a better, more thorough response.

Steps to Follow

Buying your first home using one of these loans is actually easy. The first thing you need to do is to write to or visit your state housing finance agency to request that they send you all the information on a first-time home buyer program, as well as any other programs their agency administers. Spend some time going over the guidelines and instructions. Your state housing finance agency may refer you to an office in your area. Don't worry, you're not getting the runaround. These local offices are more familiar with your town and will make your job easier.

Next, decide what kind of payments you can afford to make. The last thing I want you to do is to buy a house you can't afford and lose it to foreclosure in a year. With this in mind, determine what neighborhood you want to live in and the type of house you prefer.

Then make an offer on the property you like, subject to acquiring new financing through your state housing finance agency. The property may or may not be listed with a real estate agent. If it is listed with an agent, go through the normal purchase process. Once you have an accepted offer, tell the agent you are using the first-time home buyer plan and would appreciate her cooperation. In most cases the agent will be more than helpful.

At this point, contact a lending institution that has these loans available. You will have to do some paperwork, but no more than for a typical FHA loan application. If you meet the qualifications, you are on your way. The whole process takes about thirty to forty-five days.

Use This Program to Save $60,000

The typical loan rate under this program is less than 9 percent. Here's a way the average person can save $60,000 even with a 10 percent loan on a $50,000 home purchase.

Let's say that Bob and Sue find a cute home in a great neighborhood for only $52,650. They make a $2,650 down payment and, with the assistance of the first-time home buyer program in their area, receive a $50,000 loan at 10 percent. Their payments are about $439.00 per month. Now let me show you how Bob and Sue can save $60,000.

What would their payments be if they paid off their thirty-year loan as if it were amortized over fifteen years? $700? $800? Wrong. Their new payment would only be $537.33, or only about 22 percent more every month. For only $98.50 a month more, Bob and Sue will pay off their house in fifteen years. You see, over the life of their thirty-year loan they would normally pay $107,964 in interest charges. For about $98.00 more every month they reduce the interest charges to $46,715. The final result is a total savings of $61,249. The chart below demonstrates this best.

$50,000 LOAN AMORTIZED OVER 30 YEARS AT 10% INTEREST

	PAY IN 30 YEARS	PAY IN 15 YEARS
Monthly payment	$438.79	$537.32
Amount extra you pay each month	—	$98.53
Loan balance after 15 years	$40,850	$0
Total interest paid over life of loan	$107,964	$46,715
Interest savings 15 years vs. 30 years	$0	$61,249

What about a 12 percent thirty-year loan? Paying off your thirty-year loan as if it were a fifteen-year loan saves you even more in interest charges with higher interest (see page 108).

That's what makes these first-time home buyer loans so exciting. Because of their affordability, the money you save on interest can be applied toward paying your loan off early. Then you pay your loan off in fifteen years and save $60,000 or more in interest charges. The safety valve is that if something happens one month and you can't make the $98.00 extra payment, you can simply make only the $439 payment required.

$50,000 LOAN AMORTIZED OVER 30 YEARS AT 12% INTEREST

	PAY IN 30 YEARS	PAY IN 15 YEARS
Monthly payment	$514.31	$586.87
Amount extra you pay each month	—	$72.56
Loan balance after 15 years	$42,850	$0
Total interest paid over life of loan	$135,040	$55,636
Interest savings 15 years vs. 30 years	$0	$79,404

CONTACT YOUR LOCAL HOUSING FINANCE AGENCY

How do you find your state's housing finance agency? Housing finance agencies across the country have many different names. For instance, in Maryland the agency is referred to as the Maryland Community Development Administration. In Michigan it's the Michigan State Housing Development Authority. In Arizona the agency is a division

---

KEEP THESE POINTS IN MIND

1. You can get a low interest rate loan to buy a home through the first-time home buyer plan.
2. Although funds available vary from time to time, every state has a first-time home buyer plan.
3. This is not a low-income program. In most states, the average first-time home buyer makes $25,000 to $30,000 a year.
4. If you buy a house within a target area, most states will waive the income and "first-time purchase" requirements. (This means that you can buy more than one home through the program.)
5. Do not let a government agency receptionist tell you what you can't do, or that a particular program doesn't exist. Talk to the department managers.

of the Arizona Governor's Office of Economic Planning and Development.

Don't expect to find "Housing Finance Agency" in the telephone book. The agencies are seldom listed under such a title. To make things easier for you, the list of names and addresses of every state housing finance agency in the country is provided below.

Special Resource: State Housing Finance Agencies

Alabama Housing Finance Authority
State Capitol
Montgomery, AL 36130

Alaska Housing Finance Corporation
235 E. 8th Avenue
Anchorage, AK 99510

Arizona Governor's Office of Economic Planning and Development
1700 W. Washington
Phoenix, AZ 85007

Arkansas Housing Development Agency
16 & Main Streets
Madison Square Building
P.O. Box 8023
Little Rock, AR 72203

California Housing Finance Agency
1121 L Street
7th Floor
Sacramento, CA 95814-3908

San Francisco Office
2351 Powell Street
Suite 501
San Francisco, CA 94133

Los Angeles Office
5711 W. Slauson Ave.
Culver City, CA 90230

Colorado Housing Finance Authority
500 East Eighth Ave.
Denver, CO 80203

Connecticut Housing Finance Authority
40 Cold Spring Road
Rocky Hill, CT 06067

Delaware State Housing Authority
18 The Green
P.O. Box 1401
Dover, DE 19903

District of Columbia Housing Finance Agency
1401 New York Ave., N.W.
Suite 540
Washington, D.C. 20005

Florida Housing Finance Agency
2571 Executive Center Circle, East
Tallahassee, FL 32301

Georgia Residential Finance Authority
1190 West Druid Hills Dr.
Suite 270
Honeywell Center
Atlanta, GA 30329

Hawaii Housing Authority
1002 N. School Street
P.O. Box 17907
Honolulu, HI 96817

Idaho Housing Agency
760 West Myrtle
Boise, ID 83702

**Illinois Housing
Development Authority**
130 E. Randolph St.
Suite 510
Chicago, IL 60601

**Indiana Housing
Finance Authority**
1 North Capitol Ave.
Suite 515
Indianapolis, IN 46204

**Iowa
Finance Authority**
550 Liberty Building
418 Sixth & Grand Ave.
Des Moines, IA 50309

**Kansas Housing
Development Corp.**
503 Kansas Avenue
6th Floor
Topeka, KS 66603

**Kentucky
Housing Corporation**
1231 Louisville Rd.
Frankfort, KY 40601
(502) 564-7630

**Louisiana Housing
Finance Agency**
921 N. Lobdell Blvd.
Baton Rouge, LA 70806

**Maine State
Housing Authority**
295 Water Street
P.O. Box 2669
Augusta, ME 04330

**Maryland
Community
Development
Administration**
45 Calvert Street
Annapolis, MD 21401

**Massachusetts
Housing Finance
Agency**
50 Milk Street
5th, 6th & 7th Floors
Boston, MA 02109

**Michigan State
Housing Development
Authority**
Plaza One Building
401 South Washington
P.O. Box 30044
Lansing, MI 48909

**Minnesota Housing
Finance Agency**
333 Sibley Street
Suite 200
St. Paul, MN 55101

**Mississippi Housing
Finance Corporation**
Suite 204
Watkins Building
510 George Street
Jackson, MS 39201

**Missouri Housing
Development
Commission**
20 West 9th Street
Suite 934
Kansas City, MO 64105

**Montana Board
of Housing**
2001 11th Avenue
Helena, MT 59620

**Nebraska Investment
Finance Authority**
Gold's Galleria
Suite 304
1033 O Street
Lincoln, NE 68508

**Nevada
Housing Division**
Department of Commerce
1050 East William
Suite 435
Carson City, NV 89710

**New Hampshire
Housing
Finance Authority**
9 Constitution Drive
Bedford, N H 03102

P.O. Box 5087
Manchester, NH 03108

**New Jersey
Housing and Mortgage
Finance Agency**
CN 070
3625 Quakerbridge Road
Trenton, NJ 08625

**New Mexico Mortgage
Finance Authority**
115 Second Street, S.W.
Albuquerque, NM 87102

New York City Housing
Development
Corporation
75 Maiden Lane
8th Floor
New York, NY 10038

New York State
Division of Housing
and Community
Renewal
Two World Trade Center
Room 6060
New York, NY 10047

New York State
Housing Finance
Agency
3 Park Avenue
New York, NY 10016

New York State
Mortgage Loan
Enforcement and
Administration
Corporation
11 West 42nd Street
New York, NY 10036

State of New York
Mortgage Agency
260 Madison Avenue
9th Floor
New York, NY 10016

North Carolina
Housing Finance
Agency
424 North Blount Street
P.O. Box 28066
Raleigh, NC 27611

North Dakota Housing
Finance Agency
1012 East Central Ave.
P.O. Box 1535
Bismarck, ND 58502

Ohio Housing
Finance Agency
8 East Long Street
Suite 1200
Columbus, OH 43215

Oklahoma Housing
Finance Agency
4001 N. Lincoln Blvd.
Room 101
Oklahoma City, OK
73105

Oregon
Housing Division
Department of
Commerce
110 Labor &
Industries Building
Salem, OR 97310-0161

Pennsylvania Housing
Finance Agency
2101 North Front Street
P.O. Box 8029
Harrisburg, PA 17105-
8029

Puerto Rico Housing
Finance Corporation
Box 42001
Minillas Station
San Juan, PR 00940

Puerto Rico Housing
Bank & Finance Agency
P.O. Box 345
Hato Rey, PR 00919

Rhode Island Housing
and Mortgage
Finance Corporation
40 Westminster Street
Suite 1700
Providence, RI 02903

South Carolina State
Housing Authority
2221 Devine Street
Suite 540
Columbia, SC 29205

South Dakota Housing
Development Authority
221 South Central
P.O. Box 1237
Pierre, SD 57501

Tennessee Housing
Development Agency
706 Church Street
Doctor's Building
Room 226
Nashville, TN 37203-
5151

Texas
Housing Agency
P.O. Box 13941
Capitol Station
Austin, TX 78711

Utah Housing
Finance Agency
177 East 100 South
Salt Lake City, UT 84111

Vermont Housing
Finance Agency
239 South Union St.
P.O. Box 408
Burlington, VT 05402

**Virgin Islands
Housing Finance
Authority**
P.O. Box 7908
St. Thomas, VI 00801

**Virginia Housing
Development Authority**
13 South 13th Street
Richmond, VA 23219

**Washington State
Housing Finance
Commission**

216 1st Avenue, S.
Suite 366
Seattle, WA 98104

**West Virginia Housing
Development Fund**
814 Virginia Street, E.
Charleston, WV 25301

**Wisconsin Housing &
Economic Development
Authority**
131 W. Wilson Street
Suite 300

P.O. Box 1728
Madison, WI 53701-1728

**Wyoming
Community
Development
Authority**
139 West 2nd Street
Suite 1-C
P.O. Box 634
Casper, WY 82602

8

THE REHAB EXPRESS:
Getting Started with Low Interest Rate Loans

OTHER THAN THE GOOD LORD OR A FAITHFUL SPOUSE,
YOU COULDN'T ASK FOR A BETTER PARTNER THAN
THE U.S. GOVERNMENT.

Wayne Phillips

Using low interest rate government loans is the fastest, safest, and easiest way for anyone to save money and work with the government. We've talked about government programs that you can use to buy real estate. Now let's take a look at the millions of dollars available to rehabilitate and improve existing property at interest rates that encourage even the tightest investors and homeowners to get involved. First, let me explain why you should get involved with low interest government loan programs.

SAVE $20,000 TO $50,000

What's so great about low interest loans? Well, if you go to the bank tomorrow and borrow $50,000, you're going to pay about 12 to 14 percent interest. Over the next year, you'll pay about $7,000 in interest before you pay off one penny of that $50,000. Now ask yourself this question: "Is it worth it to get involved with the government if I can learn how to borrow the same $50,000 at 10 percent interest?" You see, doing so means you'll only pay $5,000 in interest during the next twelve months—a savings of $2,000. Isn't that $2,000 enough motivation to get involved with the government? Of course it is. And, that $2,000 is saved in only the first year. If you own the property for ten, twenty, or thirty years, your savings could add up to $20,000 to $50,000 on one property!

Now, forget about paying 10 percent interest. What if you could utilize a local community block grant government program and pay only 3 percent interest to borrow the $50,000? Instead of $7,000 in interest you would now pay only $1,500 over the next year. Your savings would be $5,500 over the cost of a conventional loan. Possible savings over the life of the loan could be $150,000! Now, that's motivation.

In this chapter you'll learn how to make money with one of the best methods available in the 1980s: low interest rate financing. You can't make money when you have to pay 12 or 14 percent interest on your loans. It's hard to make money when you have to search for motivated sellers. It's hard to make a good profit when you have to deal with banks and foreclosures. But it's easy when you use government programs to buy real estate and use low interest rate government loans to refinance or rehabilitate the properties.

I learned about the kind of money you can make with government rehabilitation loans by accident. A few years ago, I purchased a thirty-one-unit apartment building for a super bargain price, only to find out later that the building needed thirty-one new furnaces and water heaters. In desperation, I requested a loan from my bank and was promptly turned down. Only after I got involved with a local city government rehabilitation program did I get the money I needed quickly and easily. The city gave me a twenty-year loan for $119,800 at 8 percent interest. What's so exciting is that it only cost $90,000 to make all the necessary repairs. The remaining $30,000 cash was my "compensation" for doing the work. (See chapter 9 for details.) When I learned that cities nationwide are allocated billions of dollars each year to rehabilitate local real estate, I knew I could use these programs to become financially free.

YOU NEED TWO THINGS

Since that first project a few years ago, I've learned a lot about government loans and real estate. I know now that to become wealthy with real estate you need two things.

First, you must have the ability to borrow big bucks. You need money to live on while you invest in real estate. The kind of money you can fold up, put into your back pocket, and use to pay your bills. A lot of real estate investors won't tell you that the only time they make money is when they sell their properties for profit. I don't want to have to sell my real estate to make a living. I don't like buying and selling or "flipping" properties. I like owning real estate. I want to own a lot of real estate so I can leave it to my children. It takes cash to do this and the ability to borrow big bucks.

The second thing you need to make money in real estate is staying power. You must have the ability to get through the tough times as well as the good. Translated into plain English, this means that you must have cash flow (money coming in each month). These two things, the ability to borrow big bucks and cash flow, can be achieved with government programs.

Today, real estate investors and homeowners face a number of barriers that can hinder their ability to make a profit. Volatile interest rates, high acquisition costs, little or no cash flow, and balloon payments are just a few of them. Through the use of government purchase and rehabilitation programs, you can avoid these pitfalls by purchasing properties for pennies on the dollar and fixing them up with low interest rate loans. It's like having your cake and eating it too.

Rehabilitation and development of existing properties is the wave of the future for real estate. Our government strives to provide decent and affordable housing for all Americans. Yet the cost of building new housing is prohibitive for most homebuyers and investors. Since the government cannot always afford to build new projects either, it provides the money necessary to rehabilitate our country's existing housing. That's why I've developed my "rehab express" concept. It is a proven step-by-step method to help you take advantage of rehab opportunities.

THE REHAB EXPRESS CONCEPT

Take a look at these steps that I use to work with government rehab programs. See how you can apply them to your own needs.

1. Locate the ultimate motivated seller (Uncle Sam).

The ultimate motivated seller is our government. This is where you'll find the best real estate deals around (see previous chapters). There are three levels of government that sell real estate, federal, state, and local.

2. Acquire property for pennies on the dollar.

There are several ways to acquire property from the government for pennies on the dollar. You can buy a house that is in need of as little as $1,000 worth of work and then improve the property, using the FHA 203k program we discussed in chapter 6. Another way is to buy property that Uncle Sam has acquired through tax sales and foreclosures. Have the government loan you the money necessary to fix up the property so you increase the value and improve the neighborhood.

3. Obtain low interest rate fix-up loans.

Money is available at all three levels of government, federal, state, and local. Your best loan deals will come from local governments. Do not go to HUD. HUD doesn't make low interest rehab loans. Most of the low interest rate rehab loans are available through state and local housing authorities. Local housing finance agencies, community development authorities, and city housing authorities are the types of agencies you want to contact. This is where you'll find the special low interest rate loan programs and rent subsidy programs. These programs are covered in chapter 9.

4. Become a contractor and hire others to work for you.

Why be a contractor? Being a contractor allows you control over your real estate rehabilitation. When you surrender control of a property to someone else, you're not going to get the best results because no one gives the same care or devotion to your deal as you do. Whether you are working on one house or 500 units, you need to keep control. When I received my first government rehab loan, I took on the role of an owner-contractor and hired plumbers, electricians, roofers, and painters to do the rehab work. A contractor could have done the hiring, overseen the operation, and pocketed a substantial amount of money for his services. Instead, I became the contractor for the project. I made sure the work was done on time and to my specifications. When the job was done, I received the contractor's fee—normally 15 to 25 percent of the rehab loan amount. It's easy to see the benefits of becoming your own contractor. First, you schedule the work. Second, if you don't like the way the plumber or roofer is doing the job, you can get someone else. Third, you are the one who gets the contractor's fee when the rehabilitation project is complete. But, most important, you can guarantee yourself a profit by having the work done for less than the money you're borrowing. That brings us to the next step in the rehab express.

5. Pull in tax free cash during the rehabilitation.

This is the way to put cash in your pocket while the work is being completed. If you have a $100,000 loan from the government to rehabilitate a property, you will receive the money in "draws." This means that when you do 10 percent of the work, you'll receive a $10,000 draw. Now, let's say that having all of the roofs done is considered to be 10 percent of the rehab. It may only cost you $8,000 to do the roofs. You receive your first $10,000 draw, pay the roofer $8,000, and the remaining $2,000 goes to the contractor (you) for the contractor's services. Over the entire rehabilitation period you can earn several thousand dollars this way.

6. Complete the rehabilitation and sell the tax benefits for big dollars.

Did you know that there are special tax write-offs on rehabilitated property? For some properties, a rehabilitation investment can provide five-year write-offs for investors. Investors in high income tax brackets will pay you cash for these write-offs. Recently, I sold $300,000 worth of tax benefits ($60,000 a year for five years) to one limited partner for $130,000 cash.

Historic properties are even better. People who buy a historic property can receive a 25 percent investment tax credit. This means that if an investor buys a historic property for $100,000 she will be able to deduct $25,000 from her tax bill that same year. It seems incredible that our government would do these things. But Congress has created certain incentives so people like you and me will get up off our duffs, get out there into the real world, work hard, and improve some of our older neighborhoods to make a buck.

You may not need a $60,000 tax write-off or a $25,000 investment tax credit, but there are many wealthy people who do. (I discuss historic properties in chapter 13.)

7. Repeat the process on bigger deals.

When you are about half finished with one property, start looking for the next project. Have your funding and rehab money lined up so you can go immediately onto the next deal. This way you are never without cash. On one property you may be collecting a contractor fee, while on another you're pulling in a great cash flow from rents.

We are currently lining up several large rehabilitation projects, to be completed over the next few years. When they're finished, we expect to be bringing in $1 million a year in income and $4 million in tax benefits. No bad for ex-musicians like my brother, my wife, and me. It's hard to believe that a few years ago I was playing drums for a living and never thought about making more than $1000 a month.

SEVEN STEPS TO FINANCIAL FREEDOM

Let's quickly recap the seven steps of my rehab express.

1. Locate the ultimate motivated seller: Uncle Sam.
2. Acquire properties for pennies on the dollar.
3. Obtain low interest rate fix-up loans.
4. Become the owner-contractor to lock in all rehab costs and guarantee yourself a profit by using subcontractors.
5. Pull in tax-free cash during the rehab.
6. Complete the rehabilitation and sell the tax benefits for big dollars.
7. Repeat the process on bigger deals.

TURN PROBLEMS INTO PROFITS

I got involved with these government programs because I needed money to get out of a serious property problem. I never dreamed of the wealth that could be created. Not only did I solve a big problem, but I went on to find other buildings to rehabilitate with government money and pocketed big profits.

Do you have a single-family home or duplex that needs repair, but have no money? Turn to the government. Low interest rehabilitation loans are available nationwide. If you're ready to learn how to get these low interest rate loans for your own real estate, turn the page.

KEEP THESE POINTS IN MIND

1. You can get rehab loans at as low as 0 to 5 percent.
2. You can increase your income by 25 percent using low interest rate loans.
3. Low interest rate loans are available at the local government level.
4. The government makes these rehab loans so property owners will bring their real estate up to current building standards.
5. Use my rehab express concept to make the most of these fantastic low interest loans, while you help others and yourself.

9

RICHES THROUGH REHABILITATION

THE HIGHEST REWARD FOR A PERSON'S TOIL IS NOT
WHAT THEY GET FOR IT, BUT WHAT THEY BECOME BY
IT.

John Ruskin

Rehabilitation loans are available through a wide variety of government programs. There are programs specially designed for homeowners, investors, and developers who want to rehabilitate older, run-down but structurally sound properties. Interest rates for the loans range from as low as zero percent to as high as a few percentage points over the prime rate. Some of these loans are available at the federal and state levels of government, but most of the rehabilitation programs are administered from the local level. Decide what you want to accomplish, then find the government program to achieve your objective. The government loan program you use will depend upon:

1. Your goals and objectives; in other words, the type of property you wish to own (e.g., your own home, apartments, offices, housing for the elderly or disabled, low-income housing)

2. The type of property you may already own (residential, commercial, historic)

3 What you want to do with the property (e.g., rehabilitate, fill vacancies)

This chapter will cover some of the major rehabilitation loan programs available at the federal, state, and local levels. (For a summary reference chart of the programs, see the appendix to this book.)

FINDING A SUPER BARGAIN

Let me tell you a story. During the summer of 1980 my brother Richard, my wife Cathie, and I came across a thirty-one unit garden apartment complex in Baltimore, Maryland. It was a nice building in a decent neighborhood. The seller had inherited the building a short time before, and being the person he was, he really didn't want to be a landlord. The last thing he wanted to do was put up with all of the responsibilities that went with owning rental property.

But he had another reason for wanting to sell. He was paying the heat and hot water for all thirty-one apartments and couldn't handle the expense. As a result, he was asking $400,000 for the property with a $50,000 down payment. However, when we discovered his motivation and took a look at his situation, we found out that he really didn't need a lot of cash. By the end of the negotiations we had bought the entire building for $200,000 with $2,000 down and a loan at 8 percent for 30 years. On October 6, 1980 we settled the deal. What a super bargain!

Or so we thought. It didn't take long until we realized that in order to provide heat for the tenants we would have to put 5,000 gallons of heating oil each month into the building's antiquated heating system. We figured if we could remove the old heating system and install individual heaters in each unit, that would take care of the situation. The only problem was that we couldn't get any money to convert the system to a modern one. If we didn't convert it, we would lose the building. We could not go on paying $10,000 for heating oil each month.

A Desperate Situation

We made a few calls and figured that it would cost about $75,000 to do the conversion work. So we decided to go to our friendly banker and apply for a $75,000 property improvement loan to get the money to install thirty-one separate gas water heaters and forced-air furnaces. With all of our paperwork in hand, we demonstrated to our banker that we had more than enough positive cash flow to handle the additional debt.

Do you know what happened? He turned us down. I couldn't believe it. The project would not only increase the value of the building, but would make it more profitable in the long run, and the bank turned us down. In frustration we went to several other lenders in the city, explained our intentions, and showed them how our plan would work out. We were turned down every time.

By then a week had passed, and we were getting a little worried because in two more weeks we would have to put another 5,000 gallons of oil into that darn tank again.

The Government to the Rescue

About that time I discovered an interesting thing. Every state in our country has a department of economic or community development office to facilitate the rehabilitation of housing within that state. So I visited the state office in our state capital to inquire if there were any loans available for renovating heating systems like mine in existing apartment buildings. Do you know what the department said?

They said yes! Maryland had just floated a bond issue to provide for the renovation and rehabilitation of existing apartment buildings in the greater Baltimore metropolitan area. To get the details I had to contact my local community development department in Baltimore.

First thing Monday morning we marched into the municipal building downtown to see how we could get the money to get us out of this predicament. The manager in the department told us they did have investor loans, at 8 percent interest for twenty years. She gave us an application and told us to submit it with some necessary supporting documents. She then mentioned that after we returned the completed loan application package, they would send an estimator out to look at the proposed project with us. He would do a feasibility study to see if the building could support the loan. If the feasibility study proved favorable, the estimator would see what kind of housing code violations would have to be corrected before the government would issue the loan for the heating system. This was because the program was developed to correct the code violations in older apartment buildings in the city.

We returned the next day with all the necessary paperwork, ready to get the show on the road. The woman at the front desk was flabbergasted. Most people took two to three weeks to do their paperwork. She was shocked to see someone replying so promptly. After looking over our paperwork, she said she would assign an estimator to review the property in about a week or two.

That wouldn't be good enough, we told her. We had an urgent problem that needed immediate attention. We didn't have time to wait. Not only did we have to feed that heating system again, but it was on its last legs. We let her know this, and she told me she would do what she could to help us out.

The next day, I was notified that there had been a cancellation and the estimator could meet me that afternoon. I grabbed the opportunity, and that afternoon met Dave, the estimator, to go over the property. Dave was an elderly gentleman who knew just about every piece of real estate in town and could tell you stories about each. He told me that he had known the builder of this apartment and knew it was built well.

Dave was a blessing. He told me that we could install the separate heat and hot water systems. But in order to accomplish this, we would have to put fire-resistant Sheetrock around each furnace. I agreed to do that. He then suggested that we also paint the building, reglaze the windows, and replace part of the roof. He also added that I should put on metal security doors with an intercom. After the inspection, Dave said he would review the proposal, price out the work that needed to be done, and get it back to the main office that afternoon so it could go before the loan committee on Thursday.

On Friday of that same week I received a phone call from the community development agency. The loan committee had approved a loan for $119,800 at 8 percent! We were on our way.

Becoming a Contractor

To make a long story short, when we signed a few more papers at the housing department, they asked who my contractor was. The department told me that if I was the contractor, I would hire the roofers, plumbers, electricians, and painters to do the work on the apartment. After a certain amount of the work was completed, I would be paid a portion of the $119,800 loan. If I hired a contractor, he would hire the roofers, plumbers, electricians, and painters, and he would be paid for the services. When I found this out I replied, "How do I become a contractor?"

They sent me back to Dave, who told me how to get an owner-contractor license. At that time I didn't know anything about contracting. Dave took me under his wing, and with his help I was licensed within a week. I later learned that in most states you can be the contractor on your own properties without having to get a license.

Catch 22

Everything seemed great. I was my own contractor now and was ready to get to work on my apartment building. The only drawback to this loan program was that the department didn't just hand me a check for $119,800 and say, "Get to work." Instead, they put the money into an escrow account and would advance the funds as the work was completed.

But before the heating people, plumbers, electricians, and carpenters would start working, we needed to give them each a deposit. How were we going to get the money? We had $119,800 in the bank, but couldn't touch it until the work was in progress. And the construction people said they wouldn't start the work until they had a deposit. It was a classic "Catch 22" situation.

At that point we went back to our banker—the same one who had refused our loan before—and asked to borrow $75,000 to do the rehabilitation. Just as our banker was about to refuse our loan request once more, my brother handed him a letter of commitment for a $119,800 loan at 8 percent payable over twenty years. We told him we needed the money to pay the construction deposits so that we could get the job started.

What we were asking for, though we didn't know it, was a "bridge loan"—a temporary IOU to do interim construction. Banks do this type of lending all the time. Once our banker knew what we were trying to do, he gave us a ninety-day IOU for $75,000. Now we had the cash to get started.

That was the easiest and fastest loan we ever received in our lives. In less than ten minutes the same banker who had turned us down several weeks before gave us a loan for $75,000. Three months later we completed all the work on the project. Dave had set up a series of ten $12,000 draws on the rehab loan to be given to us when each 10 percent of the work had been completed. When all of the work had been finished, we had done the rehabilitation for $87,000, and paid $3,000 in interest on our $119,800 loan from the city and IOU from the bank. After paying back the IOU and the interest charges, we still had $30,000 left. I didn't know whether to return it or use it to pay off some of our loan.

Dave told me the money was mine to keep. It was my contractor's profit. Uncle Sam allows us to make a profit. What's more, because I had borrowed the money, it was tax free. And the income from the thirty-one rentals would be enough to make the loan payments.

So there I was with $30,000 tax free in my hands, looking at our beautifully refurbished, thirty-one-unit apartment building with thirty-one separate furances and water heaters, with no more oil bill and a positive cash flow of $3,500 per month—all for $2,000 down. That $30,000 cash was more money than I had made in a year playing drums. I tell you, I was out the next day looking for more properties with heating problems!

$850 A MONTH ON A $1,500 INVESTMENT

A short time later I located a little four-unit apartment building in a neighborhood of expensive homes. It was in pretty bad condition and needed some rehabilitation. So I marched down to the city to inquire about the availability of more rehab loans. I was told that the city had a program called the rental production rehabilitation program to provide loans for the moderate rehabilitation of residential units. With this loan, I could rehab the property and rent to low-income tenants, and the government would subsidize the rents for fifteen years; they would give me $355 monthly for each two-bedroom apartment. I got really excited when they told me I could also get a loan for $42,500 at 9 percent interest for twenty years to do the fix-up work. At the time, interest rates soared over 16 percent.

I purchased the four-plex using my "triple ten rule":

a. ten percent down
b. ten percent interest rate
c. ten years payback period on the loan.

I rehabilitated the four apartments and converted the store on the first floor into a fifth apartment. The building now earns $1,500 a month in rents, and we receive about $850 a month in cash flow. In addition, the neighbors love me, because I turned the property into something nice to look at. I put up new vinyl siding, renovated the interior, installed new windows, and landscaped the yard. I have helped five families get decent and affordable housing. Furthermore, all of the fix-up costs ($42,500) can be depreciated over five years. In other words, depreciation is over $8,000 per year, thanks to a special IRS code that President Reagan instituted with the tax laws of 1980.

The next building we rehabilitated was a five-unit property located in a target area (As we discussed, target areas are areas within your city or state that the government "targets" for special urban renewal programs.) It just so happened that this property was within the boundaries of an urban renewal target area in our city and thus eligible for a Section 312 loan.

A little research revealed that we could borrow about $138,000 at 3 percent to renovate the property completely. We would have to take out everything but the brick walls; the building needed all new plumbing, electrical wiring, floors, interior walls, appliances, heating, and air conditioning.

This was a major rehabilitation. We did all of the work for about $100,000 and received $38,000 for our services. By the time we were through with this project, we had a good feel for the rehab process.

CONTACT YOUR LOCAL AUTHORITIES

The best rehabilitation programs are available from your city housing finance agency and your city housing authority. These loan programs are funded through bond revenues, as well as through grants and loan programs from HUD. This is money that HUD gives to city housing authorities to rehabilitate the inner city and target areas. Since the city governments pay nothing for this money, they lend it out at low rates to developers and owners who can demonstrate that the funds will be used to rehabilitate housing in the area.

Congress has established two new HUD grant programs to increase the supply of multi-family housing units in urban areas for lower income people: the rental rehabilitation program and the Housing Development Action Grants (HoDAG) program.

The two programs complement each other. The rental rehab program is for moderate rehabilitation of existing housing, and HoDAG finances construction or substantial rehabilitation. Both mean low interest loans for developers and owners of apartments in target areas who wish to rehabilitate their buildings for low-income tenants.

In HoDAG projects, only 20 percent of the units must be rented to elderly or lower-income tenants. This leaves 80 percent of the units available for middle- and upper-income people. The rents from the high-income tenants will, in effect, subsidize the rents of the lower-income people. On the other hand, properties funded by the rental rehab program must reserve at least 70 percent of their units for elderly or lower-income tenants. Consequently, to attract more investors into this program, substantial rent guarantees are provided on a long-term basis. These guarantees are in the form of government rent vouchers or certificates. (For more information about rent guarantees for landlords and tenants, see chapter 11.)

Congress allocated $300 million for rental rehab and $315 million for HoDAG in 1984 and 1985.

Try These Local Programs

The urban homestead program is a national program. Its purpose is to revitalize declining neighborhoods and reduce the inventory of federally owned houses. City housing authorities sell the houses for pennies on the dollar to qualified purchasers who agree to rehabilitate the homes.

The new homeowners must agree to use the house as their primary place of residence for three years and to bring the property up to code within eighteen months. For more details about this program see chapter 5.

Section 312 rehabilitation loans are loans for the rehabilitation of residential and non-residential properties located in federally assisted (target) areas. They serve primarily low- to moderate-income people. Their main objectives are to improve the housing and facilities of these people, to conserve neighborhoods, and to prevent the displacement of low- to moderate-income persons. Lower-income residents qualify for special low interest loans to rehabilitate their homes, while other borrowers pay an interest rate based on the rate of Treasury securities. The typical rate in 1984 was 11½ to 12 percent.

While multi-family housing (five or more units) and non-residential and mixed-use properties (i.e., office buildings) are eligible for this program, its principal focus is single-family housing (one to four units), in conjunction with the local urban homestead program.

Owner-occupants with adjusted incomes not in excess of 80 percent of the median area income may obtain loans at 3 percent interest to rehabilitate their homes. The maximum loan term is twenty years. The loan amounts average approximately $27,000 per unit, but this amount is expected to increase to $33,000 by next year. More information and applications for these loans can be obtained from your local housing authorities.

Low interest rehabilitation loans are available from local city governments. These programs are funded by grants from the federal government. They provide low interest loans to homeowners so they can improve their residences. The interest rates and terms will vary from city to city, so contact your local housing finance agency and your city housing authority for details.

Three Percent Interest Matching Funds Program

Many cities are also lending money to property owners on a matching funds basis. Money is lent to a property owner wishing to rehabilitate his property at 3 to 5 percent. In return, he is expected to match the loaned amount; that is, invest an equal amount in the property. This program has proven to be very successful in several cities and is an excellent way to get additional money from the government at low interest rates.

KEEP THESE POINTS IN MIND

1. Most rehab programs are run from the city level.
2. You can acquire property for little or no money.
3. You can pull in tax-free cash as an owner-contractor.
4. Uncle Sam allows you to make a profit, from 15 to 20 percent of the loan amount.
5. Loans for rehab are at below-market interest rates, ranging from zero to 12 percent.

10

THE GOLD MINE LOAN AND THE ZERO PERCENT FORGIVENESS LOAN

INCH BY INCH, ANYTHING'S A CINCH.

Dr. Robert Schuller

Fred Lewis of Modesto, California, cashed in on a gold mine. After attending one of my seminars, this Air Force sergeant used an FHA Title I loan program to receive a $17,000 check in the mail ten days later.

Henry Dion, from Boston, Massachusetts, did the same. He came to one of my seminars on May 7. Three days later, he received a $14,000 check from the same government program.

Gene Cunningham lives in the little town of Warner Robins, Georgia. But the town was big enough for Gene to get a check for $13,875, then five days later receive another!

Dennis Paine from Philadelphia, Pennsylvania, attended my seminar on June 16 and deposited a check for $17,000 in his checking account of June 19.

What's going on here? These people used one of the most exciting and valuable loan programs in the country today: the FHA Title I Home Improvement Loan. The FHA Title I loan is such a super program, I call it the gold mine loan. It is a program that enables you to borrow money easily from local lenders to repair and improve your home or investment properties.

Throughout the country, many people have used this program to get the money they needed. After getting his gold mine loan in Philadelphia, Dennis Paine wrote:

"I am pleased to report that this gold mine loan was every bit as easy and simple to obtain as you [Richard Phillips] and Wayne have said.

"Thanks to you both for helping me get started in a successful real estate investment program."

As real estate investors and entrepreneurs, we occasionally need to get our hands on money in a relatively short period of time. The gold mine loan helps us do this. If you have a bad furnace, a leaky roof, or need other repairs, here's a way get the money to have them fixed.

HOW TO GET YOUR OWN GOLD MINE

Locate local or regional savings and loans, commercial banks, or credit unions that make FHA-insured Title I home improvement loans. Most lenders will make Title 1 loans of up to $2,500 at current interest rates, with up to eight years to repay, *unsecured*. These loans are easy to get, since they are insured by the FHA. This means that if the borrower defaults even after only one payment, the lender gets paid off by the FHA.

Often lenders will take your application over the phone and check your credit. When it's approved, they will mail you the papers to sign. Have your signature notarized and return the paperwork, and the lender usually mails you a cashier's check for the amount approved. You can borrow up to $17,500 with fifteen years to repay it, but a deed of trust on the property will be required on amounts over $2,500.

You can get financing for 100 percent of the rehab costs. If a mortgage is required, lenders many times will take a second, third, or fourth mortgage on the property. There are no points or closing costs. That's not bad at all.

How to Find Title I Lenders

The first thing to do is to write to your local or regional HUD office and ask for the person in charge of the Title I home improvement loans. This person can tell you which lenders in your town are presently making Title I loans. If that doesn't work, call the lenders in your area and ask if they make Title I loans or any other kind of home improvement loans. Credit unions are the most common source of Title I loans. By doing this, I have managed to borrow hundreds of thousands of dollars in Title I loans.

If you live in a small town, contact your regional HUD office and ask who is making Title I home improvement loans in the nearest city. You will most likely be able to obtain a loan from a lender HUD recommends.

Lenient Requirements

Before applying for your own gold mine loan, have your information ready for the lender. The lender will usually want to know the following:

- Your name, birthdate, social security number, place of work, income, length of employment.
- Address of the property where the loan is to be used (Your home or an investment property?)
- The improvements you plan to make.
- The bids you have from contractors (if any). If the lender requires a bid from a contractor and you plan to be the owner-contractor, you can get a blank proposal form from a stationery store.
- The amount you want to borrow.

To repeat: most of the time you can borrow up to $2,500, unsecured (no mortgage or deed of trust on your property). You can borrow up to $17,500 with a repayment term as long as fifteen years. Usually the loan is fully assumable. If you install solar energy systems, an additional $2,500 can be borrowed for a total possible loan amount of $20,000. Check with your local lender for the exact requirements.

The interest rate on a gold mine loan will be below market levels, and there will not be any balloon payments (a lump-sum payment due during the life of the note). Instead, the loan is paid off in equal monthly installments until it is paid in full. And because gold mine loans are fully assumable, anyone who buys your property can assume the note.

Use the Money Correctly

Be sure that the money is used on your property for improvements. If there is any money left over, you can use it for future improvements. If you use the money to buy cars, TVs, or other non-appreciating assets, you will fail in real estate. What's worse is that lying on your application is known as defrauding the government.

You Could Have One of These

Here are copies of checks people just like you received with the gold mine loan:

Zero Percent Loans That Are Forgiven

Many local government real estate agencies provide a rehab program for their residents known as the deferred payment loan or the "forgiveness loan." Like the gold mine loan mentioned previously, the forgiveness loan was established to provide property owners with money to assist them in the rehabilitation of their houses, to make them safer places to live and more energy efficient.

This loan is not strictly for low-income and elderly people, or for properties in target areas of town. This is a program that offers owners of residential properties the opportunity to repair and improve their properties at very little cost.

It is called a deferred payment loan because the loan does not have to be paid back for several years. If the deferred payment loan is at zero percent interest, you would only have to pay back the original loan amount and pay no interest. If there is an interest charge, interest payments may also be deferred until the due date. Many times the loan and the interest charges are entirely forgiven after a number of years.

Isn't that absolutely amazing? The program gives those people who could not otherwise afford to repair their homes or investment properties a chance to make necessary improvements.

Many cities offer this program not only to homeowners but to investors as well. For example, here is an excerpt from a letter that the affluent city of Costa Mesa, California mailed to its rental property owners informing them of a zero interest deferred payment program offered in their city:

> Dear Property Owner:
>
> The city of Costa Mesa has developed a Rental Rehabilitation Program and would like your participation in preserving and improving the quality of rental housing in the city.
>
> The City of Costa Mesa is offering a matching fund program to landlords. The city will match up to $5,000 against the owner's funds. The $5,000 is a zero interest deferred payment loan (due when the property transfers ownership). The owner's funds can be private or a 7 percent

low interest loan subsidized by the City. EXAMPLE: Mr. Smith owns a single-family unit which needs roofing repair and new plumbing and electrical. These improvements total $10,000. The city will offer Mr. Smith a $5,000 deferred payment loan (due and payable when property transfers ownership) and a low interest loan of $5,000 at 7 percent. The only stipulation is that the resident of the unit must be earning less than 50 percent of the median income. The tenant is entitled to a Section 8 certificate, which guarantees the rent.

These funds are to be used for property improvements, including but not limited to health and safety code items.

> Sincerely,
> Coordinator
> Community Development
> Costa Mesa, California

In essence, a property owner in Costa Mesa could borrow up to $5,000 from the city at 7 percent interest and then get an additional $5,000 at zero percent interest. That's unbelievable! These loan programs exist! They may vary a little from city to city, but they are available to those who want to get involved.

Our example is only from one city. While my brother Richard was in California to give my "Creating Wealth with Government Loans" seminar, he visited the city of Sacramento. He discovered that the state of California has a statewide deferred payment loan program!

Programs Are Available in Many Cities

In St. Louis, Missouri, one of my students received a deferred payment loan to fix up his rental property. The interest rate on the loan was 12 percent, but the loan and interest will be forgiven in ten years. All he has to do is to continue to own and rent the property.

In Houston, Texas, loans have been forgiven and considered paid off in five years.

In Levittown, New York, Catherine Leavey received a $7,000 zero percent interest deferred payment loan to repair the heating system in her house. With the $7,000 she was able to replace the heating system, install storm windows, caulk the house, and add more insulation. As part of the loan agreement she agreed to keep the house for five years, at which time the loan would be forgiven. However, she didn't have to wait five years. The loan was forgiven in three years.

The money Mrs. Leavey saved in heating bills alone could have justified a regular loan to do these repairs. The fact that her $7,000 loan was forgiven in three years made it even better.

How the Program Works

State lawmakers allocate Community Development Block Grant money to housing finance agencies, who give the money to local housing development agencies. These agencies in turn lend the money to property owners in the form of deferred payment loans with interest rates as low as zero percent. The money is used by the property owners to rehab their properties and improve the housing conditions in the area.

Who is Eligible?

Eligibility will vary from city to city. Generally, low- to moderate-income owner-occupants of one- to four-unit properties and non-occupant owners of rental properties are eligible for loans.

Terms and Conditions of Loans

The terms and conditions for this program do vary throughout the nation. In general, however, the amount available for a loan is that amount necessary to cover the cost of the rehabilitation. Usually there is a maximum amount that can be borrowed, but this also varies. Loans are available at as low as zero percent and usually must be repaid within a specified number of years. For elderly property owners, these loans are not due until the property is sold or transferred. Often after a number of years loans under this program are forgiven.

Finding Deferred Payment Loans in Your Town

Your city may not have this loan program, or it may be a little different from the examples given. Still, most cities do offer these loans, and it is worth your while to visit your local housing authority to find out what programs are available.

Wayne's Hot Tip: Ask Questions Correctly

When finding out about this and other government programs, it is important to ask questions correctly. For example, don't call your local housing authority and ask, "Do you have any zero percent loans that are forgiven after a while?" You'll probably get a negative response.

Instead, visit the office in person and speak to a department head. Mention that you understand there are low interest deferred payment loan programs offered in many cities and would like to know if such a program exists in your city. If the department head is unaware of such program, ask if another local government agency would offer such a program. If the department official does know about a deferred payment program, ask for some information.

How a question is presented is very important when working with government officials. With politeness and perseverance, the world can be yours.

KEEP THESE POINTS IN MIND

1. The gold mine loan will save you thousands of dollars in loan fees and points.
2. Credit unions are the best source of gold mine loans.
3. Any property owner can borrow up to $17,500 on each property owned.
4. Zero percent deferred payment loans require no payments until their due date.
5. Many times the loans are forgiven.
6. Deferred payment loans are often available to investors and home-owners.
7. Both the gold mine loan and deferred payment loans can be used to make repairs to your properties.

11

FEDERAL EXPRESS: Rents Paid by the Government

PEOPLE LOVE TO TELL YOU WHAT YOU CAN'T DO.
BUT I'M HERE TO TELL YOU WHAT YOU CAN DO,
BECAUSE I'M A CAN-DO PERSON.

Wayne Phillips

One of the most difficult problems for owners of rental properties is finding good tenants to fill a vacancy. Unrented properties mean less income to pay mortgages and operating expenses. On the other hand, one of the toughest problems for tenants who earn maybe $3.50 an hour is finding decent places to live with their limited income.

In 1974, HUD developed the Section 8 rent subsidy program to help low-income renters pay for decent housing and provide landlords with a supply of tenants. Today, this program has evolved to provide safe and affordable dwellings to house thousands of our nation's low-income individuals, people like single working parents, disabled persons, and senior citizens who cannot afford to pay half their income in rents.

For the renter, this program provides a way to survive without having to live from paycheck to paycheck. For a property owner, it is way to fill vacancies and have rent checks mailed each month like clockwork. It is to your benefit to know about this program and to learn how to use Section 8 rents to help others and increase your cash flow.

WHAT IS THE SECTION 8 PROGRAM?

The Section 8 rent subsidy is a government program that helps elderly or lower-income people with their rent. Local HUD housing authorities issue Section 8 certificates or vouchers to qualified renters. These certificates become the tenants' passports to subsidized housing.

Once a tenant is in his new home, the government pays that portion of the rent the tenant cannot afford. Usually the tenant will be required to spend 30 percent of his income on rent. In some cases, this amount may be only $1.00 per month. The difference between the rent the landlord charges and the amount the tenant pays is guaranteed (paid) by the government. Each month the Section 8 landlord receives a check from the housing authority for every unit he or she has rented to a Section 8 tenant.

The nice thing about this program is that the Housing Authority bases its rent payments to the property owner (you) on what is called fair market rent (FMR). FMR is established by taking the average rents in the area, based on the size of the unit (one, two, or three bedrooms). Therefore, if two-bedroom units have an established FMR of $395 per month, the housing authority will see to it that owners of two-bedroom units under Section 8 are paid at least $395 per month.

For the most part, the FMR that the housing authority assigns to rental units within a city is always equal to or higher than what you could get yourself. The rental amounts can vary within a city, and property owners are paid more if they pay the tenant's utilities.

WHAT'S SO GREAT ABOUT GUARANTEED RENTS?

First, with guaranteed rents, you have the right to choose the tenant who will live in your property. You are not forced to accept anyone.

I prefer nice elderly people, because they appreciate having a beautiful home or apartment. Keep in mind that when anyone has a nice place to live they will take care of the property.

A second good thing about the program is that property management is simplified. The Section 8 tenant moves in and the government mails you his rent each month, leaving only the renter's small portion, if any, to collect. I tell my tenants to call me only in an emergency. They are simply required to keep the place clean and live up to the rules and regulations. If they do that, they can stay in the apartment as long as they wish.

Most of the time Section 8 tenants hesitate to cause damage or trouble. The fact that they live practically rent free with their rent subsidy is a pretty good motivation to obey any rules and regulations. They also know that if they do cause trouble, they can be evicted and might possibly lose their Section 8 certificate—something that is hard to come by for renters. If they damage your property, not only are they banned from this housing assistance program, but they are also banned from any public assistance whatsoever, including social programs, welfare, and food stamps, until they repay any damages to you.

Provide your tenants with a clean place to live, with amenities that they have seldom had, and you'll have people who appreciate the fact they are getting help. As a result, you get fewer problems and less aggravation.

A final reason I like this program is that it provides me with a steady rental income stream. I know exactly how much money I'm receiving each month and how much I can put in my pocket after paying bills. In fact, you can even borrow money from the bank using next year's income as security. Why? Because the government guarantees the rents. I seldom worry about vacancies, because the demand for Section 8 housing is so great in most cities that there are always available tenants who need a place to live.

HOW TO GET INVOLVED

Do you have a rental property you would like to rent to Section 8 tenants? If so, visit your housing authority in the city in which your property is located. Mention that you are interested in helping them place tenants and would like some information. Probably you will be directed to a department official who will explain the program to you. Don't hesitate to ask lots of questions, but be courteous.

Describe your property and be sincere about wanting to provide housing for their clients. Let the official know that you are profit-motivated but want to work with the government to provide this service. Ask what the fair market rent is for an apartment like yours. Then decide if it is a better rate than you're getting now. Find out what the requirements are for you and the tenant. You'll be given a sample lease agreement, along with a list of requirements for all parties, the tenant, landlord, and housing authority.

If you are ready to sign up at this time, you will be given all the necessary information on the Section 8 program. You'll also be asked to put your apartment on a housing availability list. This is a list that Section 8 tenants look through to find housing. In some cities this list of properties is quite lengthy. Obviously, your property could sit on the list forever, lost among all the others. There is a better way.

Most housing authorities have a bulletin board to post "for rent" signs. Get some colorful construction paper and advertise your properties. Be creative. Describe your property and its amenities. Write down the amount you charge for each unit. Be sure to include a phone number so the tenants can respond.

In addition to this, make yourself visible around the Section 8 office. Get to know the people who advise the incoming Section 8 renters. Let them know you care. Make sure they know about your property and your efforts to get it rented to Section 8 tenants. Invite the director of the housing authority to visit your property. I personally invite the entire staff of the housing authority to a Christmas party every year. I do this to remind them that I exist and am still involved in their program.

WHAT TO DO WHEN THE TENANT CALLS

When tenants want to rent one of your properties, have the prospects fill out a rental application and apply your normal tenant screening process. If you feel they are not suitable for your property, you can refuse to rent to them. You are not allowed to discriminate on the basis of race, sex, religion, and so on. But you can deem the person to be irresponsible, untrustworthy, or financially unsound.

Let's say the tenant is just right. You review his application and feel he and his family will be good renters. At that point the renter (not the landlord) will turn in the request for housing to the housing authority. The housing authority will then send an inspector out to make sure your property complies with the current building standard for the city.

Don't worry. It should pass the inspection. Of course the inspector may find a couple of things wrong. Below is a list of possible common dwelling unit failures that must be repaired before a unit can be rented to a Section 8 tenant.

SECTION 8 EXAMPLES OF COMMON DWELLING UNIT FAILURES

Electrical

1. Three (3) prong, grounded electric outlets in kitchen, bathroom and for evaporative cooler.
   Four (4) prong, if two-speed motor. Weatherproof receptacle if roof-mount.
2. All electrical switches and receptacles must be tight and operating properly with good cover plates.
3. Multiple unit minimum service—60 amp and four (4) or more circuits. Single-family residence minimum service—100 amp.
4. Bulbs and globes in all light fixtures.
5. Fusestats or type "S" fuses required if panel not breakered.

Plumbing

1. Flex lines with shut-off valves on all gas appliances.
2. Hot water heater:
   a. Three-quarter (¾) inch pressure relief valve with ¾ inch discharge line six (6) inches from ground level.
   b. Vent caps must be FHA-U.L. approved.
   c. Outside units boxed in with vent top and bottom.
3. Faucets and traps free of drips and leaks.

Heating and Cooling

1. Adequate heating.
2. Central duct cooling on two (2) or more bedrooms.
3. Units with evaporative coolers must have screens on one openable window in each room or have up-duct installation.

Safety

1. Workable locks on all openable windows, bathroom doors and outside doors.
2. All floor covering good quality—NO BARE CONCRETE FLOORS (either tile or carpet).
3. Iron bars on windows must be SAFE EXIT APPROVED ONLY.
4. No double cylinder deadbolt locks unless room has other emergency exits.
5. Doors, windows, drawers and all hardware must be in good operating condition.
6. Rodents and insects properly exterminated.
7. No broken or cracked window panes.

Appearance

1. Exterior walls and trim painted and free from repair needs.
2. Interior walls and ceilings clean and free from repair needs.
3. Good roofing—free from leaks.
4. Yard free of debris.

Room Qualifications

1. Separate entrance for each bedroom off common hallway.
2. Bedrooms must have closets, closet doors and clothes rods.
3. Bedrooms 90 sq. ft.—minimum size.
4. In multi-bedroom units, common bathroom accessible from a common entrance.

CONTINUOUS EXTERIOR PERIMETER FOUNDATION—NO PIER BLOCKS

This list is not all inclusive, but indicative of inspection requirements.

When your property is approved by the housing authority, you and your new tenant will be asked to sign a rental contract provided by HUD. This contract spells out the terms of the lease and the amount of rent to be paid by the housing authority and by the tenant. Who pays the utilities and maintains the property is also covered. A sample lease is given at the end of this chapter. I have also provided a sample tenant–landlord inspection sheet. Use this to record the condition of the unit at time the tenant moves in. It is to your benefit to check the rental unit with the incoming tenant. This way you will be able to hold the tenant responsible for any damage done to the property.

It will take about forty-five to sixty days to get the first rent check. But it will be combined with the rent for the second month. Thereafter, the rents will come from the government on a monthly basis.

WHAT? NO MORE CERTIFICATES AVAILABLE?

During one of my northeast regional "Creating Wealth with Government Loans" seminars in Philadelphia, a woman stood up and claimed that she had called the HUD office and been told there were no more Section 8 certificates in Philadelphia.

Fortunately, our guest speaker that day was the woman in charge of the housing authority in Philadelphia. She answered this person's charge by stating that there were 6,000 people with certificates in need of Section 8 housing in the city. In fact, she was at our seminar to request landlords to sign up with the Philadelphia Section 8 program and get involved.

Again, we go back to a situation where someone *called* a government agency over the phone instead of visiting the office in person. (In this case the wrong agency, HUD.) Government agencies get hundreds of calls each day. Often the office receptionist doesn't know about all of the programs available or have time to answer your questions properly.

The other day a young investor visited the housing authority in a major city to inquire about Section 8 rentals and rehabilitation loans. She was told by a housing "counselor" that the program had been shut down because there was no money available.

It was quite a surprise when she read the following ad in the newspaper three days later:

APARTMENT OWNERS AND REAL ESTATE INVESTORS
Free City-Sponsored Seminar

RENTAL REHABILITATION PROGRAM

Section 8 Program

See how Rental Rehabilitation funds are put to work to support the rental rehabilitation program for the city. Learn how Section 8 eligible tenants can benefit. Learn how the landlord benefits. Tenants provided when eligible. Section 8 rental program discussed and explained.

Hear the details of 3% financing for rental property located in the housing target area. Free maps available.

CONTACT THE URBAN DEVELOPMENT & HOUSING DEPARTMENT

Not only did this city have an active Section 8 program, but they were giving free seminars because they had just been granted $585,000 to spend on the program!

This happens all the time. In most cities certificates are available, but you're not going to find out about them over the phone. Visit the office personally. Ask to speak to the person in charge of Section 8 housing. Be persistent and courteous until you get results.

GET THE GOVERNMENT OFFICIALS INVOLVED

We had a four-unit property that we wanted to rehabilitate with a 3 percent loan and rent to Section 8 tenants. However, in order to get the 3 percent rehabilitation loan, the property had to have five or more units. What we did to make five apartments was convert one of the large two-bedroom apartments into two studio apartments.

To get into the Section 8 program, we took the director of the housing authority to the property. He was so impressed with the quality of the improvements that he told his people at the housing authority to assist the Phillips brothers with any projects we might have in the future.

Government officials are only human. Most of the time they work at tedious jobs that command no respect and little pay. Patience and perseverance go a long way.

HOW ABOUT FIFTEEN-YEAR RENT GUARANTEES?

If you ask most housing authorities, they will tell you that there are no more fifteen-year rent guarantees. (In the past, there was a program under which the government promised to pay the tenant's rent for fifteen years.) This is true for houses and small apartment buildings. But there's one way to get fifteen-year guarantees. Many larger HUD-repossessed properties are offered for sale with fifteen-year rental guarantees attached as an incentive for investors to buy them. For big investors or a group of small investors pooling their resources, this is an opportunity to buy a large apartment building at a great price and get rental guarantees.

As a matter of fact, I'm working on a deal right now with fifteen-year guarantees. So the fifteen-year rental guarantees are still possible on larger HUD housing projects (twenty apartment units and larger).

TREND FOR THE FUTURE?

As part of the budget-cutting process started in 1985, the Reagan administration continued its attempt to shrink the federal role in housing and encourage programs to be funded and managed at the state and municipal (city) level. From this goal came the idea that a new Section 8 voucher program would be a cheaper and more effective alternative to the traditional low-income housing certificate program in current use. In fact, President Reagan proposed in 1985 eliminating the certificate program entirely and making the voucher plan the nation's main housing subsidy program. However, some of our country's legislators were hesitant to change from the certificate program to the yet-untested voucher program. So they chose instead to conduct a large-scale five-year test of the Section 8 voucher program to test its effectiveness.

What is the difference between the voucher and the certificate? The most obvious difference between the two forms of rental assistance is the voucher's so-called shopping incentive.

As we discussed previously, under the certificate program a family must occupy a property that costs no more than the HUD-determined fair market rent (FMR). The family contributes 30 percent of its adjusted income toward the cost of the unit, no more, no less. The Housing Authority pays the landlord the difference between that amount and the rent the landlord actually charges for the unit (usually the FMR).

The family has no incentive to look for cheaper housing, because any savings realized by moving to a less expensive unit would belong to HUD. (HUD simply pays a lower rent.) Likewise, even if they wanted to rent a more expensive property and pay more of their income in rent, they couldn't. The Housing Authority simply will not subsidize properties that rent for more than the FMR.

A voucher family may live in any home they choose, as long as it meets the current standards. The housing authority pays the landlord the difference between the FMR for the unit and 30 percent of the family's income, regardless of the rent actually charged for the unit. The family pays the balance.

Under the voucher program, the housing authority always pays the same amount of subsidy, regardless of the actual rent. If a voucher family finds housing that rents for less than the FMR, the family gets to pocket the savings instead of the government. Of course, this gives them a strong incentive to shop for cheaper housing. On the other hand, if they want to move to a unit with rent in excess of the FMR, they are able to do so without losing their subsidy. They will have to pay the additional rent themselves. Landlords across the nation may request higher rents from voucher tenants since they know these tenants are allowed to pay higher rents.

The government feels that the new voucher program will be cheaper to run because the vouchers have fewer strings attached than the old certificates. The housing agencies that manage this program at the local level will also realize greater savings with the voucher program. From an administrative standpoint, it is suspected that the costs of operation will be shifted from the federal level to the local housing authorities.

Of the 15,000 vouchers distributed on a trial basis, roughly two-thirds were distributed in conjunction with local rental rehabilitation programs, to help maintain the affordability of rental rehab projects

---

SECTION 8 BENEFITS

1. The program helps low-income renters pay their rent. It provides property owners with renters. Property owners fill vacancies more easily.
2. Rent subsidies can make investment property attractive to new investors.
3. Rent collection is achieved with few problems. The government mails the tenants' rent checks directly to you, the property owner.
4. Section 8 tenants are expected to live by the same rules and regulations as other tenants. Otherwise they can lose their Section 8 certificates. Landlords are reimbursed for any damage caused by a tenant.
5. The Section 8 program is easy to join.
6. The government pays generous fair market rents for Section 8 tenants.

for low-income tenants. The remainder were distributed to twenty large housing authorities in major cities to test their results. Although the test was supposed to run for five years. Congress issued 38,500 new vouchers in 1985 along with 54,500 new Section 8 certificates, in addition to the millions of existing certificates.

Obviously, a wave of change has come across the rent subsidy system. One can be sure that rent subsidies in one form or another are here to stay. How they are administered may vary from time to time. Housing for lower and moderate-income families is a very sensitive subject. Fortunately for tenants and landlords, however, this is one area of government funding that legislators hesitate to eliminate.

KEEP THESE POINTS IN MIND

1. Use the Section 8 rent guarantee program to help others and increase your cash.
2. Section 8 is a HUD program administered through local housing authorities. Contact the housing authority for information, not the HUD office.
3. Don't be discouraged by a receptionist who tells you a particular rent subsidy program is not available. Personally visit the housing authority. Establish a working relationship with employees. Let the director know you want to get involved and help him or her out.
4. If your property needs substantial repairs before it can be approved for Section 8 rentals ($1,000 or more per unit), look into the possibility of getting a low interest rate rental rehabilitation loan from the city.
5. How can you go wrong with guaranteed rents from our government?

CITY OF PHOENIX DEPARTMENT OF HOUSING AND URBAN REDEVELOPMENT

SECTION 8 HOUSING ASSISTANCE PAYMENTS PROGRAM
EXISTING HOUSING PART I OF THE
LEASE AGREEMENT BETWEEN TENANT AND LANDLORD

The Lease Agreement made and entered into this _____ day of _____ , 19 _____ , between
_____ hereinafter referred to as
"Landlord" and _____
hereinafter referred to as "Tenant."

WITNESSETH, that the parties herein, for the consideration set forth, do covenant and agree each with the other to the following terms and conditions:

1.1 The Landlord hereby leases to the Tenant all those certain premises, with the appurtenances, situated at _____
_____ and described as follows, viz: _____
commencing on the _____ day of _____ and ending on the _____ day of
_____ at a monthly rental which is stated in 1.2 below, subject to adjustment as hereinafter provided.

1.2 The total contract rent shall be $ _____ per month; $ _____ shall be the amount the Tenant shall pay. The HUR Department shall pay on behalf of the family an assistance payment of $ _____ per month. This amount shall be subject to change by reason of changes in the Tenant income, composition or in the Allowance for Utilities and Other Services or in the Contract Rent, as determined by HUR effective as of the date stated in a notification of such change by HUR to the Tenant and Landlord.

For the purpose of prorating rent, the daily rent shall be calculated on a thirty (30) day month.

1.3 The utility services will be provided as follows: (T) Tenant Furnished   (O) Owner Furnished.   Electric _____
Gas _____ Water _____ . Said rent shall be payable monthly to the Landlord or his designee, in advance, on or about the first day of the month for which payment is due, or as otherwise agreed upon in writing.

1.4 A Security Deposit of $ _____ shall be required against any damage except reasonable wear done to the premises by the Tenant, his family, guest or agent; to pay when billed the full amount of any such damage in order that the deposit will remain intact. Upon termination of the Lease Agreement, the deposit is to be refunded to the Tenant or be applied to any such damage or rent delinquency.

1.5 The tenant shall not assign this Lease Agreement to any other persons not listed in this paragraph, nor permit the use of the premises for any purpose other than as a private dwelling solely for the Tenant and his family, consisting of the following named persons:

_____

_____

_____

1.6 Entire Agreement: This Lease, including Part II hereof, contains the entire agreement between the parties hereto, and neither part is bound by any representations or agreements of any kind except as contained herein. No changes in the Lease shall be made except in writing signed by both the Owner and Tenant.

The rights of the Owner to receive Housing Assistance Payments as set forth in this Lease shall be subject to the Housing Assistance Contract and his compliance with all provisions of that Contract.

1.7 The sole financial obligation of HUR shall be to make Housing Assistance Payments on behalf of the Tenant. Neither HUR nor the Federal Government has assumed any obligation whatsoever for the amount of rent payable by the Tenant or the satisfaction of any claim by the Landlord against the Tenant, except in accordance with Section 13 of the Housing Assistance Payments Contract.

1.8 Unless terminated as provided herein, this Lease Agreement shall be for one year. The tenant may terminate this Lease Agreement, with HUR APPROVAL, upon 30 days written notice in advance to the Landlord. (See Attachment No. 1). The Landlord shall neither (i) terminate the tenancy during the term of the Contract and Assisted Lease, nor (ii) refuse to enter into a new Assisted Lease with the tenant unless the Landlord decides not to enter into a new Contract with respect to the unit, except for:

    (1) serious or repeated violation of the terms and conditions of the Lease;
    (2) violation of applicable Federal, State or Local Law; or
    (3) other good cause.

The Lease Agreement shall be renewed upon expiration, for successive terms of one year at a time or the term of the Annual Contributions Contract pertaining to the Lease Agreement, whichever is shorter.

_____   _____   _____   _____
TENANT   DATE   OWNER   DATE

_____   _____   _____   _____
SPOUSE   DATE   OWNER   DATE

REV. 5/83

Page 1 of 3

CITY OF PHOENIX DEPARTMENT OF HOUSING AND URBAN DEVELOPMENT
SECTION 8 HOUSING ASSISTANCE PAYMENTS PROGRAM
EXISTING HOUSING PART II OF THE
LEASE AGREEMENT BETWEEN TENANT AND LANDLORD

2.1 The Landlord shall permit HUR and the Government, or any of their duly authorized representatives, to have access to the premises and, for the purpose of audit and examination, to have access to any books, documents, papers and records of the Landlord that are pertinent to compliance with this Lease Agreement.

2.2 Tenant for himself and his heirs, executors and administrators agrees as follows:

    (a) To pay the rent herein stated promptly when due, without any deductions whatsoever, and without any obligation on the part of the Landlord to make any demand for the same.

    Tenant further agrees that if he should fail to pay rent herein stipulated promptly when due and fails to pay rent within 14 days after written notice by the Landlord of nonpayment of his intention to terminate the Lease Agreement, the Landlord may terminate this Lease Agreement.

    (b) If Tenant defaults in making any payment required by this Lease Agreement and a court action is commenced for the collection of said payment, then Landlord and Tenant agree that attorneys' fees will be awarded to the prevailing party.

    (c) No alteration, addition, or improvements shall be made in or to the premises without the consent of the Landlord in writing.

    (d) Tenant agrees not to waste utilities furnished by the Landlord; not to use utilities or equipment for any improper or unauthorized purpose; and not to place fixtures, signs, or fences in or about the premises without the prior revocable permission of the Landlord in writing.

    (e) Tenant agrees to conduct himself and require his guests on the premises to conduct themselves in a manner that will not disturb his neighbors peaceful enjoyment of the premises. Some general rules or regulations that apply but are not limited to: (1) serious or repeated interference with the rights of other Tenants; (2) serious or repeated damage to the premises or property; (3) illegal use of the premises; and (4) failure to control the behavior of his children.

    (f) Tenant agrees to keep the premises in a clean, safe and sanitary condition, and to comply with all laws, health and policy requirements with respect to said premises and appurtenances, and to save the Landlord harmless from all fines, penalties, and costs for violations or noncompliance by Tenant with any of said laws, requirements, or regulations, and from all liability arising out of any such violations or noncompliance.

    (g) To permit the Landlord, or his agents, or any representative of any mortgage on the property, or when authorized by the Landlord the employees of any contractor, utility company, municipal agent, or other to enter the premises for the purpose of making reasonable inspections and repairs. The Landlord shall not abuse the right of access to harass the tenant. The Landlord shall give the tenant at least 2 days notice, except in the case of an emergency, of his intent to enter and enter only at reasonable times. The Tenant reserves the right to have a representative present for any inspection of these premises.

    (h) To have no animals or pets of any kind on the premises, other than those expressly permitted in writing by the Landlord.

    (i) In the event that the Tenant, because of increase in family income, becomes ineligible for Section 8 Housing Assistance Payments Program and cannot continue in the Program, the Tenant shall so notify the Landlord in writing prior to the beginning of the next month of his tenancy. If, prior to conclusion of such month plus thirty (30) days, this Lease Agreement between Landlord and Tenant shall be terminated.

    (j) The Tenant, by the execution of the Lease Agreement, admits that the dwelling unit described herein has been inspected by him, and meets with the approval of the Tenant. The Tenant acknowledges hereby that said premises have been satisfactorily completed, and that the Landlord will not be required to repaint, replaster, or otherwise perform any other work, labor or services which it has already performed for the Tenant. The Tenant admits that the premises are in a tenantable condition, and agrees that at the end of the occupancy hereunder to deliver up and surrender said premises to the Landlord in as good condition as when received, reasonable wear and tear excepted.

2.3 Landlord hereby agrees as follows:

    (a) To make all structural and exterior repairs, including specifically, repairs to the roof, plumbing, exterior walls, screens, steps, walks, fences and painting, and repair or replacement of heating equipment, cooking range and refrigerator, as any such become necessary, during the term of this Lease Agreement or any extension thereof.

    (b) To pay all real estate taxes both general and special assessed or imposed upon the demised premises and/or the building of which the demised premises is a part during the term of the Lease Agreement.

    To carry and pay all premiums upon fire and extended coverage insurance and Landlord and Tenant liability insurance as Landlord may deem appropriate to place upon the premises.

    (c) The Landlord warrants that he has the right to execute this Lease Agreement and there are no outstanding liens and encumbrances that will interfere with the Tenant's possession of the premises in accordance with the terms of the Lease Agreement.

    (d) The Landlord warrants that the premises leased hereunder comply with the local Phoenix Housing and Urban Redevelopment Department regulations and HUD Housing Quality Standards and that the mechanical equipment and the utilities are in good serviceable condition.

    (e) That the Landlord shall not in his representations of termination of any occupancy or provision of services, or in any other manner in relation to this Lease Agreement, discriminate against any person on the grounds of race, color, creed, national origin or sex.

192-805D REV 5 83

(f) In return for the Tenant's continued fulfillment of the terms and conditions of this Lease Agreement, the Landlord covenants that the Tenant may at all times while this Lease Agreement remains in effect have and enjoy for his sole use and benefit the property hereinabove described.

2.4 The Landlord shall provide maintenance and services as follows:

(a) Custodial services (including, but not limited to, cleaning of hallways, garbage storage areas, and all common areas, and provisions of an adequate supply of trash and garbage disposal). Detached dwellings are exempt from providing this service.

(b) Grounds maintenance (including, but not limited to, exterior custodial services and maintenance of lawns and outdoor plantings, including lawn cutting and reseeding). Detached dwellings are exempt from providing this service.

(c) Prompt response to Tenant service calls (including, but not limited to, calls with respect to refrigerators, ranges, plumbing, heating, electrical and hot water fixtures and systems and broken, or damaged doors, screens or windows).

(d) Repainting and redecorating dwelling space and non-dwelling space surfaces on a three-year cycle.

(e) Prompt replacement of light bulbs and other lighting equipment in common (including outdoor) areas. Detached dwellings are exempt from providing this service.

(f) Exterminating services on a regularly scheduled basis, but not less frequently than annually.

(g) Repair of walkways and parking lot surfaces.

(h) Where applicable, repair of garbage disposal, dishwashers, air conditioners and laundry equipment.

(i) Where applicable, regular maintenance and prompt repair of elevators, incinerators, compactors and laundry equipment and facilities plus other maintenance services as are generally supplied to tenants in the housing market area.

(j) Security services and equipment as are generally supplied to tenants in the housing market area.

TENANT — LANDLORD INSPECTION

Tenant will fill out the following inventory for a record of his comments on the move-in condition.

The Landlord may do the same in the appropriate column if he so desires.

*Required Items

ROOM	ITEM	MOVE-IN CONDITION Tenant	MOVE-IN CONDITION Landlord
Living Room	Drapes		
	Floor		
	Walls		
	Windows		
Kitchen	Curtains		
	Floor		
	Walls		
	Range*		
	Refrigerator*		
	Cabinets		
	Countertop		
	Sink		
	3 Prong Grounded Outlets*		
	Windows		
Bath	Curtains		
	Floor		
	Walls		
	Tub/Shower		
	Door Lockable*		
	Windows		
	3 Prong Grounded Outlets*		
Bedroom 1	Curtains		
	Floor		
	Walls		
	Closet Space		
	Windows		
Bedroom 2	Curtains		
	Floor		
	Walls		
	Closet Space		
	Windows		
Bedroom 3	Curtains		
	Floor		
	Walls		
	Closet Space		
Hall	Windows		
	Floor		
	Walls		
General Landlord			
	100 AMP*		
	Hot Water Heater*		
	Cooling Working*		
	Heating Working*		
	Screens (Evap. Coolers)		
	Windows		
	Roof		

This is **not** the HUR inspection. No lease or contract is effective until after the HUR inspection approval. The HUR Department shall determine the effective date.

This documentation along with the list of Common Dwelling Unit Failures may be used only as a guide to the Tenant and Landlord to help them determine if the unit would pass Section "8" requirements.

The Section "8" inspector will inspect the dwelling when the Landlord feels it is ready for inspection.

12

HOW TO QUALIFY FOR A GOVERNMENT LOAN

MONEY IS LIKE AN ARM OR LEG—USE IT OR LOSE IT.

Henry Ford

Whether you want to borrow $5,000 or $5,000,000, you have to know what it takes to qualify for a loan. If you can't qualify for a government loan, you're not going to get it. Part of the process is knowing how to fill out government paperwork. Sometimes it is not you personally who qualifies for the government program, it is a property or a tenant— but you get the money. You also need to know how to put together a loan proposal. You will learn all this in this chapter.

WHAT GOES INTO A LOAN PROPOSAL?

Whenever you apply for a government loan, I recommend that you put together a formal loan proposal that gives the government all the information pertinent to the loan. This will strengthen your loan application and give you credibility. To do this, you have to do your homework. You have to know what goes into a good proposal and how to present your information.

Go to the government agency you are applying through and find out what that particular office wants to see in a loan proposal. What information is required? Find out the loan procedures. Is there a set time period or a deadline they expect you to meet? Find out when the loan committee reviews loan applications. How do you submit the finished proposal?

In other words, find out what the government wants and give it to them. This is an important key to success with the government. The government will always give you a list of guidelines and rules to follow. Don't leave any lines blank or let any questions go unanswered. The thicker your proposal, the better. But don't just add fluff; include information that the government wants. If you have any questions or don't understand a particular loan requirement, ask the person in charge of your loan to explain. Clarify any questions before you turn in your application. Ask questions before you submit your loan proposal. Afterwards, it may delay your loan.

AVOID THIS MISTAKE

Before submitting the proposal have every document copied, even letters. Make notes of all telephone conversations you have with government officials. Write down the day and time you called and the name of the person you spoke with. The government loves to lose paperwork. They don't do it intentionally, but it happens.

We almost fell victim to a government paperwork snafu when we applied for a loan increase during one of our rehab projects. The same office that had issued us the initial loan had no record of the documents we had filed with them earlier. They had no record of our request for the loan increase either. Fortunately, my brother Richard always insists on noting every interaction we have with government officials. We showed them the records of our phone conversations with key people within the department. We showed them so much documentation that they could not refute our information. What could have delayed our loan request was avoided due to our good recordkeeping.

Don't Forget These Items

Below is a list of documents I included in a recent loan application. This is typical of what should be in a good loan proposal:

A. Background of Redevelopers—Phillips Brothers
  1. Redeveloper's Statement for Public Disclosure
  2. Redeveloper's Statement of Qualifications and Financial Responsibility
  3. Project Team: Architect—Construction Management—Engineers
  4. Rehabilitation and Development Experience
  5. Proposed Redevelopment of Project
  6. Financial Information—Operating Data Sheet
B. Project Highlights
  1. Building Design
  2. Letters of Intent from Project Team
  3. Work Schedule
  4. Highest Best Use Survey
  5. Impact on Employment in Area
  6. Conclusion
C. Summary

Qualifying for the Loan

One of the most important sections of your rehabilitation loan proposal will be the financial data. This is the information that the government loan committee will use to decide if you are capable of paying back the loan. A key component of the financial section of your loan proposal is a government form called the *operating data sheet*. It includes major criteria for your loan approval.

Qualifying for government rehabilitation loans is simply based on a mathematical formula. This is drawn from the data on your operating data sheet. That's the most important thing to learn. Don't be over-concerned about dollar amounts or the rental income; it's the formula that's important. By formula I mean a ratio, the ratio of income to expenses or the debt service ratio. It tells the loan committee if you should be able to repay the debt.

If you want to qualify for a government loan, this ratio has to be within certain limits. I am going to show you how to get the ratio within those limits. If you don't understand how to do this, you are never going to get a loan from the government.

FILLING OUT THE OPERATING DATA SHEET

Take a look at the completed operating data sheet on page 158. This sheet is probably the most important aspect of your loan proposal. It demonstrates your ability to repay the loan. For our example, we will apply for a $100,000 government loan to rehab a ten-unit apartment building.

Let's start at the top of the operating data sheet, where you see the heading "A. Before rehabilitation (Annual income last 12 months.)" On the first line, under "Number of Type Unit," we put the number 5. After that we put the number 1 in the "Bedrooms Per Unit" column. This means the building has five one-bedroom apartments. The amount $150.00 goes in the next column, because that is what the units in our example would rent for in their current condition. In the fourth column, labeled "Income Received," we put a zero. This is because the building has not had anyone living in it for the last twelve months. Finally, in the fifth column, "Received if Full Occupancy," we put $9,000, meaning that if we have five one-bedroom apartments renting for $150.00 a month each, we would have an income of $9,000 a year

(5 one-bedroom units × $150 per mo. × 12 months = $9,000).

The same process is used to complete the second line of section A. Here, we fill in the information for the five two-bedroom units that rent for $200 each. In the fifth column we enter the amount $12,000

(5 two-bedroom units × $200 per mo. × 12 months = $12,000).

The five two-bedrooms will rent for more than the five one-bedrooms. Now look at line five, "Total Rentals Income." We filled in $21,000 ($9,000 + $12,000) in column five. If we had other income, from a laundry or video games, for example, we would put the amount on line six. Since we have no other income, we enter a zero. Line nine

GOVERNMENT LOAN
OPERATING DATA SHEET
COMMERCIAL AND MULTIPLE RESIDENTIAL PROPERTIES

Name of Applicant: _____

Property Address: _____

A. BEFORE REHABILITATION (Annual Income Last 12 Months)					B. AFTER REHABILITATION (Estimated Annually)			
Number of Type Unit	Bedrooms Per Unit	Monthy Rent Per Unit	ANNUAL RENT		No. of Each Type Unit	Bedrooms Per Unit	Monthly Rent Per Unit	Annual Rent Full Occupancy
			Income Received	Received if Full Occupancy				
TOTAL RENTALS INCOME								
Other Income (Specify)								
TOTAL INCOME BEFORE REHABILITATION								
						TOTAL ESTIMATED INCOME		

C. EQUIPMENT AND SERVICES INCLUDED IN RENT

(Before and After Rehabilitation)

ITEMS	Before	After
Range (Gas or Electricity)		
Refrigerator (Gas or Electricity)		
Attic Vent Fan		
Laundry Facilities		
Venetian Blinds		
Water (Cold)		
Water (Hot)		

ITEMS	Before	After
Gas		
Electricity		
Heat (Specify fuel)		
Janitor Service		
Air Conditioning		
Ground Maintenance		
Garbage and Rubbish Removal		
Other (Specify)		

D. ANNUAL OPERATING EXPENSES:

	Before Rehab.	After Rehab.
ADMINISTRATIVE EXPENSE: Management		
Superintendent		
OPERATING EXPENSE: Elevator Maintenance		
Heating		
Janitorial Materials		
Lighting—Misc. Power		
Water		
Gas		
Garbage Removal		
Payroll		
MAINTENANCE EXPENSE: Decorating		
Repairs		
Exterminating		
Insurance		
Furniture & Furnishings		
Miscellaneous		
TOTAL OPERATING EXPENSES		
RESERVE FOR REPLACEMENTS		
TOTAL EXPENSES & RESERVE		

PROJECTED ANNUAL OPERATING STATEMENT

E. PROJECTED ANNUAL OPERATING STATEMENT

Estimated Annual Income from Schedule B _____

Minus

Vacancy rate _____

Effective Gross Income _____

Minus Operating Expenses & Property Taxes

Operating Expenses (from Schedule D) _____

Property Taxes _____

Net Income Before Debt Service _____

Debt Service (amount necessary for payment of P & I on all mortgages outstanding on property _____

Debt Service Coverage _____

GOVERNMENT LOAN
OPERATING DATA SHEET
COMMERCIAL AND MULTIPLE RESIDENTIAL PROPERTIES

Name of Applicant:
(Insert Your Name or

Partnership Name)

Property Address:
(Insert Address)

A. BEFORE REHABILITATION (Annual Income Last 12 Months) | **B. AFTER REHABILITATION (Estimated Annually)**

Number of Type Unit	Bedrooms Per Unit	Monthly Rent Per Unit	ANNUAL RENT Income Received	Received if Full Occupancy	No. of Each Type Unit	Bedrooms Per Unit	Monthly Rent Per Unit	Annual Rent Full Occupancy
5	1	150.00	0	9,000	5	1	300.00	18,000
5	2	200.00	0	12,000	5	2	355.00	21,300
TOTAL RENTALS INCOME				21,000				
Other Income (Specify)				0				
TOTAL INCOME BEFORE REHABILITATION			0	$21,000				39,300
							TOTAL ESTIMATED INCOME	39,300

C. EQUIPMENT AND SERVICES INCLUDED IN RENT

(Before and After Rehabilitation)

ITEMS	Before	After
Range (Gas or Electricity)		X
Refrigerator (Gas or Electricity)		X
Attic Vent Fan		
Laundry Facilities		
Venetian Blinds		
Water (Cold)		X
Water (Hot)		

ITEMS	Before	After
Gas		
Electricity		
Heat (Specify fuel)		
Janitor Service		
Air Conditioning		
Ground Maintenance		X
Garbage and Rubbish Removal		X
Other (Specify)		

D. ANNUAL OPERATING EXPENSES:

	Before Rehab.	After Rehab.
ADMINISTRATIVE EXPENSE: Management		3,851
Superintendent		
OPERATING EXPENSE: Elevator Maintenance		
Heating		
Janitorial Materials		
Lighting—Misc. Power		400
Water		1,080
Gas		
Garbage Removal		
Payroll		1,200
MAINTENANCE EXPENSE: Decorating		
Repairs		515
Exterminating		
Insurance		500
Furniture & Furnishings		
Miscellaneous		100
TOTAL OPERATING EXPENSES		7,646
RESERVE FOR REPLACEMENTS		1,000
TOTAL EXPENSES & RESERVE		8,646

PROJECTED ANNUAL OPERATING STATEMENT

E. PROJECTED ANNUAL OPERATING STATEMENT

Estimated Annual Income from Schedule B	$39,300
Minus	
Vacancy rate	$786
Effective Gross Income	38,514
Minus Operating Expenses & Property Taxes	
Operating Expenses (from Schedule D)	8,646
Property Taxes	950
Net Income Before Debt Service	28,918
Debt Service (amount necessary for payment of P & I on all mortgages outstanding on property	$23,785
Debt Service Coverage	1.22

is for "Total Income Before Rehabilitation." Insert the total in columns four and five on line nine. In our case they are zero and $21,000 respectively.

Let's move on to section B, "After Rehabilitation." Note that the first two columns are the same as in section A. In column three we are to put the monthly rent per unit. How do you estimate what the monthly rent will be per apartment? You could check to see what the neighbors charge for similar apartments or ask a real estate agent. A fool-proof way to figure the fair market rent for any property is to simply contact the housing authority in the city where the property is located and ask what the Section 8 fair market rent is for the neighborhood. They will be happy to tell you.

In our example, the maximum rent allowed for one-bedroom apartments in this neighborhood is $300.00. The rent for two-bedroom apartments is $355.00. So we put $300.00 on line one of column three and $355.00 on line two of column three. We end up with a total estimated income of $39,300:

$$5 \text{ one-bedroom units} \times \$300 \text{ per mo.} \times 12 \text{ months} = \$18,000$$
$$5 \text{ two-bedroom units} \times \$355 \text{ per mo.} \times 12 \text{ months} = \underline{21,300}$$

$$\text{Total estimated income} = \$39,300$$

It is important to use these government rent figures, because this is a fool-proof way to get your rent estimates approved.

Hot Tip: How to Get Higher Rents

We use the government rent figures because, after this building is fixed up, we plan to rent it to section 8 tenants. In the last chapter, we discussed how to get involved with this program. I just want to tell you a little secret here that I have discovered the hard way.

It is possible to get up to 120 percent of the fair market rent for your apartments. To do this, you will have to become acquainted with the program director of the housing authority. He is the only one who can authorize additional rent. If you can *honestly* justify to the program director that the rent of $300.00 per month for the one-bedroom apartments is not enough to cover rehab costs, the director can permit you $360.00 per month. The housing authority will never tell you this, but you can request higher rents.

It is important to remember that you are not going to be able to establish such a relationship with the director over the phone. You have to visit the office in person. You have to let him know that you want to buy property and rent it to elderly, disabled, or low-income persons to help them out. However, though you may be able to get higher rents at a later date, be sure to use the regular rent figures when filling out the operating data sheet—not the 120 percent values.

Hot Tip: Install Used Appliances

In section C we check off the equipment and services we plan to provide after the rehabilitation is completed. Cross off the "Before" column; it's not important.

The government requires you to install certain appliances. However, it is not required that they be new, only that the appliances be clean and in good operating condition. Buying used appliances will save you thousands of dollars over time. I highly recommend this.

Figure the Operating Expenses

Section D is for the annual operating expenses. We're not going to figure the before-rehabilitation expenses, only the after-rehabilitation expenses. The figures used are estimates of the annual expenses for this building. The only exception is the management fee. You are allowed to pay yourself a management fee equal to 10 percent of the effective gross rental income. Of course, you can hire a management company and pay them. But if you plan to manage the property yourself, include your 10 percent fee. In our case this amounts to $3,851 ($38,514 × .10). Be sure to use dollar amounts for expenses, not percentages. The government wants dollar figures.

Our total expenses add up to $8,646. The total expenses in section D must be between 21 and 24 percent of the total estimated income in section B. This is the percentage the government wants to see. Our $8,646 just happens to be 22 percent of $39,300, so we are in the ball park. That is why the government wants to see dollar figures: the person reviewing the loan application will do these same calculations.

Now we are ready for section E, "projected annual operating statement." It is the most crucial section of the operating data sheet. Our example gives the numbers we calculated in the previous sections for income and expenses.

What vacancy rate percentage should you use? Use 7 percent of the gross incomes for *federal* loan projects, 2 percent of the gross income for state and local projects. Do not use anything else. The federal government bases its calculations on a 7 percent vacancy factor, regardless of the figure you enter. Since this loan is through a *local* government program, we used the permissible 2 percent vacancy figure to get an amount of $786.00 (.02 × $39,300). The resulting effective gross income is $38,514. Subtracting operating expenses and property taxes, we reach "net income before debt service."

Now we need to know what the debt service will be on all the loans on the property, including the amount we plan to borrow. The payments on the current mortgages can be figured by adding up all of the payments per year. The government will tell us the interest rate and annual payments for the new $100,000 loan. We add this amount to the amount for the existing mortgages, and put the resulting number on the "debt service" line of section E. We figure our payments to be $23,785.

What is the Correct Debt Service Ratio?

Now we are ready to calculate the debt service ratio. It's very simple to do. Take your net income and divide it by your debt service. In other words, divide $28,918 by $23,785. The result is 1.2. To be approved a loan is required to have a debt service ratio of 1.1 or higher. It is as simple as that. If you end up with a ratio of .95 or 1.0 you won't qualify. If you have a 1.2 or higher, then you're OK.

Why a 1.1 Ratio?

A debt service ratio of 1.1 or better demonstrates to the government that you will have enough income from rents to pay all expenses and all debt. I don't know how the government came up with a figure of 1.1. I only know that this is the figure they plug into the computer when they process your loan application. The higher the number, the better your chances of getting the loan. In general, if you have a debt service ratio of 1.55 you are not going to have much of a problem getting a loan, if everything else in your proposal checks out.

If you have a ratio of less than 1.1, you need to go over your expenses to reduce them or else find out how to raise your income. Perhaps you are borrowing too much money. Some states, such as California, have such high property costs that extremely high existing mortgage payments make it next to impossible to get the ratio within the 1.1 to 1.5 range. To compensate for this, some states will use special bond money to create affordable loans. They are called "write-down" loans because you have to pay back only a portion of the amount you initially borrowed. Contact your local government for details on the write-down program. (These loans are usually only for large housing projects where investors need to borrow over $500,000, and not all states offer this program.)

Submit Your Proposal Personally

When you have everything together, make copies and personally deliver the proposal to your loan officer. Get a written receipt. Find out when the loan committee will meet to discuss your proposal. Then, two to three days after submitting your proposal, call your loan officer and ask if he or she has had a chance to look at your package yet. Make sure everything is in order. Ask if there is anything else you can do to expedite the processing.

Follow These Steps

These are the steps that I have used to borrow millions of government dollars at low interest rates. They work. If you do your homework and provide the government with what it wants to see, you will get what you want—your loan.

To sum up the loan process, here are the steps to follow:

1. Decide which government loan program suits your needs.
2. Find out what the government wants on a loan application.
3. Give the government the information it wants in a formal loan proposal.
4. Do your homework. Fill in every detail.

5. Use income and expense figures that are within government guidelines.
6. Have a debt service ratio of 1.1 or better.
7. Make photocopies of all documents.
8. Submit your proposal personally to the loan officer.
9. Check with your loan officer regularly to see how the loan is progressing.
10. Most important, be prepared. Be persistent.

KEEP THESE POINTS IN MIND
1. Each government agency has its own loan guidelines for you to follow.
2. Government rehab loans can be placed on properties with many existing loans.
3. Projected, not current, income qualifies the building for the loan.
4. For best results put together a loan proposal for every government loan you apply for.

13

PRESENT-DAY PROFITS WITH OLDER AND HISTORIC PROPERTIES

HE THAT WILL NOT APPLY NEW REMEDIES MUST EX-
PECT NEW EVILS.

Sir Francis Bacon

Throughout this book we have emphasized that you can't make money in real estate when you pay market prices for property and high interest rates. We have discussed several ways to use government programs to buy properties at bargain prices and get low interest rate loans. Now let's look at yet another way to use the government to make money.

WHY HISTORIC PROPERTIES?

Historic properties offer fantastic investment opportunities, because you can acquire run-down historic properties for little or nothing, then borrow low interest money from the government to restore them. The end result is affordable monthly payments lower than your former rent—or positive cash flows for income-producing historic properties.

In addition, special tax benefits can result in direct tax savings for you, or the benefits can be sold to investors, dollar for dollar, for cash in your pocket.

WHAT IS HISTORIC RESTORATION?

Restoration involves the substantial improvement of historic property. This improvement can include the conversion of the property for a new use that increases its value for profit. The end result may be housing, offices, retail shops, theaters, art galleries, or whatever is an economically feasible use for the restored building.

There are a number of different ways you, the developer, can realize a return on a historic rehabilitation project. These include:
- Profit from the sale of a renovated property when the sale price exceeds the purchase and rehab costs.
- Actual cash flow generated by the operation of your properties.
- Fees earned for organizing and managing the project for someone else.
- Syndication fees earned through the sale of shares in the project to limited parters.
- Tax losses (e.g., depreciation) that shelter other income.
- Tax credits, which can be used to offset federal tax liability.

YOU, THE DEVELOPER

A developer is any person who builds, restores, or rehabs real estate or oversees these activities. Your role as developer is to determine the feasibility of the development project. That is, does it make financial sense? What the developer also brings to the project is the ability to acquire, organize, and manage the required investment capital and professional services. The ultimate goal is profit, and this should be your motivation.

WHY PRESERVE?

For one third of the cost of new construction, you can rehab or restore a property in need of fix up. When people think of the preservation of historic buildings, they usually think of single landmarks. Today, the opportunities associated with preserving historic districts and entire neighborhoods are recognized by both preservationists and investors.

It is now realized that not every old building can exist solely as a relic of the past. Old buildings must be integrated into the social and economic fabric of the twentieth century. This means finding contemporary uses for these buildings and making the necessary changes to them to accommodate these uses.

Often old buildings are more "sensitive" than modern buildings in terms of design and construction. More care, craftsmanship and pride went into their development. Many have features that would be too expensive to duplicate today. Some of the craftsmanship is lost. More and more, people are recognizing this artistic heritage and are willing to pay a premium to live and work in its surrounding.

Many cities have areas of vacant industrial buildings, from which businesses have moved to the suburbs or the sunbelt states. These areas are waiting for new economic use, since it is obvious that the old industries are not going to return. The areas of Soho in New York City and the river banks of St. Louis are obvious examples, where nineteenth and early twentieth century warehouses have been turned into art galleries, restaurants and offices.

In cities across the country, people are seeking the type of creative living space available in these buildings. Adapting older buildings such as outdated warehouses, government buildings, schools and older homes to new uses provides an opportunity for a developer to exercise creative and entrepreneurial skills. Here are some other reasons for preserving historic buildings:

Saves Energy

Though recent years have seen a drop in oil prices, predictions for the future vary. Since most large cities have already grown to limits beyond practical commuting distance and the funds for new roadways are scarce, redeveloping in existing city centers seems most practical.

Creates Jobs

The Economic Development Administration reports that for every million dollars spent, renovation creates 109 new jobs, while new construction results in only 69 jobs. Rehabilitation thus produces 64 percent more jobs at one third of the cost.

Helps Small Investors

Restoring historic properties can be done with only limited resources. Much of the rehab work can be done personally by the investor.

Federal, state, and local governments provide incentives that make restoration enormously profitable for those who undertake this work. Current tax laws make it possible for small investors even in rental houses to take advantage of tax credits that were formerly available only to owners of commercial property.

The involvement of small investors is evidenced by the size of rehabilitation projects that have taken advantage of the Investment Tax Credit (ITC) offered by the federal government as a result of the 1981 Economic Recovery Tax Act. Rehabs of less than $100,000 in construction costs have accounted for 45 percent of the projects qualifying for the ITC. Rehabs of $100,000 to $500,000 account for an additional 35 percent. These are small projects in terms of real estate rehab. This clearly indicates that small-scale entrepreneurs are taking advantage of rehab development opportunities.

Advantages over New Construction

Rehabilitation also has great advantages over new construction in terms of the conservation of natural resources. Rather than destroying wildlife and farmland to develop new projects in outlying areas, a rehabilitation project utilizes an existing building with access to streets, water and sewer systems, and fire and police service. Also, as mentioned before, rehab costs only one third as much as new construction.

Today's Opportunities with Historic Properties

In the past few years, rehabilitation of old buildings has accounted for about one third of all non-residential construction, an amount that has doubled in the last decade. This amount will grow even more as the government rehab incentives become more widely known. The total dollar amount spent for all "remodeling" approaches $100 billion annually. In the area of historic rehabilitation, the growth is more phenomenal. Tax incentives brought about by the Tax Reform Act of 1976 were not nearly as advantageous as the current law, yet encouraged private investment of more than $2.2 billion in 4,350 historic preservation projects.

Passage of the 1981 Economic Recovery Act is producing even more dramatic growth. The Treasury Department estimates that construction eligible for the 25 percent historic rehab tax credit increased to an average of $2 billion annually in 1985, a fourfold increase in three years.

In the residential market, there will be 50 million new households formed in the 1980s, compared to 30 million in the 1970s. During the last ten years, more units were added to the nation's rental housing stock though adaptive reuse, housing rehab, and the division of large houses into smaller units than through the construction of new units. With the great demand for housing, the need for recycling of old buildings will continue through the 1980s, providing fantastic profit opportunities and affordable housing.

The 25 Percent Investment Tax Credit

For years the Internal Revenue Code favored new construction over rehabilitation. New buildings could be depreciated faster than rehabs. This encouraged demolition and rebuilding rather than renovation, causing an enormous number of beautiful old buildings to be lost for economic reasons. Buildings that were irreplaceable treasures fell to the wrecker's ball, not because they lacked value, but because of the way Congress had written the tax laws.

Incentives related to historic properties were first passed in 1976.

These incentives provided for a sixty-month amortization period for certified rehab expenses and accelerated depreciation for substantially rehabilitated certified historic properties. In 1978 a 10 percent tax credit was added.

The Economic Recovery Tax Act of 1981 (ERTA) went even further to encourage historic preservation. The incentives were simplified and substantially improved. The 10 percent tax credit was replaced by a three-tiered credit for the rehabilitation costs of certain buildings. For non-residential income properties over thirty years old, a 15 percent tax credit is now offered; for non-residential income properties over forty years old, a 20 percent credit is allowed; and for certified historic structures, both commercial and residential, a 25 percent tax credit is available.

ERTA also improved the depreciation rule. While the old law required depreciation over the useful life of the property, ERTA allows the rehabilitated property to be depreciated over only fifteen years. (See chapter 14 for additional real estate tax information.)

QUALIFYING A BUILDING FOR THE ITC

Use of the 15 percent credit for buildings at least thirty years old and the 20 percent credit for buildings at least forty years old is limited to non-residential industrial and commercial buildings, which are used for income-producing purposes.

The 25 percent credit, however, applies to both depreciable non-residential and residential building. For the 25 percent credit, the building must be certified by the Secretary of the Interior as historic. To get a building certified is not as hard as it may seem. The building must be listed on the National Register of Historic Places or be within the boundaries of a certified historic district.

In addition, a historic building must be rehabilitated to certain standards in order to qualify for the ITC. Basically, these standards are that the rehabilitation must maintain the historic character and style of the building. Usually rehab plans must be approved by the historic preservation offices in your area.

If a building lies within a historic district but is not certified as "historic," the building is eligible for the 15 or 20 percent credit if it meets the age requirement. An older building can be certified by review of the National Park Service Historic Preservation office. Once certified, it will be eligible for the 25 percent tax credit.

HOW THE TAX CREDIT WORKS

A tax credit reduces a taxpayer's liability dollar for dollar. The distinction between a tax credit and a tax deduction is worth noting. A tax credit comes off the bottom line of the investor's tax bill (the amount required in taxes). On the other hand, a deduction is subtracted from the taxpayer's income before taxes are calculated. Thus, to an investor in the 50 percent bracket, a $1000 tax deduction is worth only $500, whereas a $1000 tax credit is worth $1000.

Historic properties offer great tax credit opportunities. For example, let's say that you find a certified historic property available for $10,000. You figure it will cost $100,000 to restore the building. Since the building qualifies for local low interest rehabilitation money in your city, you get a 3 percent rehabilitation loan from the government. With this money you rehabilitate the property. You also receive a $25,000 tax credit:

$$\begin{array}{r} \$100,000 \text{ rehabilitation cost} \\ \times \qquad .25 \text{ ITC} \\ \hline \$ 25,000 \text{ tax credit} \end{array}$$

The $25,000 ITC is a direct tax savings. If you owe $10,000 in income taxes, you could use $10,000 of your $25,000 ITC to reduce your tax liability to zero. You would also have the right to carry forward the remaining $15,000 ITC over the next fifteen years, and would save up to $15,000 that you would have had to pay in income taxes during those years. Not a bad deal, is it? But even better, you can elect to go back to the last three years and have the IRS refund taxes you've already paid, up to the remaining ITC balance (in our example, $15,000). The IRS must also pay you interest on the taxes to be refunded. Now, how's that for a deal?

But what happens if you don't pay taxes, are in a low income tax bracket, or have not paid taxes in the last three years, and need tax write-offs like a hole in the head? Well, here's the reason that historic properties are for everyone—rich, poor, self-employed, unemployed, even bankrupt.

In 1984, nearly $5 billion was paid to people like you by persons in the 50 percent tax bracket to buy investment tax credits available with historic properties. This amount increased from $4 billion in 1983. In 1985, persons in the 50 percent tax bracket put over $6 billion into the hands of people ready, willing, and able to take advantage of the historic property opportunities available right now in every city, town, and state throughout the United States.

To get involved in this program you need to locate certified public accountants or certified financial planners who have clients in high tax brackets. Show them information about your historic property. The CPAs that deal in real estate syndications can provide investors in high tax brackets who will pay you dollar for dollar for your investment tax credit on a historic property.

In addition to the $25,000 ITC that the investor receives, he or she will normally get 50 percent of the ownership. The CPA or CFP will require about a 15 percent fee for finding the money for you. In the end, you will have half-interest in a beautifully restored historic property and about $21,000 in your pocket.

Here's how it works:

Restore historic property	$100,000	rehabilitation cost
	× .25	ITC
	$ 25,000	Investment tax credit

Sell ITC for $25,000		$25,000	
	less	$ 4,000	CPA finder fee
You receive		$21,000	cash (plus 50% ownership)

PRESERVING OUR FUTURE

Times change and people change, but the way people think about money hasn't changed. They still want to make money. Real estate investors go where the economic incentives are. As long as there are investment incentives for historic preservation, old properties will be salvaged and resurrected as the beautiful structures they originally were.

Renovating historic properties is one of the most exciting and rewarding ways to attain wealth and success while providing a valuable service to the community and our culture. Get involved. You'll probably make a few dollars while doing something to preserve our heritage.

KEEP THESE POINTS IN MIND:
1. Buy historic properties for very low prices and use low interest rate loans to renovate them.
2. Only properties that are certified as historic are eligible for the 25 percent tax credit.
3. Contact your local office of historic preservation to find historic buildings in your area.
4. All work on historic buildings must be approved by the Department of the Interior, via your local office of historic preservation.
5. There is a 15 percent tax credit for non-residential and commercial buildings at least thirty years old. A 20 percent tax credit is available for non-residential and commercial buildings at least forty years old.
6. After completing a historic renovation, sell the 25 percent tax credit to persons in high tax brackets for cash in your pocket.

SPECIAL RESOURCE: STATE HISTORIC PRESERVATION OFFICES

Alabama
State Historic
   Preservation Officer
   and Executive Director
*Alabama Historical
   Commission*
Rice-Semple-Hardt House
725 Monroe St.
Montgomery AL 36130

Alaska
State Historic
   Preservation Officer
*Office of History and
   Arehaeology*
*Division of Parks and
   Outdoor Recreation
Department of Natural
   Resources*
Olympia Bldg.
555 Cordova St.
Pouch 7001
Anchorage AK 99510

Arizona
State Historic
   Preservation Officer
Arizona State Parks
1688 W. Adams St.
Phoenix AZ 85007

Arkansas
State Historic
   Preservation Officer
*Historic Preservation
   Program
Department of Natural
   and Cultural Heritage*
200 Heritage Center
225 E. Markham St.
Little Rock AR 72201

California
Deputy State Historic
   Preservation Officer

*Office of Historic
    Preservation*
*Department of Parks and
    Recreation*
830 S St.
P.O. Box 2390
Sacramento CA 95811

Colorado
State Historic
    Preservation Officer
*Office of Archaeology
    and Historic
    Preservation*
State Historical Society
*Department of Higher
    Education*
Colorado Heritage Center
1300 Broadway
Denver CO 80203

Connecticut
Director
*State Historical
    Commission*
59 S. Prospect St.
Hartford CT 06106

Delaware
Bureau Chief
*Bureau of Archaeology
    and Historic
    Preservation*
*Division of Historical
    and Cultural Affairs*
Department of State
Old State House
The Green
Dover DE 19903

District of Columbia
Chief,
*Historic Preservation
    Division*

*Department of Consumer
    and Regulatory Affairs*
North Potomac Bldg.
614 H St., N.W.
Washington DC 20001

Florida
Director,
*Division of Archives,
    History, and Records
    Management*
Department of State
R. A. Gray Bldg.
500 Bronough St.
Mail to: The Capitol
Tallahassee FL 32301

Georgia
Chief,
*Historic Preservation
    Section*
*Division of Parks and
    Historic Sites*
*Department of Natural
    Resources*
704 Trinity-Washington
    Bldg.
270 Washington St.,
    S.W.
Atlanta GA 30334

Hawaii
Chairman and State
    Historic Preservation
    Officer
*Department of Land and
    Natural Resources*
Kalanimoku Bldg.
1151 Punchbowl St.
P.O. Box 621
Honolulu HI 96809

Idaho
Idaho State Archivist and
    Historic Preservation
    Officer
State Historical Society
Department of Education
610 N. Julia Davis Dr.
Boise ID 83702

Illinois
Associate Director
*Bureau of Lands and
    Historic Sites*
*Department of
    Conservation*
405 E. Washington St.
Springfield IL 62706

Indiana
Assistant State Historic
    Preservation Officer
    and Director
Historic Preservation
*Department of Natural
    Resources*
202 N. Alabama St.
Indianapolis IN 46204

Iowa
Executive Director
*State Historical
    Department*
Historical Bldg.
E. 12th St. and Grand
    Ave.
Des Moines IA 50319

Kansas
Executive Director
State Historical Society
Memorial Bldg.
120 W. 10th St.
Topeka KS 66612

Kentucky
State Historic
    Preservation Officer
*Heritage Council
Education and
    Humanities Cabinet*
Capital Plaza Tower,
    12th Fl.
Frankfort KY 40601

Louisiana
State Historic
    Preservation Officer
*Office of Cultural
    Development
Department of Culture,
    Recreation, and
    Tourism*
Great Fosters Office
    Plaza
666 N. Foster Dr.
P.O. Box 44247
Baton Rouge, LA 70804

Maine
Director
*Maine Historic
    Preservation
    Commission
Department of
    Educational and
    Cultural Services*
55 Capitol St.
Mail to: State House,
    Station 65
Augusta ME 04333

Maryland
Director
*Maryland Historical
    Trust
Department of Economic
    and Community
    Development*

John Shaw House
21 State Cir.
Annapolis MD 21401

Massachusetts
Executive Director and
    State Historic
    Preservation Officer
*Historical Commission
Office of the Secretary of
    State*
294 Washington St.
Boston MA 02108

Michigan
Director and State
    Historic Preservation
    Officer
*History Division
Department of State*
208 N. Capitol St.
Lansing MI 48918

Minnesota
Director
Historical Society
Historical Bldg.
690 Cedar St.
St. Paul MN 55101

Mississippi
Director
*Department of Archives
    and History*
100 S. State St.
P.O. Box 571
Jackson MS 39205

Missouri
Director
*Division of Parks and
    Historic Preservation
Department of Natural
    Resources*

1915 Southridge Dr.
P.O. Box 176
Jefferson City MO 65102

Montana
Director
*Montana Historical
    Society
Department of Education*
Veterans-Pioneers
    Memorial Bldg.
225 N. Roberts St.
Helena MT 59620

Nebraska
Director
Historical Society
1500 R St.
P.O. Box 82554
Lincoln NE 68501

Nevada
Supervisor
*Division of Historic
    Preservation and
    Archeology
Department of
    Conservation and
    Natural Resources*
106 Nye Bldg.
201 S. Fall St.
Capitol Complex
Carson City NV 89710

New Hampshire
Commissioner
*State Historic
    Preservation Office
Department of Resources
    and Economic
    Development*
Prescott Park, Bldg. 2
105 Loudon Rd.
P.O. Box 856
Concord NH 03301

New Jersey
Acting Administrator
Office of New Jersey
   Heritage
Department of
   Environmental
   Protection
John Fitch Plz.
C.N. 402
Trenton NJ 08625

New Mexico
State Historic
   Preservation Officer
Historic Preservation
   Division
Office of Cultural Affairs
Department of Finance
   and Administration
101 La Villa Rivera
   Bldg.
224 E. Palace Ave.
Santa Fe NM 87501

New York
Commissioner
Office of Parks,
   Recreation, and
   Historic Preservation
Executive Department
Agency Bldg. 1
Empire State Plz.
Albany NY 12238

North Carolina
Director
Division of Archives and
   History
Department of Cultural
   Resources
Archives–Library Bldg.
109 E. Jones St.
Raleigh NC 27611

North Dakota
Director
Division of Archaeology
   and Historic
   Preservation
State Historical Society
North Dakota Heritage
   Center
Bismark ND 58505

Ohio
State Preservation Officer
Division of Historic
   Preservation
The Ohio Historical
   Society
Interstate 71 at 17th Ave.
Columbus OH 43211

Oklahoma
Executive Director
Oklahoma Historical
   Society
Wiley Post Historical
   Bldg.
2100 N. Lincoln Blvd.
Oklahoma City OK
   73105

Oregon
Manager
Historic Preservation
   Office
Parks and Recreation
   Division
Department of
   Transportation
Vick Bldg., 3rd Fl.
525 Trade St., S.E.
Salem OR 97310

Pennsylvania
Executive Director
Historical and Museum
   Commission

William Penn Memorial
   Museum and Archives
   Bldg.
3rd and Forster Sts.
P.O. Box 1026
Harrisburg PA 17108

Rhode Island
Chairman
Rhode Island Historical
   Preservation
   Commission
Old State House
150 Benefit St.
Providence RI 02903

South Carolina
State Historic
   Preservation Officer
   and Director
Department of Archives
   and History
1430 Senate St.
P.O. Box 11669
Columbia SC 29211

South Dakota
Director
Office of Cultural
   Preservation
Deparment of Education
   and Cultural Affairs
State Library Bldg.
800 N. Illinois St.
Pierre SD 57501

Tennessee
Executive Director
Tennessee Historical
   Commission
Customs House
701 Broadway
Nashville TN 37203

Texas
Executive Director
Texas Historical
Commission
1511 Colorado St.
P.O. Box 12276,
Capitol Sta.
Austin TX 78711

Utah
Director
Division of State History
Department of
   Community and
   Economic
   Development
Rio Grande Railroad
   Depot
300 Rio Grande St.
Salt Lake City UT 84101

Vermont
Director
Historic Preservation
Division
Agency of Development
and Community
Affairs
Pavilion Office Bldg.
109 State St.
Montpelier VT 05602

Virginia
Executive Director
Virginia Historic
Landmarks
Commission

221 Governor St.
Richmond VA 23219

Washington
State Historic
   Preservation Officer
Office of Archaeology
and Historic
Preservation
111 W. 21st Ave.
Mail Stop KL-11
Olympia WA 98504

West Virginia
Director
Historic Preservation
Division
Department of Culture
and History
Science and Culture
   Center
Capitol Complex
Charleston WV 25305

Wisconsin
State Historic
   Preservation Officer
State Historical Society
of Wisconsin
816 State St.
Madison WI 53706

Wyoming
State Historic
   Preservation Officer
   and Director
Recreation Commission

Herschler Bldg., 2nd Fl.
122 W. 25th St.
Cheyenne WY 82002

American Samoa
Historic Preservation
   Officer and Director
Department of Parks and
Recreation
P.O. Box 700
Pago Pago AS 96799

Guam
Director
Department of Parks and
Recreation
P.O. Box 2950
Agana GU 96910

Puerto Rico
State Historic
   Preservation Officer
State Historic
Preservation Office
Office of the Governor
La Fortaleza
P.O. Box 82
San Juan PR 00901

Virgin Islands
Director
Planning Office of the
Virgin Islands
Office of the Governor
P.O. Box 2606
Charlotte Amalie,
St. Thomas VI 00801

14

SELLING TAX BENEFITS FOR CASH

I'M PROUD TO BE PAYING TAXES IN THE U.S. THE
ONLY THING IS, I COULD BE JUST AS PROUD FOR HALF
THE MONEY.

Arthur Godfrey

Tax shelters.

Everyone has heard of them. March 1, 1913 marked both the beginning of income taxation and the birth of tax shelters. Since then, we have developed thousands of ways to legally, morally, and ethically shelter our income from taxation.

The government uses our desire to avoid taxes by designing the tax laws to encourage certain types of activities. Real estate investing is one of them. Investing in rental real estate is one of the most widely used and safest forms of tax shelter.

Tax Incentives for Private Production of Rental Housing

Changes in the treatment of income from rental properties under the Economic Recovery Tax Act (ERTA) have greatly increased profitability of rental housing, with important implications for urban areas and their large rental stock. New provisions in the tax code increase the rate at which both new and existing properties can be depreciated by allowing investors to use an 18-year capital recovery period.

The accelerated depreciation rate was increased from 125 percent to 175 percent of declining balance for existing rental properties and decreased from 200 percent to 175 percent for new units. Low-income rental housing can now be depreciated using the 200 percent declining balance method. Other provisions established a 10-year amortization of construction period property tax and interest expenses and reduced the amount of capital gain taxed as ordinary income on a sale of the property.

At current rates, it is estimated that with 13 percent mortgage interest, these tax changes make possible a long-term reduction in rents of approximately 40 percent through increased supply of rental units. Most investment analysts maintain that, in the long term, at least some of the special tax benefits available to rental housing relative to competing investment opportunities are passed through to renter households in the form of reduced rents.

Included in ERTA was an increase in the investment tax credit for certified historic rehabilitation from 10 to 25 percent; under the new law a 20 percent tax credit is permitted for rehabilitation of nonresidential buildings at least 40 years old and a 15 percent credit for rehabilitation of buildings at least 30 years old. These credits were included specifically to "help revitalize the economic propects of older locations and prevent the decay and deterioration of distressed urban areas."

Success of this particular tax subsidy program is evident from the fact that nearly 2,000 projects qualified for the historic rehabilitation tax credit during the first three quarters of FY 1983 alone, representing total investment of some $1.3 billion. More than one-third of the rehabilitated historic housing has been made available to low- and moderate-income households.

—President's National Urban Policy Report 1984

Tax Benefits and Incentives

Tax benefits are one of the means that Uncle Sam uses to influence the supply, location, direction, and quality of housing, especially rental housing. He puts out policy statements like the one opposite. What this adds up to for you on April 15, only your tax consultant can tell you. But there certainly are many tax benefits available that can put money in your pocket.

There are four major tax shelters available through investment real estate. They are:

1. Interest deductions
2. Capital gains treatment of profits from the sale of real estate.
3. Depreciation
4. Investment tax credits (ITC).

There are many fine books on the subject of real estate taxation. But what I want to do is show you how to save on your income taxes easily, get back the last three years of income taxes you have already paid, or, better yet, sell tax benefits for cash.

We will discuss each of these in turn.

Interest Expense Reduces Income Taxes

The interest paid on home mortgages is a major tax deduction for most homeowners. Owners of rental properties can deduct not only the interest expense on rental property mortgages, but also the expenses of day-to-day operations. The additional beauty of rental property is that the rents you receive from your tenants pay these expenses.

Shelter Profits with Capital Gains

In the world of taxation, if you buy something for one price and sell it for a higher price, the profit you receive is added to your regular (ordinary) income and taxed at the rate for your total income bracket.

Let's say you sell antiques for a hobby in addition to your regular $25,000-a-year job. This year was a very good year, and you made a $10,000 profit from the sale of your antiques. Your total income subject to taxes now would be $35,000, which puts you in about the 33 percent tax bracket. Roughly speaking, that means $3,300 of your $10,000 profit would have to go to the government in the form of income taxes.

On the other hand, the treatment of profit from the sale of real estate is much different. Real estate that is held for six months or longer is subject to long-term capital gains treatment. This means that only 40 percent of the profit is added to your regular income.

Suppose you invest in real estate to help shelter your income. This year you sell a rental house you've owned for two years and make a $10,000 cash profit. Although you made $10,000 cash, in the eyes of the IRS only 40 percent of the $10,000 ($4,000) is taxable income. This $4,000, not the full $10,000, is the amount that is added to your regular income for a total of $29,000. Your tax bracket would be about 30 percent, so only $1,200 of your $10,000 profit goes to the government in taxes ($4,000 × .30 = $1,200). You could also exchange your property rather than sell it. This would allow you to defer the capital gains tax.

It is easy to see the advantage of real estate capital gains as a tax shelter. Only 40 percent of your profit is taxable instead of 100 percent. You are only required to hold onto the property for over six months. Otherwise, 100 percent of your profits is taxed.

How Depreciation Saves You Money

Depreciation is not a cash outlay. It is a non-cash expense that the IRS lets you deduct to account for the "aging" of your real estate each year. Depreciation deductions are based on the entire cost of the depreciable real estate. This includes the loan amounts, not just the owner's cash investment. Depreciation is not allowed on your residence or on land, only on investment real property (such as apartments, rental houses, or commercial buildings).

For example, if the cost of an apartment building (less the value of the land under it) you own is $180,000, the government will allow you to deduct at least $9,400 a year to account for the depreciation and aging of your property. This depreciation expense can reduce your ordinary taxable income. This in turn results in a lower tax bill for the year.

The depreciation schedules for investment property have changed several times over the last few years. The amount of depreciation you could take would depend upon when you purchased your investment property.

Here is a general summary of the depreciation changes.

DATE PROPERTY PURCHASED	RECOMMENDED DEPRECIATION PERIOD
Prior to 1982	30 years
1982 to 1984	15 years
1984 to 1985	18 years
1985 to present	19 years

One law that hasn't changed recently is the Tax Reform Act of 1984. This law grants a sixty-month write-off for rehab expenses on low-income property. We will discuss this later.

Let's say you purchased a four-unit apartment building in January of 1986 for $120,000. Your accountant figures that the land (not depreciable) under the building is worth $20,000, while the improvements (the actual building) are worth $100,000. The nineteen-year straight line depreciation write-off comes to 5.3 percent. This means you deduct approximately $5,300 per year for nineteen years. Even if your property has a breakeven or positive cash flow during these years, you would still show an approximate annual loss of $5,300 for depreciation for the IRS. This amount could be deducted from your other income (e.g., wages, self-employment, or other investment income) to lower your taxable income and reduce your taxes. If you were in a 50 percent tax bracket, the $5,300 a year in depreciation write-off would save you $2,650 in taxes every year for nineteen years.

The amount and number of years of tax shelter you can expect to receive from depreciation depends upon several factors. They include:

1. Rate and method of depreciation. You could use accelerated depreciation to get more depreciation write-off in the earlier years of ownership instead of the conventional straight line depreciation we used in our example.
2. The taxpayer's income tax bracket without any real estate investments.
3. The amount of cash flow left over from income after all cash expenses

are paid (interest, insurance, property taxes, and operating expenses).

Let's look at another example. Suppose an investor we'll call Allen bought an apartment building in 1985 for $680,000. Allen's accountant figures that the land under the building is worth $110,000, so the building and improvements are worth $570,000. Over the next ten years Allen uses the IRS-approved nineteen-year straight line depreciation schedule. At the end of the 10 years he will have received a total of $300,000 in depreciation benefits ($570,000 ÷ 19 years × 10 years = $300,000). In general, the amount of taxes he will save depends on Allen's tax bracket. The chart below shows how much the $300,000 in depreciation could save him in taxes over the ten years.

If his tax bracket is:	25%	30%	40%	50%
$300,000 of depreciation saved him:	$75,000	$90,000	$120,000	$150,000

In other words, every dollar of depreciation Allen gets from his real estate reduces his income by that dollar. This means that one less dollar of income will be subjected to taxation. In the 50 percent tax bracket, he saves 50 cents in taxes. (If he was in a 30 percent bracket, 30 cents would be saved, and so on.) Therefore, $300,000 in depreciation would reduce his income by $300,000 and result in paying $150,000 less in taxes. This is cash that would have otherwise gone to the government— money that Allen can use to send his kids to college or do whatever he wants.

Are you beginning to see the fantastic benefits of depreciation in real estate ownership? To get the best tax benefits from rental property ownership, find properties where you break even or have positive cash flow; that is, where rental income is equal to or more than cash expenses each month. This way, even if you are putting cash in your pocket each month, you wouldn't owe any taxes if the depreciation offsets (shelters) the positive cash flow.

Although tax reforms have changed depreciation periods for most investment properties, low-to-moderate-income housing depreciation has not changed. You are allowed a shorter fifteen-year depreciation period. This gives you larger write-offs each year. In our previous example, if Allen's investment had been an apartment building for lower-and moderate-income renters, he could have depreciated his property over 15 years instead of 19 years. At the end of the 10 years he could have received a total of $380,000 in depreciation benefits ($570,000 ÷ 15 years × 10 years = $380,000). The amount of tax savings Allen would reap under these circumstances are shown below:

If his tax bracket is:	25%	30%	40%	50%
$380,000 of depreciation will save him:	$95,000	$114,000	$152,000	$190,000

Quite a savings. Even though Allen depreciates the property over a shorter number of years (15 years instead of 19 years), the large annual tax savings he receives early in the depreciation period justifies the depreciation he doesn't receive after 15 years.

Following is an example of the depreciation schedule to be used for low- and moderate-income housing:

COST RECOVERY TABLES FOR REAL ESTATE
LOW INCOME HOUSING

(To find the applicable percentage, use column for the month in the first year the property is put in service)

Month Placed in Service

	1	2	3	4	5	6	7	8	9	10	11	12
Year 1	13	12	11	10	5	8	7	6	4	3	2	1
2	12	12	12	12	12	12	12	13	13	13	13	13
3	10	10	10	10	11	11	11	11	11	11	11	11
4	9	9	9	9	9	9	9	10	10	10	10	10
5	8	8	8	8	8	8	8	8	8	8	8	9
6	7	7	7	7	7	7	7	7	7	7	7	7
7	6	6	6	6	6	6	6	6	6	6	6	6
8	5	5	5	5	5	5	5	5	5	5	6	6
9	5	5	5	5	5	5	5	5	5	5	5	5
10	5	5	5	5	5	5	5	5	5	5	5	5
11	4	5	5	5	5	5	5	5	5	5	5	5
12	4	4	4	5	4	5	5	5	5	5	5	5
13	4	4	4	4	4	4	5	4	5	5	5	5
14	4	4	4	4	4	4	4	4	4	5	4	4
15	4	4	4	4	4	4	4	4	4	4	4	4
16			1	1	2	2	2	3	3	3	4	4

Compare the depreciation schedules to be used for real estate other than low- and moderate-income property:

COST RECOVERY TABLES
19-YEAR REAL PROPERTY
STRAIGHT LINE METHOD

	Month Placed In Service											
	1	2	3	4	5	6	7	8	9	10	11	12
Year 1	5.0	4.6	4.2	3.7	3.3	2.9	2.4	2.0	1.5	1.1	.7	.2
2	5.3	5.3	5.3	5.3	5.3	5.3	5.3	5.3	5.3	5.3	5.3	5.3
3	5.3	5.3	5.3	5.3	5.3	5.3	5.3	5.3	5.3	5.3	5.3	5.3
4	5.3	5.3	5.3	5.3	5.3	5.3	5.3	5.3	5.3	5.3	5.3	5.3
5	5.3	5.3	5.3	5.3	5.3	5.3	5.3	5.3	5.3	5.3	5.3	5.3
6	5.3	5.3	5.3	5.3	5.3	5.3	5.3	5.3	5.3	5.3	5.3	5.3
7	5.3	5.3	5.3	5.3	5.3	5.3	5.3	5.3	5.3	5.3	5.3	5.3
8	5.3	5.3	5.3	5.3	5.3	5.3	5.3	5.3	5.3	5.3	5.3	5.3
9	5.3	5.3	5.3	5.3	5.3	5.3	5.3	5.3	5.3	5.3	5.3	5.3
10	5.3	5.3	5.3	5.3	5.3	5.3	5.3	5.3	5.3	5.3	5.3	5.3
11	5.3	5.3	5.3	5.3	5.3	5.3	5.3	5.3	5.3	5.3	5.3	5.3
12	5.3	5.3	5.3	5.3	5.3	5.3	5.3	5.3	5.3	5.3	5.3	5.3
13	5.3	5.3	5.3	5.3	5.3	5.3	5.3	5.3	5.3	5.3	5.3	5.3
14	5.2	5.2	5.2	5.2	5.2	5.2	5.2	5.2	5.2	5.2	5.2	5.2
15	5.2	5.2	5.2	5.2	5.2	5.2	5.2	5.2	5.2	5.2	5.2	5.2
16	5.2	5.2	5.2	5.2	5.2	5.2	5.2	5.2	5.2	5.2	5.2	5.2
17	5.2	5.2	5.2	5.2	5.2	5.2	5.2	5.2	5.2	5.2	5.2	5.2
18	5.2	5.2	5.2	5.2	5.2	5.2	5.2	5.2	5.2	5.2	5.2	5.2
19	5.2	5.2	5.2	5.2	5.2	5.2	5.2	5.2	5.2	5.2	5.2	5.2
20	.2	.6	1.0	1.5	1.9	2.3	2.8	3.2	3.7	4.1	4.5	5.0

These tables represent a simplified way you can accurately calculate the annual depreciation deduction on your properties. To use these tables multiply the depreciable basis of your property by the appropriate percentage to get the annual deduction. For example, let's assume the property was purchased in January and depreciated over 19 years. If the depreciable basis of your building is $570,000 the first year's depreciation deduction would be $28,500 ($570,000 × .05); years 2–13 would be 30,210 annually ($570,000 × .053), and so on.

TAX CREDITS: ICING ON THE CAKE

In 1981, we submitted a proposal to refurbish a historic building in Baltimore, Maryland. The total development costs were to exceed $1.1 million. Yet we stood to gain about $280,000 through the special 25 percent tax credit for historic buildings. You see, with development costs of $1,115,494.00 on this certified historic property, we would receive a 25 percent tax credit for those fix-up costs. That's $278,873.50 we could take directly off our taxes in one year!

Chances are, however, that you may never have to pay that much in taxes in one year. So what are you going to do with a $280,000 tax credit? You are going to sell it. Sell the tax credit to a person or a group of persons who *will* use it to save $280,000 on their taxes. If you give them half-interest in the property plus a $280,000 credit, don't you think you could sell that tax credit for a quarter of a million dollars or more? You bet your bottom dollar you could, and fast! We'll go over selling tax credits later on.

How Tax Credits Work

Historic property is not the only type of real estate that can quality for tax credits. Non-residential properties that are thirty years old can qualify for a 15 percent tax credit on any rehab work done to them. Also, 20 percent of rehab work done on buildings over forty years old can be deducted from your taxes in the form of a tax credit.

Remember, the nice thing about a tax credit is that it reduces your tax bill dollar for dollar. This is in contrast to the depreciation deductions discussed previously, where a deduction is subtracted from your income before taxes are calculated. Tax credits are applied directly to the amount you owe in taxes. Therefore, if you are an investor in the 50 percent tax bracket, a $100 tax deduction means $50 off your tax bill. A $100 tax credit reduces your tax bill by $100.

Tax Credits Affect Depreciation Benefits

With buildings qualifying for the 15 or 20 percent tax credits, the amount of the credit is deducted from the property's cost basis for purposes of computing depreciation. Normally, if you were to spend $100,000 to rehab a property that you paid $90,000 for, you would add the $100,000 to the $90,000 purchase price and depreciate the entire $190,000 balance (less the cost of the land). However, if you take a 20 percent tax credit, that 20 percent would be deducted from the rehab cost of $100,000, and only $80,000 would be added to the cost basis. So you would depreciate only $170,000 the first year ($80,000 + $90,000).

If a historic building qualifies for a 25 percent tax credit, you deduct only half of the credit (12½ percent) from the depreciable basis. This provides an added incentive to rehabilitate some of our country's historic properties. Not only is the 25 percent tax credit larger than the other credits, but you are allowed to depreciate 87½ percent of the rehab costs.

Comparing the Benefits

Does this all sound too confusing? It isn't really. Let's take a look at the three types of tax credits and compare the benefits you would receive for rehabilitating a 30 year old, a 40 year old, and a historic property.

Thirty year old property $100,000 is spent on the rehab. The investment tax credit is 15 percent, or $15,000. The total amount of the credit is first subtracted from the $100,000 rehabilitation basis, and then the remaining $85,000 is depreciated over fifteen years. (Only fifteen-year straight line depreciation can be used.) This amounts to a $5,666 depreciation deduction per year. Assuming a 50 percent tax bracket, the deduction provides a $2,833 tax savings. Added to the $15,000 tax credit, this results in a $17,833 tax savings in cash the first year.

Forty year old property The same $100,000 spent on a forty year old building would receive a 20 percent tax credit, or $20,000. Depreciation would be based on $80,000 over fifteen years, for a deduction of $5,333 with an after tax value of $2,666. Total tax savings are $22,666 in the first year.

Historic property A rehab investment of $100,000 would receive a $25,000 tax credit in the first year. One-half of the credit is subtracted from the rehab portion of the basis ($100,000 − $12,500 = $87,500). This amount divided by fifteen years results in a deduction of $5,833 and tax savings of $2,916. Total tax savings in the first year would be $27,916 in cash. The benefits are summarized in the chart below:

	30 YEAR OLD BUILDING 15% ITC	40 YEAR OLD BUILDING 20% ITC	HISTORIC BUILDING 25% ITC
Amount invested	$100,000	$100,000	$100,000
Tax credit	15,000	20,000	25,000
Depreciation savings (1st year)	2,833	2,666	2,916
Total tax savings	$ 17,833	$ 22,666	$ 27,916

This simple example reveals the powerful after-tax effect of the investment tax credit. The beauty of rehabilitating real estate is that you can use a low interest government loan to rehabilitate the property and then take a 15, 20, or 25 percent tax credit on the rehab costs. This explains why property rehabilitation is one of the most valuable tools for investors needing legitimate tax shelters. The benefits of depreciation and tax credits come when you file your yearly income tax return and owe nothing in taxes.

Get Back All of the Taxes You've Paid

Now suppose you go through your income and expenses for the year and estimate that unless you do something, you will owe about $10,000 in taxes on April 15. You have a little house that is 35 years old and surrounded by law and medical offices. If renovated, it would make a fine office for two or three lawyers. You know that if you rehabilitated the property, you could get a 15 percent tax credit on all the money you put into it. Also, the building would be worth much more when you finish. With this in mind, you decide to go through with the rehabilitation project.

You spend $100,000 on the renovation and get a tax credit for

$15,000. The $15,000 credit is applied toward your $10,000 tax bill to reduce it to zero. Since you can't reduce your taxable income below zero, what happens to the remaining $5,000? You may use the $5,000 to get a cash refund for taxes already paid over the last three years. The $5,000 can also be credited toward your future taxes for up to seven years, to eliminate or reduce any taxes on future income.

Hold the Property for Five Years

Obviously, each year you take an investment tax credit, the amount of depreciation available decreases. This takes away some of the on-going write-off you would normally get in later years. Therefore, it might seem very tempting to buy a property, rehab it, take the tax credits, and sell the building within a few years. Tempting as it many seem, it won't work. In order to receive the full tax credit, you have to own the building for at least five years after the rehab work is completed. You are allowed to take the full credit each year you own the building, but if you sell before five years have passed, you will have to repay 20 percent of the credits you have already received for each year you no longer owned the property.

This means that if you owned a property and received a 15 percent tax credit for four years, but then you sold the property, you would have to repay 20 percent of the credits you had already received. So, if you did $100,000 worth of rehabilitation and received $60,000 in tax credits before selling the building four years later, the IRS would ask you to repay 20 percent of the amount received, or $12,000. Holding onto the building for one more year would result in no re-payment and would save you $12,000. If you had to sell before the five years were up, here is how much you would have to repay:

Years Held	Percentage to Repay
Less than 1 year	100
1–2 years	80
2–3 years	60
3–4 years	40
4–5 years	20
5+ years	0

Rehab Must Exceed Cost of Property for Credit

One more thing to keep in mind when rehabilitating a historic property is that the cost of the rehab must exceed the adjusted cost basis of the property by at least one dollar. (The adjusted basis is computed by adding the purchase price of the property not including the land value to the cost of capital improvements, and subtracting any depreciation already taken.) Thus, a property with a cost of $50,000 would require at least $50,001 of rehabilitation to quality for the tax credit. If property prices are high in your area, it might be difficult to meet this requirement because of the high initial cost of the building. Here are four ways you might overcome this problem.

1. *Facade easement.* By donating a portion of your older building as a facade easement, you can reduce the cost basis of the property by the dollar value of the easement. This reduces the amount needed to be spent on the rehab to qualify for the investment tax credit. Historic building fronts (facades) are also donated to charities or government agencies in order to take advantage of the Federal income tax deduction for charitable contributions.
2. *Capitalization of construction interest and taxes.* Another technique would be to capitalize the construction interest and taxes. These expenses would normally be amortized over an eight-to-ten-year period, but by capitalizing them, you can treat them as rehab costs.
3. *Tax deferred exchange.* By exchanging another building you may already own for the present property, you can transfer the old and presumably lower cost basis to the new property.
4. *Long-term lease.* Investors who lease and rehabilitate a property can qualify for tax credits. So, rather than buying a building, you may want to lease it for a long-term period (at least fifteen years). This way you may use the owner's existing basis instead of a higher new purchase price.

FIVE-YEAR WRITE-OFFS FOR RENTAL PROPERTY

Another great tax benefit comes as a result of the Internal Revenue Code (IRC) rule 167-K. This rule allows you to write off the cost of rehabilitation on low- and moderate-income property over a period of five years, creating a 20 percent write-off per year. Let's look at how you would utilize IRC 167-K in conjunction with the popular Section 8 rental rehabilitation loan and rental rehabilitation program.

Let's say you get a good deal on a small run-down apartment building. The cost is $75,000 on flexible terms—ten percent down ($7,500). The building is not old enough to quality for a 15 or 20 percent tax credit, but as you have learned, the IRC 167-K program allows five-year depreciation of rehab costs. With the assistance of a rental rehabilitation program in your city you get a $50,000 low interest rate rehabilitation loan (5 percent). The Section 8 rental income will cover the building's debt service, maintenance, property taxes, insurance, and other expenses. Therefore, the write-offs, which you may use to reduce your taxable income, will come as a result of depreciation and the five-year expensing of your rehabilitation costs allowable under IRC 167-K. To see the results take a look at the chart below:

*YEAR	DEPRECIATION	167-K WRITE OFF	TOTAL TAX WRITE-OFF
1	9,750	10,000	19,750
2	9,000	10,000	19,000
3	7,500	10,000	17,500
4	6,750	10,000	16,750
5	6,000	10,000	16,000
6	5,250		5,250
7	4,500		4,500
8	3,750		3,750
9	3,750		3,750
10	3,750		3,750
11	3,000		3,000
12	3,000		3,000
13	3,000		3,000
14	3,000		3,000
15	3,000		3,000
Total	75,000	50,000	125,000

*Property purchased in January 1985.

Now let's say you sell the property for $150,000 in the sixteenth year.

Sale price	$150,000
less tax due*	30,000
Balance	120,000
less Debt (approx.)	88,125
less Original investment	7,500
Net profit	$24,375

* Tax calculation—property sold for $150,000:

**$150,000	Long term capital gain
× .40	Capital gains tax
$ 60,000	Taxable profit
× .50	Your tax bracket
$ 30,000	Taxes due

** Note: The long-term capital gain is equal to the sales price less any remaining basis (cost) on the property. After 15 years, the property is depreciated to zero; therefore the capital gain equals the sales price ($150,000 − 0 = $150,000 gain).

As you can see, if you sold the property in the sixteenth year for $150,000 cash, you would have an approximate profit of $24,375 after paying all taxes. The depreciation deduction would have saved you $62,500 in taxes during the years you owned the property (assuming a 50 percent tax bracket). What if you don't need $4,166 a year in write-offs? Sell them to someone who does.

SELL TAX BENEFITS FOR BIG DOLLARS

In chapter 8, I introduced my rehab express concept. The sixth step of the rehab express is to sell the tax benefits of your projects to persons in high tax brackets. Here's one way to do it. First, educate yourself about the programs and properties available in your area. Then buy a two-family historic property. Borrow $100,000 from your local office of historic preservation at 5½ percent annual interest or lower, and proceed to fix the property up.

Once you have completed the rehabilitation, you are automatically entitled to a 25 percent investment tax credit. That is a direct savings of $25,000 on your tax bill. If you will have to pay $10,000 in taxes this year, you could use $10,000 of the $25,000 tax credit, and you would owe nothing in taxes. The remaining $15,000 tax credit is carried forward for the next fifteen years, and will save you up to $15,000 in taxes. Or you can go back to the last three years, and collect up to $15,000 you may already have paid. The government will give it back to you with interest.

But what if you don't pay that much in taxes? You say to yourself, "I need tax benefits like I need a hole in the head." What you do is find the CPAs (certified public accountants) who have clients in the 50 percent tax bracket. Look for a CPA who owns rental real estate and understands its investment opportunities and tax benefits. That CPA will find an investor for you who will pay $25,000, dollar for dollar, for the $25,000 investment tax credit. In exchange for the cash you will most likely have to give the investor half-ownership in the property to make it worthwhile. But in the end the investor will own 50 percent of a nicely rehabilitated property and can utilize its tax benefits. You maintain control of half-interest and pocket the cash from the sale of the benefits—a great arrangement for both of you. The CPA will probably charge a 15 percent fee to put the deal together. But for $3,750 (25,000 × .15 = $3,750), you will end up with a 50 percent controlling interest in a beautifully restored single-family historic property and over $21,000 cash in your pocket.

How many properties do you know of that are fifty years of age or older? There are thousands of properties that are in certified historic areas across the country. Restoring them is an easy way to make money. Very few people are taking advantage of the opportunities.

Have your accountant help you put together a little package or memorandum on the special tax write-offs and depreciation benefits available on a property you have rehabilitated. Here is a list of the information we send out to investors who are interested in buying the tax benefits of one of our projects:

1. Project description
2. Section 8 rental rehabilitation program description
3. IRS Code 100,027.2 information (Low-income housing five-year amortized costs)
4. SEC Regulation D, Rule 504 information*
5. Background of general partner
6. Article by general partner
7. Appraisal

---

* Regulation D explains the rules and regulations regarding putting together a privately offered limited partnership.

8. Work write-up
9. Settlement sheet—loan from city
10. Legal documents—loan from city
11. Settlement sheet—other loans
12. Legal documents—other loans
13. Section 8 documents/guarantees
14. Income/expense sheets—first year
15. Questionaire—to be filled out by investor
16. Insurance policy
17. Certificate of limited partnership

Find a Need

In 1982 I bought sixteen houses for about $6.25 apiece and with the help of a government loan spent $300,000 to rehabilitate all of them. Since the $300,000 was used to rehabilitate moderate-income housing, I was allowed to depreciate those costs over five years (as opposed to fifteen years). That meant $60,000 a year in depreciation benefits, or $30,000 a year in tax savings for somebody in a 50 percent tax bracket. I contacted a certified public accountant who had numerous clients in high tax brackets, and using the procedure discussed in this chapter, proposed that some of them invest in my seventeen houses.

Why would wealthy people want to invest in moderate-income housing? First, each house had guaranteed rents coming in from the government, so an investor would know what the rents would be and that there would be few vacancies. Second, the properties were fixed up as if they were brand-new and would have to be kept in good condition every year to retain the guaranteed rents. Third, if the tenants damaged a property, the government would reimburse the property owner. Fourth, an investor would own 50 percent of the rehabilitated properties, now worth $408,000, and would receive 99 percent of the write-offs, including the $60,000 in yearly depreciation benefits.

Solve Other People's Problems

Not long ago, in another situation, we found a need and filled it. We were trying to buy an apartment building from a group of doctors. We became acquainted with one doctor and offered him a deal, using some imagination. I'm sure that there has been an occasion or will be an occasion when you can do something similar to this.

Dr. A. owned a small apartment building in partnership with several other doctors. He had been trying to sell this property for some time, but to no avail. The other doctors wanted too high a price with too much money down. After talking with Dr. A., we decided that he would be better off if he sold the property at a high price to us with no money down. We would then go in and rehab the property. Dr. A. would become a limited partner with us, and we would pass on the tax savings to him in lieu of his share of the down payment.

The doctor now receives $1,000 a month, tax free, for selling us his property. This $1,000 a month is tax-free money to him, because it is sheltered by the excess depreciation that we've passed on to him. We own a rehabilitated building with all the benefits of ownership. Not a bad investment.

EVERYONE BENEFITS

In this chapter we have taken a look at some of the ways national housing goals are achieved, some with tax law incentives. Whether you want to assure your own best housing, increase your holding of real estate investments, or whether you want to get into the action of rehabilitating our nation's housing, whatever the path, the invitation is wide open. Government loans and tax shelters are the tools at hand. All you have to do is to make the moves to turn your knowledge into action and use the tools to gain the success for your own goals.

KEEP THESE POINTS IN MIND

1. Real estate is one of the safest tax shelters available today.
2. Depreciation is a non-cash expense that reduces your taxable income.
3. Write-offs reduce your taxable income; tax credits are applied directly against your tax bill.
4. The rehabilitation costs on low-to-moderate-income housing can be depreciated over five years.
5. Four major tax advantages of owning investment real estate are:
   • Interest deductions
   • Capital gains treatment for real estate profits
   • Depreciation
   • Investment tax credits.
6. Thirty-year-old non-residential property is eligible for a 15 percent tax credit.
7. Properties that are forty years old or older can qualify for a 20 percent tax credit.
8. Certified historic properties qualify for 25 percent tax credits.
9. To qualify for 15 and 20 percent rehabilitation tax credits:
   • Rehab must be on non-residential properties.
   • The rehab costs must exceed the cost basis of the property by at least one dollar.
   • You must hold onto the property for five years (to receive the full credits).
10. If you don't need as much tax shelter as the rehabilitated property provides (from depreciation, expenses, or tax credits), sell the tax benefits to an investor in a higher tax bracket.

15

HOUSING FOR THE ELDERLY: The Future Is Now

WELL DONE IS BETTER THAN WELL SAID.

Ben Franklin

Through my conversations with government officials and my travels throughout the nation to buy real estate, I have discovered the money-making trend for the rest of the 1980s and into the '90s. Unlike some trends in our society, this one is as obvious as a full moon on a clear night. Yet the best part of this opportunity is that it is little used. That is what makes it so powerful.

What is this opportunity? Housing for the elderly. The elderly are the largest and fastest growing age group in the United States. The millionaires of tomorrow will be made today through housing for the elderly. Take a look at the facts:

Currently there are 17 million Americans over the age of sixty-two. By 1995, 51 percent of the population will be fifty years old or older.

According to recent government statistics, 69 out of every 100 Americans over the age of sixty-five exist on incomes of less than $1,200 a month.

Politicians realize that "the future is now" and the word is out: Full steam ahead with programs for the elderly. In a time of government cutbacks, the administration is developing numerous programs to fulfill its commitment to support housing for the elderly.

What this translates to for you, the investor, is 1) low interest loans for building or rehabilitating housing for elderly persons, and 2) rent subsidies and guarantees for tenants who are elderly. If you want to help other people, this is an opportunity for you. For now, forget about becoming a millionaire overnight. How would you like to increase your income by 25 percent a year? And by doing so, watch your fortune grow? You can do this by helping elderly people.

WIDE VARIETY OF PROGRAMS AVAILABLE

The wide range of housing programs for the elderly includes three basic categories: mortgage insurance on loans for home ownership; direct loans for rental housing; and rent payment assistance programs. Many of the programs discussed in this chapter are for elderly (sixty-two years old or older) and handicapped persons exclusively. Others are programs that are designed for low-income persons that also include the elderly. (Remember that 69 percent of all elderly persons earn less than $1,200 a month.) With this in mind, let's take a look at some of the fantastic programs available.

HOME OWNERSHIP LOANS

Because of age and low income, many elderly persons cannot qualify for conventional home loans. In 1983, the government stepped in to provide home mortgage insurance on loans specifically for elderly persons. Through this action, lenders can make more loans to elderly persons and have lowered the qualification requirements. Right now you may have a friend or relative who could use one of these loans to buy a home he or she could not otherwise afford. There are several types.

Manufactured Home Parks

At the request of the Reagan Administration, HUD was allowed to insure loans for manufactured home parks for the elderly. This enabled thousands of elderly citizens to get loans necessary to purchase manufactured homes within manufactured home parks for the elderly.

Home Loans for Retirement Villages

Another initiative permitted HUD to insure mortgages on single-family homes in retirement villages. This action allowed elderly persons to buy houses in subdivisions and planned communities that restrict ownership to those above a certain age who wouldn't qualify for other traditional loan programs.

Home Equity Conversion Mortgage for the Elderly

Almost 12.5 million homes are owned by Americans over sixty-five years old; 80 percent of these are mortgage free. While home equities (the value of a house minus mortgage debt) are over $600 billion, inflation has eroded the buying power of people on fixed incomes. The story is a painful one for many older Americans who are "house rich, but cash poor." To help them draw on their equity and supplement their retirement incomes without having to sell their homes, various home equity conversion plans are being studied nationwide.

At present, home equity conversion is available to homeowners in only a few states. In New York, persons over sixty years old can take out a loan often referred to as a "reverse annuity mortgage" (RAM) on their property. Under arrangements negotiated with local banks, homeowners receive payments that may start with a lump sum, not exceeding 25 percent of the loan amount. The remainder is paid to the homeowner on a regular monthly basis. Upon the death of the homeowner the house is sold, and the loan is repaid. In Nassau County a family service association helps older persons analyze their financial situation and go over the various options.

REHABILITATION AND CONSTRUCTION LOANS

The government has developed many programs to encourage investors to rehabilitate and build housing for the elderly. It realizes that only with economic incentives to investors will enough housing for the elderly get built and rehabilitated. A few of the government programs geared toward elderly persons are listed below.

Deferred Payment Loans

This program is unbelievable! The government will make loans to investors to rehab housing for low-income and elderly persons. What makes this loan program different from others is that payments on the principal portion of the loan are deferred to a later date, usually eight to ten years later. However, each year a percentage of the loan principal is forgiven, so when the deferred portion of the loan becomes due, there is no principal left for the investor to pay back!

In Glendale, Arizona, this program has been very successful for rehabilitating some of the city's housing for low-income and elderly people. The city lends rehab money to owners of rental housing at zero percent interest for ten years. Payments on the loan principal are deferred until the loan is due, ten years later. Since the interest rate is zero, there are no interest payments, either. Each year 10 percent of the principal portion is forgiven, so at the end of ten years there is no balance remaining to pay. A similar program can be found in Washington, D.C., and other cities. Isn't that amazing? Think what you could do with this type of loan in rehabilitating one of your rental properties—a loan that has no interest payments and would be deferred, then forgiven after ten years. I can think of a lot of things I could do. What about you?

Money That is Given Away

Each year the government gives away over $2 billion. Just gives it away to people who deserve it. Throughout the country, the government grants money to local government agencies that in turn give or lend the money to local citizens, including the elderly. Utilities, weatherization, safer homes, and better living conditions are just a few of the many reasons elderly persons are given grants of money. In Baton Rouge, Louisiana, low-income elderly persons can receive up to $7,000 in grants to maintain and improve their homes and make them safer places to live.

Investors in Chesapeake, Virginia, can receive up to $5,000 per apartment unit to improve and rehabilitate housing for low-income and elderly persons. That is $5,000 per unit that an investor gets *for free* to improve the property he owns. If he owns an eight-unit building, the city could grant him up to $40,000 to make necessary improvements and then rent to low-income and elderly persons. Wouldn't you like someone to give you $40,000 so you could fix up your real estate? I discuss a few more elderly grant programs at the end of this chapter.

Section 202: Rehab and Construction Loans

The Section 202 program provides direct, low interest rate loans to finance the construction or rehabilitation of residential projects and related facilities for the elderly and handicapped. This program was intended to serve elderly persons whose income was above the "low-to-moderate-income" public housing level, but not enough for them to afford decent rental housing in the private market. Therefore, to encourage the construction and rehabilitation of housing for elderly persons, HUD will make up to fifty-year loans at 9¼ percent to persons wishing to provide housing for the elderly.

A loan at 9¼ percent might not seem inexpensive until you look at what is typically available in the conventional loan market. There you would be lucky to get a commercial loan for ten to fifteen years at a variable interest rate of around 11 to 13 percent. Let me tell you, if I had the choice between a fifty-year fixed interest government loan at 9¼ percent and a variable rate ten-year commercial loan starting at 13 percent, I would pick the government loan. Not only are the terms on the government loan more reasonable, but the qualifications are less stringent. The lower interest rate makes my cash flow better, plus I can pay myself a fee for being the contractor on the project.

Section 231: Mortgage Insurance for Housing for the Elderly

This program authorizes HUD to insure forty-year loans for construction or rehabilitation of rental housing (apartments) for the elderly. This is HUD's main program designed solely for rental housing for the elderly. However, most apartment buildings rehabilitated with this loan are very large and not practical for a beginning investor.

Section 221 (d) (3) and (4): Loans for Multi-family Housing

As mentioned earlier, these are programs to insure loans used to rehab or build low-to-moderate-income properties of five units or larger. While these programs are not specifically for the elderly, they are an alternative to the Section 231 program.

A new wave of housing has been created using this program to bridge the gap between totally independent living arrangements and the health-care-oriented nursing home. These apartment projects provide meals and other minor services to the elderly tenants.

Section 223 (f): Loans to Purchase or Refinance Multi-family Housing

This program insures forty-year loans to purchase or refinance existing properties, including housing for the elderly, where money is needed to make minor repairs. Before this program was implemented in 1974, loans were only provided for major rehab work or new construction.

Section 232: Loans for Nursing Homes/ Intermediate Care Facilities

Developers who want to build or rehabilitate long-term care facilities can get loans through this mortgage insurance program. The emphasis here is on housing for residents who need skilled nursing care and related medical services.

RENTAL ASSISTANCE PROGRAMS FOR ELDERLY TENANTS

What happens when thousands of units have been rehabilitated for elderly people and the elderly can't afford the rent to live in them?

Well, if you're the government, you help them pay their rent with rent subsidies. If you are an investor or owner of an apartment building, you rent to elderly tenants on a rent subsidy program, and their rent checks are mailed directly to you.

Section 8 Rent Subsidies for Elderly Tenants

This is the most important rent subsidy program in our country today. As you learned in chapter 11, the Section 8 program provides rental assistance for low-to-moderate-income families. Unfortunately, many people associate Section 8 tenants with ghetto or slum properties, so most landlords do not get involved. Nothing could be further from the truth. That's why you *should* get involved. Did you know that as of August 1984 there were 2,231,061 units under this program? Of those units, approximately 40 percent were occupied by the elderly. That means the government paid the rent on almost 900,000 apartments occupied by elderly persons. About 100,000 additional Section 8 units were added in 1985, including 14,000 units provided as a result of the Section 202 housing for the elderly loan program. In a day of ever-increasing housing costs, this is an invaluable and much needed program for those elderly persons on a small fixed income.

What really is exciting is that almost half of the Section 8 tenants move yearly. That means over a million Section 8 renters are looking for apartments each year. Thousands of those renters will be elderly. The choice is yours. You can rent your apartments to Section 8 tenants with incomes below a certain level, or you can rent to Section 8 elderly people.

Getting Started with Housing for the Elderly

Although the rehab and construction loan programs mentioned previously are the backbone of our nation's housing for the elderly, they are geared mainly to major developers and investors. What if you are just starting out? How can you get involved in this kind of housing if you don't own any real estate? There is something that is relatively easy to do and is readily available. It can be put to work right now to increase your income 20 to 30 percent a year, starting in thirty to forty-five days.

The best way for you to get started with this money-making trend is to purchase a small fix-up type apartment building, such as a four-plex. Let's take the example of Joan in Atlanta. Joan was able to locate a four-unit apartment building in a decent neighborhood. Two of the two-bedroom apartments were rented. The other two units, also two bedrooms each, were vacant because of the poor condition of the building. Since the building needed about $25,000 worth of fix-up, Joan was able to negotiate a purchase price of $75,000 with a down payment of $10,000 and a $65,000 seller-financed loan at 10 percent, with monthly payments of $570.70 until paid in full. Once she owned the apartment, Joan used her local rental rehabilitation program (discussed in chapter 9) to get a $15,000 4 percent rehabilitation loan. This loan would provide a portion of the money she would use to convert the run-down apartments into housing for elderly tenants.

In order to borrow the $15,000 at 4 percent, Joan agreed to match the $15,000 government loan with an additional $15,000 bank loan. It was easy for Joan to get the $15,000 bank loan, because she would rent to section 8 elderly tenants and the increased rental income would cover the extra debt. With the total of $30,000, the units were rehabilitated and rented to elderly Section 8 tenants. All of the units rented quickly, because of the improvements Joan made and her preference for elderly Section 8 tenants.

Here is a financial outline of what Joan receives each month:

Rents received @ $395/unit		$1,580.00
less		
Payment on $65,000 loan	570.70	
Payment on $15,000 bank rehab loan (13% interest)	189.90	
Payment on $15,000 goverment rehab loan (4% interest)	50.00	
Operating expenses	450.00	1,260.60
Total profit after expenses		$ 319.40

The interesting part of Joan's story is still to come. Joan was the owner/contractor of this rehabilitation project. Using the cost guidelines issued by the city, Joan bid the rehab costs for her four units at $30,000. After paying all of her subcontractors, Joan came away with $5,400 in cash—her compensation as contractor. This returned to Joan much of her original down payment of $10,000. But where is the benefit from rehabilitating the apartments into housing for the elderly? As you remember, Joan paid $75,000 for the four units. By rehabilitating the units, raising the rents, and renting the entire building to Section 8 elderly tenants, she raised the value of her fourplex to $120,000. Combine that with a positive cash flow of about $320 a month. It's obvious that Joan has created quite a money machine for herself. In summary, Joan bought the building for $75,000, put $10,000 down, and rehabilitated the property with a $30,000 matching funds rental rehabilitation loan. She pulled out $5,400 in cash as her contractor's compensation. Then Joan rented the property to Section 8 elderly tenants, receiving $1,580 in rents from the government every month—problem free. Finally, after paying all her bills, Joan receives about $320 positive cash flow each month from a building that is now worth $120,000. Joan feels great, because she worked with her government to provide renovated housing for some wonderful elderly people who otherwise couldn't afford such nice apartments. Her profit is a motivation to do it again and provide more housing for the elderly persons in her community.

What Elderly Persons Like in an Apartment

Once you decide to rehabilitate a property for elderly tenants, there are several things you can do to make your property more valuable and more attractive to elderly people shopping for a place to live.

Security. One of the most important features you can provide for elderly tenants is a safe and secure building. Solid-core front and back doors with deadbolt locks especially are preferred by the elderly. A small peephole in the front door can enable tenants to know who is at their door without opening it. See to it that the building has adequate outside lighting. A well-lit building discourages crime. If the property has an intercom system, make sure it is in working order and that the elderly tenants know how to use it.

Convenience. An apartment located close to shopping, hospitals, doctors, and public transportation will be especially preferred by elderly persons. This should be kept in mind when you purchase your investment property. One way to encourage elderly persons to rent an apartment that is not located within walking distance of public transportation is to provide a weekly shuttle service to the nearest bus or train stop.

Comfort. Doors that stick, drawers that won't open, heaters that don't heat, cold tile floors—these are a few of the complaints that elderly people may have about their homes. Put yourself in their shoes. Many elderly people have arthritis or don't have the strength to do the things you take for granted. Check things like doorknobs, locks, water faucets, stove fixtures, windows, and curtain rods to make sure they can be operated easily. Install doors and drawers that open smoothly. Test every appliance for working condition. Install carpet over tile floors for additional warmth and comfort.

I have rented many apartments to elderly people, simply because I took the time to add a few of the features above—items that don't cost much but mean a lot to an elderly person. Take the time to cater to your elderly customer. Point out the special things you have done to the property. Let your prospective elderly resident know that you care. It will pay off in the long run.

HOW TO FIND ELDERLY RENTERS

The best way to find elderly residents is to advertise your apartment in places where elderly people socialize. Put notes on the bulletin boards of several churches, synagogues, senior citizen centers, grocery stores, and pharmacies. Let the elderly know that you have an apartment that qualifies for Section 8 rent subsidies. Mention the special amenities you have added to make elderly residents more comfortable.

THE OPPORTUNITIES ARE NOW

Think about it. As Americans get older, their need for decent, affordable housing will increase. Even without government assistance, hundreds of elderly residential care projects, like the Sierra Guest Homes in California, are springing up to meet the growing demand for housing for the elderly.

Utilizing the spirit of American enterprise, the government is providing fantastic economic incentives to see that enough housing for the elderly is provided. Combine this fact with the rehabilitation techniques discussed in this book, and you have yet another road to wealth, which also serves a need in our society—housing for the elderly.

SPECIAL RESOURCE: GRANTS AT THE LOCAL LEVEL

COMMUNITY DEVELOPMENT BLOCK GRANTS (CDBG)

Another area in which the government is helping the elderly is through local programs funded by federal grants. The Community Development Block Grant (CDBG) program is a major source of funds enabling cities to conduct a wide range of community development activities. Approximately $2.5 billion of CDBG money is given each year to 735 cities and urban counties. About $1 billion goes to states to be distributed to small cities with populations under 50,000. Local governments either give away or lend money at low interest rates to provide low- and moderate-income housing. This means that owners of rental housing in specific areas can apply for these low interest rate loans to improve their properties. Elderly citizens benefit directly by having nicer housing and better services in the community.

Here are a few examples of the kinds of projects funded with CDBG grants that directly benefit the elderly.

- Seattle, Washington, provides zero to 9 percent loans to low-income families for home renovation. CDBG funds have also been used for zero-interest loans. In 1979, over half of these loans went to elderly persons. CDBG funds were also used to build a senior citizen community center and community health clinic.
- The East Side Housing Action Committee of Milwaukee, Wisconsin, offers free repair and maintenance services to elderly persons and low-income households.
- Brookline, Massachusetts, has used CDBG funds for a combined grant and rebate program. The program also provides free technical advice to homeowners to help them inspect their properties. In 1979 and 1980, about 40 percent of the grants and 13 percent of the rebates went to elderly homeowners.
- Detroit, Michigan, provides minor home repair for elderly persons in revitalization neighborhoods.

- Senior Housing in Minneapolis–St. Paul is a CDBG-funded program designed to deal with the special problems of elderly homeowners. The organization provides information to callers about housing programs, helps elderly persons complete forms for loans and grants for home repair, publishes a list of responsible contractors, and provides small home-repair loans.
- The Council on Aging in the County of Santa Clara, California, provides a shared-housing service to elderly tenants that matches older persons who have housing with other persons who need low-rent housing.
- In Banks County, Georgia, a county jail was rehabilitated for use as a senior center. It is also used for food stamp distribution, and as a courtroom and large meeting room.
- Davidson County, Georgia, rehabilitated a health center and senior center.
- Lafayette, Colorado, used CDBG funds to build a ten-unit rental housing project for the elderly.
- Twenty substandard rental units were rehabilitated with CDBG funds in Greenville, Georgia. An abandoned train depot was transformed into a senior citizen center.
- Rehabilitation grants were given to twenty-nine elderly and fourteen non-elderly homeowners in Powder, Georgia. This is CDBG money that was given to these people so they could repair their homes. Isn't that great?

URBAN DEVELOPMENT ACTION GRANTS (UDAG)

These are grants given to cities across the nation to help them improve blighted and distressed areas. Similar to CDBGs, UDAGs are primarily for urban renewal. In 1984, 457 projects used $602 million of UDAG money. Here are a few examples.

- In Cleveland, Ohio, UDAG funds were used to build a 100-bed, 50,000-square-foot skilled and intermediate care facility with a multipurpose senior center.
- In Manitou Springs, Colorado, UDAG funding was used to convert a historic downtown hotel into fifty-six apartments for the elderly.
- In Old Forge, Pennsylvania, a sixty-unit addition was built onto an existing ninety-eight bed nursing care facility.

In many of the cases involving CDBG and UDAG money, contractors, developers, and investors were given the opportunity to do the projects. Many cities need elderly housing and services. The money is available if you are ready to get involved.

KEEP THESE POINTS IN MIND
1. How to get started with housing for the elderly:
    - Locate a small rental property near shopping, churches, public transportation, doctors.
    - Make an offer on the property, subject to getting a low interest rate rehab loan from your local community development agency.
    - Get bids from subcontractors to do the work on your project.
    - Close the deal and take over ownership.
    - Get the rehab work completed. Remember to cater to elderly-needs.
    - Find Section 8 elderly tenants by advertising at churches, stores, health clinics.
    - Take care of final paperwork and make sure your new tenants are comfortable in their new homes.
2. The demand for housing for the elderly is increasing rapidly.
3. Use the "ghetto" misconception people have about Section 8 tenants to your benefit. You can be the one to rent to the Section 8 elderly people who need housing.
4. Section 8 renters can rent in any part of any town. They are not limited only to target areas.

16

THE ONE HUNDRED BEST GOVERNMENT PROGRAMS

FAILURE IS THE OPPORTUNITY TO BEGIN AGAIN MORE INTELLIGENTLY.

Henry Ford

As you finish this book and prepare to get started with government loans, you should have no doubt that the government has provided a vast number of programs designed for you to use. Whatever your business, hobby, or occupation, there is a government program or loan for you.

Recently, Congress allocated over $56.3 billion to state and local governments, agencies, non-profit organizations, profit organizations, and individuals to support specialized endeavors. Much of this money each year is used by individuals wishing to pursue interests that benefit themselves and society. Some of the programs are loans (or loan insurance), while other programs give you direct cash grants. Still others provide government property at great value. Of course, there are many more than one hundred government programs in our nation today. However, here are one hundred of the best programs available to individuals. I call them one hundred of the Best Government Goodies.

HOUSING PROGRAMS

1. *Interest Reduction for Homes for Lower Income Families*
   What You Get: Direct payments and guaranteed or insured loans of up to $11,013 annually per unit to make home ownership more possible for lower income families. Payments are made to lenders to subsidize a lower interest rate for home loans.
   Who to Contact: Director, Single Family Development Division, Office of Single Family Housing, Department of Housing and Urban Development, Washington, D.C. 20410.

2. *Rehabilitation Mortgage Insurance*
   What You Get: Guaranteed or insured loans of up to $92,000 to help families improve, purchase and improve, or refinance and improve existing residential structures that are more than one year old.
   Who to Contact: Director, Single Family Development Division, Office of Single Family Housing, Department of Housing and Urban Development, Washington, D.C. 20410.

3. *Home Purchase Mortgage Insurance*
   What You Get: Guaranteed or insured loans of up to $107,000 to help families finance the purchase of proposed, under construction, or existing one- to four-family housing, as well as to refinance debts on existing housing.
   Who to Contact: Director, Single Family Development Division, Office of Single Family Housing, Department of Housing and Urban Development, Washington, D.C. 20410.

4. *Home Purchase Mortgage Insurance for Veterans*
   What You Get: Guaranteed or insured loans of up to $67,000 to help veterans finance the purchase of proposed, under construction, or existing single-family housing, as well as to refinance debts on existing housing.

Who to Contact: Director, Single Family Development Division, Office of Single Family Housing, Department of Housing and Urban Development, Washington, D.C. 20410.

5. *Home Purchase Mortgage Insurance for Disaster Victims*
What You Get: Guaranteed or insured loans of up to $14,400 to finance the purchase of proposed, under construction, or existing single-family housing for the occupant-borrower who is a victim of a major disaster.
Who to Contact: Director, Single Family Development Division, Office of Single Family Housing, Department of Housing and Urban Development, Washington, D.C. 20410.

6. *Mortgage Insurance for Low- and Moderate-Income Families*
What You Get: Guaranteed or insured loans of up to $42,000 for families displaced by urban renewal or other government action, as well as other low-income and moderate-income families. These loans may be used to finance the purchase or rehabilitation of proposed or existing low-cost one- to four-family housing.
Who to Contact: Director, Single Family Development Division, Office of Single Family Housing, Department of Housing and Urban Development, Washington, D.C. 20410.

7. *Mortgage Insurance for Homes in Outlying Areas*
What You Get: Guaranteed or insured loans of up to $75,000 to help families finance the purchase of proposed, under construction, or existing one-family non-farm housing, or new farm housing on five or more acres adjacent to a highway.
Who to Contact: Director, Single Family Development Division, Office of Single Family Housing, Department of Housing and Urban Development, Washington, D.C. 20410.

8. *Mortgage Insurance for Homes in Urban Renewal Areas*
What You Get: Guaranteed or insured loans of up to $107,000 to finance the purchase or rehabilitation of one- to eleven-family housing in approved urban renewal or code enforcement areas.
Who to Contact: Director, Single Family Development Division, Office of Single Family Housing, Department of Housing and Urban Development, Washington, D.C. 20410.

9. *Mortgage Insurance for Homes in Older, Declining Areas*
   What You Get: Guaranteed or insured loans, averaging $9,400, to help families finance the purchase, repair, construction, and rehabilitation of housing in older, declining neighborhoods.
   Who to Contact: Director, Single Family Development Division, Office of Single Family Housing, Department of Housing and Urban Development, Washington, D.C. 20410.

10. *Mortgage Insurance for the Purchase of Condominiums*
   What You Get: Guaranteed or insured loans of up to $67,500 to finance the acquisition of individual units in proposed or existing condominium projects containing four or more units.
   Who to Contact: Director, Single Family Development Division, Office of Single Family Housing, Department of Housing and Urban Development, Washington, D.C. 20410.

11. *Mortgage Insurance for Persons with Special Credit Risks*
   What You Get: Guaranteed or insured loans of up to $18,000 to help low- and moderate-income persons who cannot meet normal HUD standards buy homes. These loans may be used to finance the purchase of new, existing, or substantially rehabilitated single-family housing.
   Who to Contact: Director, Single Family Development Division, Office of Single Family Housing, Department of Housing and Urban Development, Washington, D.C. 20410.

12. *Graduated Payment Mortgage Payments*
   What You Get: Guaranteed or insured loans of up to $67,000 to facilitate early home ownership for households that expect their incomes to rise. This program allows homeowners to make smaller monthly payments initially and increase their size gradually over time.
   Who to Contact: Director, Single Family Development Division, Office of Single Family Housing, Department of Housing and Urban Development, Washington, D.C. 20410.

13. *Single-Family Home Mortgage Coinsurance*
   What You Get: Guaranteed or insured loans of up to $67,500 to help finance the purchase of proposed, under construction, or existing one- to four-family housing, as well as to refinance debt on existing housing.

Who to Contact: Director, Single Family Development Division, Office of Single Family Housing, Department of Housing and Urban Development, Washington, D.C. 20410.

14. *Mortgage Insurance for Cooperatives*
    What You Get: Guaranteed or insured loans of up to $67,500 to provide insured financing for the purchase of shares of stock in a cooperative project. Ownership of the shares carries the right to occupy a unit located within the cooperative project.
    Who to Contact: Director, Single Family Development Division, Office of Single Family Housing, Department of Housing and Urban Development, Washington, D.C. 20410.

15. *Mortgage Insurance for Homes in Military Impacted Areas*
    What You Get: Guaranteed or insured loans of up to $107,000 to help families buy homes in military impacted areas.
    Who to Contact: Director, Single Family Development Division, Office of Single Family Housing, Department of Housing and Urban Development, Washington, D.C. 20410.

16. *Mobile Home Loan Insurance*
    What You Get: Guaranteed or insured loans of up to $18,000 to finance the purchase of mobile homes as principle residences of borrowers.
    Who to Contact: Director, Title I Insured and 312 Loan Servicing Division, Office of Single Family Housing, Department of Housing and Urban Development, Washington, D.C. 20410.

17. *Property Improvement Loan Insurance*
    What You Get: Guaranteed or insured loans of up to $37,500 to help finance improvements to homes and other existing structures, and the erection of new non-residential structures that substantially protect or improve the basic livability or utility of the properties.
    Who to Contact: Director, Title I Insured and 312 Loan Servicing Division, Office of Single Family Housing, Department of Housing and Urban Development, Washington, D.C. 20410.

18. *Mortgage Insurance for Mobile Homes and Lots*
    What You Get: Guaranteed or insured loans of up to $36,500 to

finance the purchase of a mobile home and the lot to place it on. *Who to Contact:* Director, Title I Insured and 312 Loan Servicing Division, Office of Single Family Housing, Department of Housing and Urban Development, Washington, D.C. 20410.

19. *Mortgage Insurance for the Construction or Substantial Rehabilitation of Condominium Projects*
What You Get: Guaranteed or insured loans of up to $36,000 to enable sponsors to develop condominium projects in which individual units will be sold to home buyers.
Who to Contact: Office of Multifamily Housing Development, Department of Housing and Urban Development, Washington, D.C. 20410.

20. *Mortgage Insurance for Mobile Home Parks*
What You Get: Guaranteed or insured loans of up to $14,000 per mobile home to make possible the financing of construction or rehabilitation of mobile home parks consisting of five or more spaces.
Who to Contact: Office of Multifamily Housing Development, Department of Housing and Urban Development, Washington, D.C. 20410.

21. *Mortgage Insurance for Nursing Homes and Intermediate Care Facilities*
What You Get: Guaranteed or insured loans to finance the construction or rehabilitation of nursing homes and intermediate care facilities that accommodate twenty or more patients requiring skilled nursing care and related medical services, or those who are not in need of nursing home care but are in need of minimum and continuous care provided by licensed or trained personnel.
Who to Contact: Office of Multifamily Housing Development, Department of Housing and Urban Development, Washington, D.C. 20410.

22. *Mortgage Insurance for Purchase by Homeowners from Lessors*
What You Get: Guaranteed or insured loans up to $30,000 per family to help finance the purchase from lessors by homeowners of property that is held under long-term leases and on which their homes are located.

Who to Contact: Director, Single Family Development Division, Office of Single Family Housing, Department of Housing and Urban Development, Washington, D.C. 20410.

23. *Mortgage Insurance for Rental Housing*
What You Get: Guaranteed or insured loans of up to $36,000 to finance the construction or rehabilitation of rental detached, semidetached, row, walk-up, or elevator-type structures with five or more units.
Who to Contact: Director, Multifamily Development Division, Office of Multifamily Housing Development, Department of Housing and Urban Development, Washington, D.C. 20410.

24. *Mortgage Insurance for Investor-Sponsored Cooperative Housing*
What You Get: Guaranteed or insured loans of up to $36,000 to finance the construction or rehabilitation of good quality housing that will be sold to non-profit cooperatives and ownership housing corporations.
Who to Contact: Office of Multifamily Housing Development, Department of Housing and Urban Development, Washington, D.C. 20410.

25. *Rent Supplements on Rental Housing for Lower Income Families*
What You Get: Direct payments to landlords, to provide good quality rental housing to low-income families at a cost they can afford. These payments are made to the owners of approved multi-family rental housing projects to supplement the partial rental payments made by eligible tenants.
Who to Contact: Director, Office of Multifamily Housing Management and Occupancy, Department of Housing and Urban Development, Washington, D.C. 20410.

26. *Supplemental Loan Insurance for Multi-family Rental Housing*
What You Get: Guaranteed or insured loans to finance additions and improvements to any multi-family project, group facility, hospital, or nursing home insured or held by HUD.
Who to Contact: Director, Multifamily Development Division, Office of Multifamily Housing Development, Department of Housing and Urban Development, Washington, D.C. 20410.

27. *Mortgage Insurance for the Purchase or Refinancing of Existing Multi-family Housing Projects*
    What You Get: Guaranteed or insured loans for the purchase or refinancing of existing multi-family housing projects, whether conventionally financed or subject to federally insured mortgages at the time of application for mortgage insurance.
    Who to Contact: Director, Multifamily Development Division, Office of Multifamily Housing Development, Department of Housing and Urban Development, Washington, D.C. 20410.

28. *Mortgage Insurance for Rental and Cooperative Housing for Low- and Moderate-Income Families at Market Interest Rate*
    What You Get: Guaranteed or insured loans of up to $35,480 to provide good quality rental or cooperative housing within the price range of low- and moderate-income families.
    Who to Contact: Director, Multifamily Development Division, Office of Multifamily Housing Development, Department of Housing and Urban Development, Washington, D.C. 20410.

29. *Mortgage Insurance for Housing for the Elderly*
    What You Get: Guaranteed or insured loans of up to $34,846 to finance the construction or rehabilitation of detached, semidetached, walk-up, or elevator-type rental housing designed to provide quality rental housing for the elderly or handicapped, consisting of eight or more units.
    Who to Contact: Director, Multifamily Development Division, Office of Multifamily Housing Development, Department of Housing and Urban Development, Washington, D.C. 20410.

30. *Mortgage Insurance for Rental Housing in Urban Renewal Areas*
    What You Get: Guaranteed or insured loans of up to $36,000 to finance proposed construction or rehabilitation of detached, semidetached, row, walk-up, or elevator-type rental housing, or to finance the purchase of properties that have been rehabilitated by a local public agency.
    Who to Contact: Director, Multifamily Development Division, Office of Multifamily Housing Development, Department of Housing and Urban Development, Washington, D.C. 20410.

31. *Assistance for Troubled Multi-family Housing Projects*
    What You Get: Grants and direct payments from $20,000 to $1,700,000 to restore or maintain the financial soundness, assist in the management, and maintain the low- to moderate-income character of certain projects assisted or approved under the National Housing Act (1934) or under the Housing and Urban Development Act (1965).
    Who to Contact: Director, Management Operations Division, Office of Multifamily Housing Management and Occupancy, Department of Housing and Urban Development, Washington, D.C. 20410.

32. *Lower Income Housing Assistance (Section 8)*
    What You Get: Direct payments to help lower income families obtain decent, safe, and sanitary housing in private accommodations and to promote economically mixed existing, newly constructed, and substantially and moderately rehabilitated housing.
    Who to Contact: Public Housing and Indian Programs, Department of Housing and Urban Development, Washington, D.C. 20410.

33. *Section 312 Rehabilitation Loans*
    What You Get: Direct loans of up to $200,000 for the rehabilitation of residential, commercial, and other non-residential properties.
    Who to Contact: Community Planning and Development, Office of Urban Rehabilitation, Department of Housing and Urban Development, 451 7th Street, S.W., Washington, D.C. 20410.

34. *Mortgage Insurance for Experimental Homes*
    What You Get: Guaranteed or insured loans, ranging from $30,000 to $35,000, to help finance, by providing mortgage insurance, the development of homes that incorporate new or untried construction concepts designed to reduce housing costs, raise living standards, and improve neighborhood design.
    Who to Contact: Assistant Secretary for Policy Development and Research, Department of Housing and Urban Development, 451 7th Street, S.W., Washington, D.C. 20410.

35. *Mortgage Insurance for Experimental Projects Other Than Housing*
    What You Get: Guaranteed or insured loans to help finance the development of group medical facilities or subdivisions or new communities that incorporate new or untried construction concepts designed to reduce construction costs, raise living standards, and improve neighborhood design.
    Who to Contact: Assistant Secretary for Policy Development and Research, Department of Housing and Urban Development, 451 7th Street, S.W., Washington, D.C. 20410.

36. *Mortgage Insurance for Experimental Rental Housing*
    What You Get: Guaranteed or insured loans averaging $2,314,814 to help finance the development of multi-family housing that incorporates new or untried construction concepts designed to reduce housing costs, raise living standards, and improve neighborhood design.
    Who to Contact: Secretary for Policy Development and Research, Department of Housing and Urban Development, 451 7th Street, S.W., Washington, D.C. 20410.

37. *Historic Preservation Grants-In-Aid*
    What You Get: Grants ranging from $500 to $500,000 given to state governments to perform many tasks that expand and maintain the National Register of Historic Places, including matching acquisition and development grants-in-aid through the states to public and private parties for the preservation of historic properties.
    Who to Contact: Your state historical preservation office (see Chapter 13).

U.S. DEPARTMENT OF AGRICULTURE PROGRAMS

38. *Farm Ownership Loans*
    What You Get: Guaranteed or insured loans ranging from $16,000 to $200,000 to assist eligible farmers and ranchers, including farming cooperatives, partnerships, and corporations, to become

owner-operators of not larger than family farms; to make efficient use of land, labor, and other resources; to carry on sound and successful operations on the farm. These loans are available to eligible applicants with limited incomes and resources who are unable to pay market interest rates and have special problems, such as undeveloped managerial skills.
Who to Contact: Administrator, Farmers Home Administration, Department of Agriculture, Washington, D.C. 20250.

39. *Low- to Moderate-Income Housing Loans*
   What You Get: Guaranteed or insured loans ranging from $1,000 to $60,000 to help rural families finance the construction, repair, or purchase of housing. Loans may also be used for sewage facilities, water supply, weatherization, and buying a site on which to place a dwelling for applicant's own use.
   Who to Contact: Single Family Housing, Farmers Home Administration, Department of Agriculture, Washington, D.C. 20250.

40. *Recreation Facility Loans*
   What You Get: Guaranteed or insured loans ranging from $20,000 to $100,000 to help eligible farm and ranch owners convert all or part of the farms they own or operate to income-producing outdoor recreational enterprises that supplement farm income. Recreational enterprises that may be financed include campgrounds, horseback riding stables, swimming facilities, tennis courts, shooting preserves, vacation cottages, lodges and rooms for visitors, lakes and ponds for boating and fishing, docks, nature trails, and winter sports areas.
   Who to Contact: Community Programs, Farmers Home Administration, Department of Agriculture, Washington, D.C. 20250.

41. *Rural Rental Housing Loans*
   What You Get: Guaranteed or insured loans ranging from $27,000 to $2,000,000 to finance the construction, improvement, or repair of rental or cooperative housing suited for independent living in rural areas.
   Who to Contact: Administrator, Farmers Home Administration, Department of Agriculture, Washington, D.C. 20250.

42. *Very Low Income Housing Repair Loans and Grants*
    What You Get: Direct loans and grants ranging from $200 to
    $5,000 to give very low income rural homeowners an opportunity
    to make essential repairs to their homes to make them safe and
    to remove health hazards to the family or the community. These
    include repairs to the foundation, roof, or basic structure as well
    as water and waste disposal systems and weatherization.
    Who to Contact: Administrator, Farmers Home Administration,
    Department of Agriculture, Washington, D.C. 20250.

43. *Business and Industrial Loans*
    What You Get: Guaranteed or insured loans ranging from $11,000
    to $50,000,000 to assist public, private, or cooperative organi-
    zations, Indian tribes, or individuals in rural areas to obtain loans
    to improve, develop, or finance business, industry, and employ-
    ment.
    Who to Contact: Administrator, Farmers Home Administration,
    Department of Agriculture, Washington, D.C. 20250.

44. *Rural Rental Assistance Payments*
    What You Get: Direct payments to reduce the rents paid by low-
    income families occupying eligible rural rental housing, rural
    cooperative housing, and farm labor housing projects financed
    through the Farmers Home Administration. Rental assistance
    may be used to reduce the rents paid by low-income elderly
    citizens or families and domestic farm laborers and families whose
    rents exceed 25 percent of an adjusted annual income that does
    not exceed the limit established for the state.
    Who to Contact: Administrator, Farmers Home Administration,
    Department of Agriculture, Washington, D.C. 20250.

45. *Economic Emergency Loans*
    What You Get: Guaranteed or insured loans of up to $400,000
    to help bona fide farmers, ranchers, and aquaculture operators
    continue operations during an economic emergency that has caused
    a lack of agricultural credit due to national or areawide economic
    stress.
    Who to Contact: Emergency Loan Division, Farmers Home Ad-
    ministration, Department of Agriculture, Washington, D.C.
    20250.

46. *Above-Moderate-Income Housing Loans*
What You Get: Guaranteed or insured loans ranging from $1,000 to $59,000 to help above-moderate-income families purchase, construct, or improve decent, safe, and sanitary housing when loans would not be made available without a guarantee.
Who to Contact: Single Family Housing, Farmers Home Administration, Department of Agriculture, Washington, D.C. 20250.

47. *Great Plains Conservation*
What You Get: Direct payments of up to $25,000 to conserve and develop the Great Plains soil and water resources by providing technical and financial assistance to farmers, ranchers, and others in planning and implementing conservation practices.
Who to Contact: Administrator, Soil Conservation Service, Department of Agriculture, P.O. Box 2890, Washington, D.C. 20013.

48. *Plant Materials for Conservation*
What You Get: Donation of property and goods to assemble, evaluate, select, release, and introduce into commerce new and improved plant materials for soil, water, and wildlife conservation, and environmental improvement.
Who to Contact: Administrator, Soil Conservation Service, Department of Agriculture, P.O. Box 2890, Washington, D.C. 20013.

49. *Rural Abandoned Mine Program*
What You Get: Grants ranging from $5,000 to $196,000 to promote the development of soil and water resources of unreclaimed mined lands so as to protect people and the environment from past coal mining practices.
Who to Contact: Director, Conservation Operations Division, Soil Conservation Service, Department of Agriculture, P.O. Box 2890, Washington, D.C. 20013.

U.S. DEPARTMENT OF COMMERCE PROGRAMS

50. *Trade Adjustment Assistance*
What You Get: Direct loans and guaranteed or insured loans of up to $3,000,000 to provide trade adjustment assistance to firms,

businesses, and industry associations and communities adversely affected by increased imports.

Who to Contact: Deputy Director, Office of Private Investment, Economic Development Administration, Department of Commerce, 14th Street and Constitution Avenue, N.W., Washington, D.C. 20230.

51. *Operating Differential Subsidies*
What You Get: Direct payments ranging from $2,400 to $6,390 per day to promote the development and maintenance of the U.S. Merchant Marine by granting financial aid to equalize the cost of operating a U.S. flagship with the cost of operating a competitive foreign flagship.
Who to Contact: Assistant Administrator for Maritime Aids, Maritime Administration, Department of Commerce, Washington, D.C. 20230.

52. *Minority Business Development*
What You Get: Grants ranging from $10,000 to $3,000,000 to provide free financial, management, and technical assistance to economically and socially disadvantaged individuals who need help in starting and/or operating a business. Primary objectives of the assistance are to increase the gross receipts and decrease the failure rates of the client firms.
Who to Contact: Chief, Grants Administration Division, Minority Business Development Agency, Department of Commerce, Washington, D.C. 20230.

GENERAL SERVICES ADMINISTRATION PROGRAMS

53. *Disposal of Federal Surplus Real Property*
What You Get: Surplus property and goods that are sold to the general public without restrictions at a price equal to the estimated fair market value of the property.
Who to Contact: Office of Real Property, Federal Property Resource Service, General Services Administration, Washington, D.C. 20406.

54. *Sale of Federal Surplus Personal Property*
    What You Get: Surplus property and goods that are no longer needed by the government sold in an economical and efficient manner to obtain the maximum net return from sales. The General Services Administration conducts the sale of personal property for most of the civil agencies; the Department of Defense handles the sale of its own surplus property.
    Who to Contact: Director, Sales Division, Office of Personal Property, Federal Property Resource Service, General Services Administration, Washington, D.C. 20406.

DEPARTMENT OF DEFENSE PROPERTY

55. *Surplus Property Sales*
    What You Get: Property that is no longer needed by the Department of Defense put up for sale to the public. Prospective bidders must request an application for placement on the bidders' list. This application provides a place to indicate the types of property and the regional sales offices in which the bidder is interested. When the types of property selected on the application are placed for sale in the region selected, a sale catalog called an "Invitation for Bids" will be mailed. Items sold by the Department of Defense include agricultural machinery and equipment; aircraft and aircraft equipment; alarms; bearings; books; chemicals; cleaning equipment; clothing; communication equipment; construction and building materials; highway maintenance equipment; electrical equipment; engines and accessories; furnishings; live animals; lumber; material handling equipment; medical supplies; motor vehicles; musical instruments; office supplies; photographic equipment; plumbing and metal products; recreational equipment; refrigeration equipment; ropes and chains; ship and marine supplies; tools.
    Who to Contact: Request an application from DOD Surplus Sales, P.O. Box 1370, Battle Creek, Michigan 49016.

UNCLAIMED PROPERTY AUCTIONS

56. *Unclaimed U.S. Customs Property Auctions*
    What You Get: Unclaimed property that is held at each customs
    district office auctioned periodically.
    Who to Contact: In order to determine when sales will be held
    at various locations you should write to your area district director,
    U.S. Customs Office.

57. *U.S. Postal Service Property Auctions*
    What You Get: Auctions of unclaimed loose-in-the-mail items
    held at least twice each year at each dead parcel office. The
    scheduling and announcement of these sales is delegated to the
    managers of various bulk mail centers where dead parcel branches
    are located.
    Who to Contact: Write to your district's U.S. Post Office, at-
    tention General Manager, Dead Parcel Branch. The address of
    the nearest dead parcel post office branch can be requested from
    the main post office in your area.

U.S. DEPARTMENT OF HEALTH AND HUMAN SERVICES

58. *Supportive Services and Senior Centers*
    What You Get: Elderly persons receive, through state and area
    agencies, long-term care assistance; in-home services such as
    homemakers and home health aid, telephone calls, reassurance,
    and chore maintenance; and informational and referral services.
    Who to Contact: Associate Commissioner, Administration on
    Aging, Office of Human Development Services, Department of
    Health and Human Services, 330 Independence Avenue, S.W.,
    North Building Rm. 4271, Washington, D.C. 20201.

59. *Nutrition Program for the Elderly*
    What You Get: Older Americans are provided with low-cost nu-
    tritious meals in local senior citizen centers.
    Who to Contact: Nutritionist, Administration on Aging, Office

of Human Development Services, Department of Health and Human Services, 330 Independence Avenue, S.W., North Building Rm. 4639, Washington, D.C. 20201.

60. *Disability Insurance*
What You Get: Direct payments of up to $989.30 monthly to replace part of the earnings lost because of a physical or mental impairment severe enough to prevent a person from working.
Who to Contact: Office of Information, Social Security Administration, Rm. 124, Altmeyer Building, Baltimore, MD 21235.

61. *Retirement Insurance*
What You Get: Direct payments of up to $1,000.60 monthly to replace part of the earnings lost because of retirement.
Who to Contact: Office of Information, Social Security Administration, Rm. 124, Altmeyer Building, Baltimore, MD 21235.

62. *Special Social Security Benefits for Persons Age Seventy-two and Over*
What You Get: Direct payments of up to $138.10 monthly to assure some regular income to certain persons age seventy-two and over, who had little or no opportunity to earn Social Security protection during their working years.
Who to Contact: Office of Information, Social Security Administration, Rm. 124, Altmeyer Building, Baltimore, MD 21235.

63. *Survivors Social Security Insurance*
What You Get: Direct payments of up to $1,000.60 monthly to replace part of earnings lost to dependents because of worker's death.
Who to Contact: Office of Information, Social Security Administration, Rm. 124, Altmeyer Building, Baltimore, MD 21235.

64. *Special Benefits for Disabled Coal Miners*
What You Get: Direct payments of up to $508 monthly to coal miners who have been disabled due to black lung disease and to their dependents or survivors.
Who to Contact: Office of Information, Social Security Administration, Rm. 124, Altmeyer Building, Baltimore, MD 21235.

65. *Supplemental Security Income*
   What You Get: Direct payments of up to $312.30 monthly to provide supplemental income to persons age sixty-five and over and to persons blind or disabled, whose income and resources are below specified levels.
   Who to Contact: Office of Information, Social Security Administration, Rm. 124, Altmeyer Building, Baltimore, MD 21235.

66. *Low-Income Energy Assistance Program*
   What You Get: Grants available to state governments to provide low-income persons with money to offset their rising costs of home energy consumption.
   Who to Contact: Office of Information, Social Security Administration, Rm. 124, Altmeyer Building, Baltimore, MD 21235.

67. *Minority Access to Research Careers*
   What You Get: Grants ranging from $3,900 to $100,000 to assist minority institutions and to increase the number of minority students who can compete successfully for entry into graduate programs that lead to the Ph.D. degree in biomedical science fields.
   Who to Contact: Program Director, MARC Program, National Institute of General Medical Sciences, National Institutes of Health, Bethesda, MD 20014.

68. *Medical Research Programs*
   What You Get: Grants ranging from $5,000 to $300,000 for research on each of a variety of physical and mental medical disorders.
   Who to Contact: National Institutes of Health, Bethesda, MD 20014.

69. *Cancer Research Programs*
   What You Get: Grants ranging from $10,000 to $3,000,000 to study and research various details of causes, prevention, and treatment of cancer.
   Who to Contact: Chief, Grants Administration Branch, Division of Cancer Research Resources and Centers, National Cancer Institute, Westwood 8A18, Bethesda, MD 20205.

SMALL BUSINESS ADMINISTRATION

70. *Displaced Business Loans*
    What You Get: Direct loans and guaranteed or insured loans, ranging from $5,000 to $904,000, to help small businesses continue in business, purchase a business, or establish a new business if substantial economic injury has been suffered as a result of displacement by, or location in or near, a federally funded program or project having the authority to exercise the right of eminent domain on such program or project.
    Who to Contact: Director, Office of Disaster Operations, Small Business Administration, 1441 L Street, N.W., Washington, D.C. 20416.

71. *Economic Opportunity Loans for Small Business*
    What You Get: Direct loans and guaranteed or insured loans, ranging from $1,000 to $315,600, for small businesses owned and operated by low-income or socially or economically disadvantaged persons.
    Who to Contact: Director, Office of Financing, Small Business Administration, 1441 L Street, N.W., Washington, D.C. 20416.

72. *Management and Technical Assistance for Disadvantaged Businessmen*
    What You Get: Grants ranging from $15,000 to $306,250 to provide management and technical assistance through public or private organizations to existing or potential business people who are economically or socially disadvantaged; who are located in areas of high concentrations of unemployment; or who are participants in certain activities authorized by the Small Business Act.
    Who to Contact: Assistant Administrator for Management Assistance, Small Business Administration, 1441 L Street, N.W., Washington, D.C. 20416.

73. *Small Business Investment Companies*
    What You Get: Direct loans and guaranteed or insured loans,

ranging from $50,000 to $35,000,000, to make equity and venture capital available to the small business community with maximum use of private sector participation and a minimum of government interference in the free market, and to provide advisory services and capital.

Who to Contact: Associate Administrator for Finance and Investment, Small Business Development–Management, Small Business Administration, 1441 L Street, N.W., Washington, D.C. 20416.

74. *Small Business Loans*
What You Get: Direct loans and guaranteed or insured loans, ranging from $1,000 to $500,000, to aid small businesses that are unable to obtain financing in the private credit marketplace, including agricultural enterprises. Funds may be used to construct, expand, or convert facilities; to purchase building equipment or materials; or for working capital.
Who to Contact: Director, Office of Financing, Small Business Administration, 1441 L Street, N.W., Washington, D.C. 20416.

75. *Regulatory Loans*
What You Get: Direct loans and guaranteed or insured loans to help any small business make alterations to its plant, facilities, or methods of operation to meet governmental requirements if substantial economic injury has been suffered as a result of such governmental orders.
Who to Contact: Office of Disaster Loans, Small Business Administration, 1441 L Street, N.W., Washington, D.C. 20416.

76. *Office of Women's Business Enterprise*
What You Get: Grants ranging from $5,000 to $150,000 to develop effective business management skills of potentially successful women entrepreneurs in significant numbers, and improve the business environment for women-owned businesses.
Who to Contact: Planning, Evaluation and Research, Office of Women's Business Enterprise, Small Business Administration, 1441 L Street, N.W., Washington, D.C. 20416.

VETERANS ADMINISTRATION PROGRAMS

77. *Automobiles and Adaptive Equipment for Certain Disabled Veterans*
    What You Get: Direct payments of up to $3,800 to provide financial assistance to certain disabled veterans toward the purchase price of an automobile, and an additional amount for adaptive equipment deemed necessary to insure that the eligible person will be able to operate or make use of the automobile or other conveyance.
    Who to Contact: Veterans Administration, Central Office, 810 Vermont Avenue, N.W., Washington, D.C. 20420.

78. *Compensation for Service-Connected Deaths for Veterans' Dependents*
    What You Get: Direct payments of up to $121 monthly to compensate widows, widowers, children, and dependent parents for the death of any veteran who died before January 1, 1957 because of a service-connected disability.
    Who to Contact: Veterans Administration, Central Office, 810 Vermont Avenue, N.W., Washington, D.C. 20420.

79. *Specially Adapted Housing for Disabled Veterans*
    What You Get: Direct payments of up to $30,000 to assist totally disabled veterans in acquiring suitable housing units with special fixtures and facilities made necessary by the nature of the veterans' disabilities.
    Who to Contact: Veterans Administration, Central Office, 810 Vermont Avenue, N.W., Washington, D.C. 20420.

80. *Veterans' Educational Assistance*
    What You Get: Direct payments of up to $422 monthly to make service in the armed forces more attractive by extending the benefits of higher education to qualified younger persons who might not otherwise be able to afford such an education; and to restore lost educational opportunities for those whose education was interrupted by active duty after January 31, 1955 and before January 1, 1977.

Who to Contact: Veterans Administration, Central Office, 810 Vermont Avenue, N.W., Washington, D.C. 20420.

81. *Direct Loans and Advances for Veteran's Housing*
What You Get: Direct loans of up to $33,000 to provide direct housing credit assistance to veterans, service personnel, and certain unmarried widows and widowers, or veterans and spouses of service personnel living in rural areas and small cities where private capital is not generally available for VA-guaranteed or insured loans.
Who to Contact: Veterans Administration, Central Office, 810 Vermont Avenue, N.W., Washington, D.C. 20420.

82. *Direct Housing Loans for Disabled Veterans*
What You Get: Direct loans of up to $33,000 to provide certain totally disabled veterans with direct housing credit and to supplement grants authorized to assist the disabled veterans in acquiring suitable housing.
Who to Contact: Veterans Administration, Central Office, 810 Vermont Avenue, N.W., Washington, D.C. 20420.

MISCELLANEOUS PROGRAMS

83. *Air Carrier Payments*
What You Get: Direct payments, ranging from $308,000 to $19,504,173, in subsidy compensation for development of air transportation of the extent and quality required for the commerce of the United States, the postal service, and the national defense. Subsidies can be used to cover the carrier's operating loss incurred under honest, economical, and efficient management, and to provide it an opportunity to earn a fair return (after taxes) on investment used in air transportation services.
Who to Contact: Director, Bureau of Domestic Aviation, B-60, Civil Aeronautics Board, 1825 Connecticut Avenue, N.W., Washington, D.C. 20428.

84. *Payments for Essential Air Services*
What You Get: Direct payments to provide essential air transportation to eligible communities by subsidizing air service. Pay-

ments are made to air carriers that are providing essential air services, which would not be provided but for subsidy.
Who to Contact: Director, Bureau of Domestic Aviation, B-60, Civil Aeronautics Board, 1825 Connecticut Avenue, N.W., Washington, D.C. 20428.

85. *Loan Guarantees for Purchase of Aircraft and Spare Parts*
    What You Get: Guaranteed or insured loans, ranging from $1,500,000 to $89,500,000, to guarantee loans under certain conditions for the purchase of aircraft and spare parts.
    Who to Contact: Federal Aviation Administration, Office of Aviation Policy, Department of Transportation, AP03, 800 Independence Avenue, S.W., Washington, D.C. 20591.

86. *Railroad Rehabilitation and Improvement Loans*
    What You Get: Guaranteed or insured loans, ranging from $5,000,000 to $35,000,000, to finance the acquisition or rehabilitation and improvement of railroad facilities, equipment, and yard and terminal facilities.
    Who to Contact: Office of National Freight Assistance Programs, Federal Railroad Administration, 400 7th Street, S.W., Washington, D.C. 20590.

87. *Basic Research in Collaboration with Smithsonian Institution Staff*
    What You Get: Grants of up to $14,000 a year to qualified individuals at various levels of educational accomplishment so that they may utilize the resources of the facilities, collections, and professional staff of the Smithsonian.
    Who to Contact: Director, Office of Fellowships and Grants, Smithsonian Institution, Rm. 3300, 955 L'Enfant Plaza, Washington, D.C. 20560.

88. *Woodrow Wilson International Center for Scholars Program*
    What You Get: Grants to individuals in the form of a fellowship program that is designed to accentuate the aspects of Wilson's ideals and concerns for which he is perhaps best known—his search for international peace and his imaginative new approaches in meeting the pressing issues of his day.
    Who to Contact: Director, Woodrow Wilson International Center for Scholars, Smithsonian Institution, Washington, D.C. 20560.

89. *Educational Exchange—Graduate Students*
    What You Get: Grants ranging from $1,000 to $15,000 to improve
    and strengthen the international relations of the United States by
    promoting better mutual understanding among the peoples of the
    world through educational exchanges.
    Who to Contact: Institute of International Education, 809 United
    Nations Plaza, New York, NY 10017.

90. *Educational Exchange for University Lecturers and Research
    Scholars*
    What You Get: Grants ranging from $2,000 to $30,000 to improve
    and strengthen the international relations of the United States by
    promoting better mutual understanding among the people of the
    world through educational exchanges.
    Who to Contact: Council for International Exchange of Scholars,
    11 Dupont Circle, Suite 300, Washington, D.C. 20036.

91. *Foster Grandparent Program*
    What You Get: Opportunity for men and women sixty and older
    to provide companionship and guidance to emotionally, physi-
    cally, and mentally handicapped children. This program provides
    direct benefits to foster grandparents, including stipends (cur-
    rently $2.20 an hour), meals while on duty, annual physical
    examinations, volunteer insurance, recognition, and uniforms.
    Who to Contact: Chief, Foster Grandparent Program, Older
    Americans Volunteer Programs, ACTION, 806 Connecticut Av-
    enue, N.W., Washington, D.C. 20525.

92. *Retired Senior Volunteer Program (RSVP)*
    What You Get: Grants to state agencies for funding programs that
    offer persons over the age of sixty an opportunity to contribute
    their skills and services to the community.
    Who to Contact: Chief, Retired Senior Volunteer Program, Older
    Americans Volunteer Programs, ACTION, 806 Connecticut Av-
    enue, N.W., Washington, D.C. 20525.

93. *Promotion of the Arts—Design Arts Program*
    What You Get: Grants up to $20,000 available to individuals for
    projects, including research, professional education, and public
    awareness in architecture, landscape architecture, and urban, in-

terior, fashion, industrial, and environmental design. This program attempts to encourage creativity and to make the public aware of the benefits of good design.

Who to Contact: Director, Design Arts Program, National Endowment for the Arts, 2401 E Street, N.W., Washington, D.C. 20506.

94. *Claims of Prisoners of War in Vietnam*

What You Get: Direct payments ranging up to $13,000 to provide compensation to members of the Armed Forces of the United States who were held as prisoners of war for any period of time during the Vietnam conflict by any force hostile to the United States.

Who to Contact: Office of the General Counsel, Foreign Claims Settlement Commission of the United States, 111 20th Street, N.W., Washington, D.C. 20579.

95. *Second China Claims Program*

What You Get: Direct payments to individuals to provide for the determination of the validity and amounts of outstanding claims against the People's Republic of China that arose out of the nationalization, expropriation, or other taking of property interest of nationals of the United States between November 6, 1966 and May 11, 1979 in China.

Who to Contact: Office of the General Counsel, Foreign Claims Settlement Commission of the United States, 111 20th Street, N.W., Washington, D.C. 20579.

96. *National Trust for Historic Preservation*

What You Get: Matching grants ranging from $20,000 to $50,000, each coupled to a low interest loan of an equal amount, to help revitalize historic neighborhoods for the benefit of low- and moderate-income residents, especially minorities.

Who to Contact: Director, Financial Services, National Trust for Historic Preservation, 1785 Massachussetts Avenue, N.W., Washington, D.C. 20036.

97. *Foreign Investment Guarantees*

What You Get: Guaranteed or insured loans to guarantee loans and investments made by eligible U.S. investors in friendly developing countries and areas.

Who to Contact: Information Officer, Overseas Private Investment Corporation, Washington, D.C. 20527.

98. *Foreign Investment Insurance*
What You Get: Insurance ranging from $4,000 to $100,000,000 to insure investments of eligible U.S. investors in friendly developing countries and areas against the risks of inconvertibility, expropriation, war, revolution, and insurrection.
Who to Contact: Information Officer, Overseas Private Investment Corporation, Washington, D.C. 20527.

99. *Pre-Investment Assistance*
What You Get: Direct payments ranging from $10,000 to $300,000 to initiate and support, through financial participation, the identification, assessment, surveying, and promotion of overseas private investment opportunities.
Who to Contact: Information Officer, Overseas Private Investment Corporation, Washington, D.C. 20527.

100. *Direct Investment Loans*
What You Get: Direct loans ranging from $325,000 to $2,500,000 for projects in developing countries sponsored by or significantly involving U.S. small businesses or cooperatives.
Who to Contact: Information Officer, Overseas Private Investment Corporation, Washington, D.C. 20527.

KEEP THESE POINTS IN MIND:
1. Government programs change from time to time. Stay informed, and stay in tune with what government agencies are doing in your area.
2. There is a government loan or program for everyone.
3. Take a look at your own situation, and then find a government loan or program to solve your problem.
4. Government loans are available in areas besides housing.
5. Write to (don't phone) the agency you are interested in for additional information about a particular government loan or program.

17

ACHIEVING FINANCIAL INDEPENDENCE

DINOSAURS BECAME EXTINCT BECAUSE THEY COULD NOT ADAPT THEIR LIFESTYLE TO CHANGING CONDITIONS IN THE ENVIRONMENT.

Anonymous

Which government loan or program will work the best for you? The program that will work for you will depend on where you are now, what you plan to do, and how you use it. The government program that makes one person a hefty profit may not interest another. Let's consider a few of the major government programs again and see where you fit in.

- The VA repo program, which I used to buy my first home, is perhaps the finest opportunity for anyone to buy a home for little or nothing down. There is no limit to the number of VA repos you may buy, as long as you can show that you're able to make the mortgage payments.
- The HUD acquired property program, which also sells homes to people like you and me at below-market prices, has been used by many of my students to build fortunes.

- The numerous HUD-insured loan programs encourage lenders to make loans to borrowers who would not qualify for conventional loans without the government insurance.
- Government property sales have been a source of real estate and other property for thousands of my students who knew how to get on the various government bid lists.
- The first-time home buyer program is truly America's best kept secret. It gives thousands of people a chance to own a home with reasonable payments and lower interest rate loans, and yet few bankers or government officials know about it. It is also one of the most beautiful opportunities this country of ours has to offer.
- Low interest rate rental rehabilitation loans that are available right now across the nation provide money to homeowners and investors at interest rates as low as 3 percent.
- Zero percent loans and deferred payment loans are sometimes called "forgiveness" loans because the amounts borrowed are forgiven after a number of years and don't have to be repaid.
- The Section 8 guaranteed rent program provides housing for the elderly, the handicapped, single parents, and others. The government pays their rents, directly to you, the landlord.
- The gold mine loan, which I used to borrow hundreds of thousands of dollars, lets you borrow money to fix up your properties. It's a loan that is easy to qualify for, is fully assumable, and has no huge loan fees typical of other home equity loans.
- Historic and older property programs offer fantastic tax credits that can be kept or sold by you to investors for cash.

With these and the hundreds of other programs available from our government (see the appendix), there is a program whereby everyone can make money. Thousands of my students across the nation have written to tell me of their successes and their surprise at the opportunities they discover with government programs. These success stories are what this book is all about. That is the reason why you should get involved. If they can do it, so can you.

THE TOUCHSTONE: A STORY OF OBJECTIVES AND OPPORTUNITY

During the days of the great library of Alexandria, there was a terrible fire that destroyed all of the books in the land save one. Since this book was not a masterpiece or a work of great philosophy, no one had wanted the book.

Except one poor man.

In trade for two pieces of copper the poor man purchased this book so worthless to many. Upon returning to his home and reading the book, the poor man came across a parchment hidden within its pages. Written on this parchment was the secret of the Touchstone. The Touchstone was a magic pebble that was like any other stone except for two things. First, when picked up, the Touchstone would feel very warm. Second, when the Touchstone was placed against any ordinary metal, the metal would turn to gold. The magic Touchstone could only be found along the shores of the Black Sea.

By now the poor man was very excited and realized that if he could locate the Touchstone, he would become wealthy beyond his wildest dreams. He sold his meager house and belongings, placed his family in the care of his neighbors, and set off for the Black Sea. As he came to the shores of the Black Sea, the poor man was faced with millions of pebbles, all looking the same. To avoid picking up the same stone twice, the poor man devised a simple plan. He would reach down and pick up a pebble, and it if was cold, he would throw it into the sea. And he did so for the rest of that day, and the next day, and the day after, as well as through the many weeks that followed.

In fact, the poor man spent three years picking up stones on the beach and tossing them into the sea. Finally, one day, the poor man reached down, picked up a stone that was warm, *and he threw it into the sea*. He threw the Touchstone into the sea. Along with the Touchstone went his dreams and his hope of becoming the wealthiest man in the land.

Why, after three years of searching, did the poor man throw the Touchstone into the sea? He threw the Touchstone away because he had formed a habit of picking up pebbles and throwing them into the sea. He had lost the focus of his objective. His objective was to find the warm Touchstone. Yet, over the years, the poor man formed a habit of picking up stones and throwing them into the sea. And so he did the same with the warm Touchstone.

Like the poor man, many of us have formed habits that prevent us from being effective in today's real estate market. It is important not to allow the habits we've formed in the past to inhibit us in the ever-changing real estate market of the 1980s and 1990s.

Be flexible to new ideas. Open your mind to new possibilities as you encounter them in the marketplace. Just because techniques and formulas worked for us in the past doesn't mean that they will make us money today and in the 1990s. The problems in today's market-place—negative cash flows, large down payment requirements, balloon payments, unpredictable interest rates, high sale prices—cannot always be solved with yesterday's solutions. New ways must be found to tackle these modern problems. When old investment methods are used in new real estate markets, serious problems often arise. Habit-breaking ideas are antidotes to the problems that plague many of today's investors. The government programs in this book offer new solutions to these problems. I know they do, because I've had my share of real estate problems, and I've discovered that government programs solved my investment problems.

Today, I never have to worry about negative cash flows, high interest rates, balloon payments, or high purchase prices. I use the many different government programs available nationwide, and I am not concerned about any of these problems.

I suggest you get involved with one or more government programs to help you with your own goals and to solve your own problems. Learn about two or three programs and apply them. The first time will be difficult, because you are learning. But do it. Nothing you do is easy the first time. Your first kiss was the hardest, the first time you drove a car was the hardest, your first real estate purchase was or will be the hardest, and the first time you use one of these government programs will be the hardest. But it gets easier thereafter.

This book helps you along your road to wealth. It isn't a book that you should read and put on a shelf. It's not one of those motivational "let's make a million overnight" books, either. It's your reference book. A book that is to be used over and over. My goal is to give you at least one idea that you can use to go in for the winning touchdown. If this idea helps you stop throwing rent money down the drain, borrow $2,500 easily, buy the home you have always dreamed of, or make a million dollars, then all of the time and effort I've put into this book has been worthwhile.

You have in your possession a book based on years of actual experiences and mistakes. Its contents are not theory. This is what I've actually done. It's a step-by-step approach that shows you the way to get in on the government programs that are available right now. It's up to you to act on the knowledge. You are the one who is going to have to do the legwork. If you do, you will help others and improve your life. Just put people before profits, and the profits will come to you. That's what I have done and am doing. It's working for me, and if I can do it, so can you.

USE THE PIGGYBACK METHOD

If you're a little nervous about getting started, or don't know which program to use right off, use what I call the "piggyback method." Find some people who have been investing in real estate for some time and work with them. Offer to be an assistant, anything. Let them know that you want to learn and that you will be willing to work. That is exactly what I did when I was a jazz drummer. I wanted to be the best drummer in the world, so I "piggybacked" with the very successful musician Charlie Byrd to learn the ropes of the music industry. It worked. Before leaving the music business to make my fortune in real estate, I was voted seventh best jazz drummer in the world by *Downbeat* music magazine. Had I not been enticed by the wealth real estate had to offer and remained a drummer, I might have become the number one drummer in the world. I still use my piggyback method today. Whenever I start a new endeavor, I find experts in the industry and ask for assistance. I work with them and learn from their experiences.

Feel free to talk to real estate investors in your area. Visit real estate brokers, lenders, and investors. Visit government officials. After going through this book, ask them particular questions about the government programs they are involved with. Piggyback on their knowledge. Utilize their experiences. And then apply the knowledge to your own situation.

DON'T BECOME A REAL ESTATE DINOSAUR

Whatever you do, continue to learn. Keep updated on government programs in your area. As discussed earlier in this chapter, learn new ways to solve new problems. Don't rely on old investment methods that do not work in modern investment markets. Dinosaurs became extinct because they could not adapt their lifestyle to the changing environment. Like dinosaurs, old investment methods often cannot adapt to changing conditions in the environment, and so they become extinct.

Recently, I heard that several great real estate investors and seminar companies of the 1970s and early 1980s had declared bankruptcy. These men had devised investment programs that made millions for many. Unfortunately, they did not individually adapt to the challenges of the second half of the 1980s. As a result, they became real estate dinosaurs.

Don't become a real estate dinosaur. You must keep your mind open to the new, proven ways to make money now and in the 1990s. Government loans and programs are the way.

To help you through your first year of getting involved with government loans, I have included a coupon on the jacket of this book for you to mail in to receive a free copy of my "Government Loans Newsletter." This newsletter will introduce you to the real world of government loan programs, keep you updated on the millions of dollars available, and tell you where to go for the money. It will also give you a little more hands-on advice for their use. I'm giving you this opportunity because I want you to succeed. Use the loans and programs in this book as well as the ones you'll discover on your own. In time your own dreams will come true.

Thank you, and God bless.

RESOURCES

GLOSSARY OF INVESTMENT AND GOVERNMENT TERMS

Accelerated depreciation: Depreciation method that writes off the cost of an asset at a faster rate than under the straight line method.

Acceleration clause: A clause in a note, bond, or mortgage which provides that in the event of default by the debtor the entire outstanding balance shall become due and payable.

Acknowledgment: A formal declaration before a Notary Public or other duly authorized officer by a person who has executed (signed) an instrument that such execution is his or her act or deed.

Adaptive re-use: The rehabilitation of old property for a new purpose.

Adjusted basis: The original cost of a property plus the value of any capital expenditures for improvements to the property, minus any depreciation taken.

Ad valorem tax: A tax based on the assessed value of property.

Amortize: To liquidate a value on an installment basis; an amortized loan is one in which the principal amount of the loan is repaid in equal periodic installments during the life of the loan.

Amount to make the project operational (AMPO): An allowance that can be included in a mortgage insured by HUD/FHA to provide a nonprofit sponsor with working capital during the initial period of a project.

Annual housing survey (AHS): Yearly HUD/Census Bureau study of housing units and trends in movements of owners and renters.

Annuity: A series of payments of a fixed amount for a specified number of years.

Appraisal: Estimate of the real or market value of a property; that is, what the owner could reasonably expect to get upon sale. Estimates are made by appraisers.

Appreciation: Increase in the value of property.

Areawide Housing Opportunity Plan (AHOP): A program designed to reduce the geographic concentration of low-income persons by expanding housing opportunities throughout a broad area.

Assessed valuation: The valuation placed on a property by a local public officer for the purposes of taxation. This is usually less than the market value of the property.

Assessor: The elected county official who has the responsibility of determining assessed values of property.

Assumption of Mortgage: What occurs when the responsibility for repaying existing indebtedness secured by a property is "assumed" by a second buyer.

Auction: The system of dispensing property through public or private brokers and agents to buyers through bids for the most advantageous purchase price.

Balloon payment: When a debt is not fully amortized, a final payment larger than preceding payments, that pays a note off in full.

Bankrupt: A person legally declared unable to pay debts owed.

Before-tax income: Gross income minus all expenses except income taxes.

Below-market interest rate (BMIR): Interest rate that applies to certain mortgage insurance programs (e.g., Section 202 and Section 221 [d] [3]), where the interest rate on the mortgage is below that charged for conventional financing in the area. It's purpose is to assist low- and moderate-income families to rent or purchase dwelling units.

Bid: The highest price one is willing to pay for a property at a given time.

Bill of sale: A written instrument that passes title to personal property. Common with personal property sold by government agencies to private buyers.

Blighted area: A declining area in which real estate values are seriously affected by destructive economic forces, such as encroaching inharmonious property usages and/or rapidly depreciating buildings.

Broker: A licensed person employed on a fee or commission basis as an agent to bring parties together and assist in negotiating contracts between them.

Builder's and sponsor's profit and risk allowance (BSPRA): A credit against the required equity contribution in HUD/FHA insurance programs granted to the developer for services in sponsoring and building the project.

Building code: A systematic set of health and safety regulations on the construction of buildings within a municipality.

Building line: A line set by law a certain distance from the boundaries of a lot beyond which an owner cannot build on the lot; when this is the street line, it is known as a "setback line."

Capital asset: An asset with a life of more than one year that is not bought and sold in the ordinary course of business.

Capital gain or capital loss: Profit or loss from the sale of a capital asset. A capital gain, under current federal income tax laws, may be either short term (held six months or less) or long term (held more than six months). A short-term capital gain is taxed at the reporting individual's full income tax rate. A long-term capital gain is subject to a lower tax. Capital gains tax laws are complicated. Consult your tax adviser for more specific information.

Capitalization: In appraising, determining the value of property by considering net income and percentage of reasonable return on the investment.

Capitalization rate: The rate of interest that is considered a reasonable return on an investment; used in the process of determining value based upon net income.

Carry back; Carry forward: For income tax purposes, carrying profits and losses back seven years or forward three years to reduce federal income taxes.

Cash flow: Money left over from a project's gross income after all operating and debt expenses have been deducted. Some developers include depreciation and tax calculations when computing cash flow.

Chain of title: A history of title transfers from one owner to another and the encumbrances affecting the title as far back in time as records are available.

Collateral: Assets used to secure a loan.

Commission: An agent's compensation for performing the duties of an agent in real estate transactions; usually a percentage of the selling price of property or a percentage of rentals.

Commitment: A pledge, promise, or firm agreement. A letter of commitment is often provided by lenders to borrowers as a promise to loan an agreed-upon amount.

Community Development Block Grant (CDBG): Under Title I of the Housing and Community Development Act of 1974, a system of unified block grants developed, under which communities of over 50,000 people are entitled to receive funding and other communities may apply for discretionary funding. The purpose is to encourage more broadly conceived community development projects and expand housing opportunities for low- and moderate-income persons.

Community property: Property accumulated through the joint efforts of husband and wife.

Compound interest: Interest paid on the original principal and also on the accrued and unpaid interest.

Concurrent ownership: Situation when title to a particular piece of real estate is owned by two or more persons at the same time. Examples are joint tenancy, tenancy in common, and community property.

Condemnation: The act of taking private property for public use; declaration that a structure is unfit for use.

Condition: A stipulation in a contract that some event must occur or a requirement must be met before the completion of the terms can be achieved.

Conditional commitment: A commitment, as by the FHA, of a definite loan amount for some future unknown buyer of satisfactory credit standing.

Condominium: A multi-unit dwelling, each of whose residents enjoys exclusive ownership of an individual unit, holding a fee-simple title thereto, while retaining rights to use the common areas.

Consideration: That which is bargained for and given in exchange for a promise by another party. This may be money, personal services, or even love and affection.

Construction loan: A short-term loan that enables a developer to pay contractors' bills and other expenses incurred before and during the construction period (also known as an *interim loan*).

Constructive notice: Notice given by the public records.

Contract: A legally enforceable agreement, either written or oral, between two or more parties to do or not to do certain things.

Conveyance: The transfer of title of land from one to another; an instrument that carries an interest in the land from one person to another.

Cooperative: A multi-unit dwelling where title to the building and land are vested in a corporation or trust and each tenant-owner holds a block of stock in the corporation or a certificate of beneficial interest in the trust, together with a proprietary lease of an apartment in the building.

County clerk: An elected official with whom documents of public record are filed.

Debt capital: Money loaned at an agreed interest rate for a fixed term of years.

Debt-coverage ratio: The ratio of net yearly income to total yearly debt service.

Debt service: A borrower's periodic payment comprising repayment of principal and payment of interest on the unpaid balance.

Deed: A written instrument which, when properly executed, acknowledged, and delivered to the buyer (grantee), conveys the title to real estate from one owner to another. Common types of deeds are:

- **Warranty deed:** A deed in which the seller (grantor) warranties that the property being conveyed is free from all liens and encumbrances (loans) other than those specified therein, and the grantor will warrant and defend the title against the lawful claims and demands of all persons whomsoever.
- **Quitclaim:** Deed in which the grantor conveys any interest which the grantor may have in the property, but does not warrant any interest.
- **Sheriff's deed:** Document given to the holder of a sheriff's certificate at the conclusion of a foreclosure period of redemption.

Default: Failure to fulfill a duty or promise, usually the failure to make a payment called for by a note or mortgage.

Delinquency: Failure to make timely payments under a loan agreement.

Density: The ratio of land area to the number of structures built upon it.

Density zoning: Population-controlled zoning.

Deposit: Money given as security for the performance of a contract, which is forfeited if the depositor fails to carry out the terms of the contract.

Depreciation: A sum representing a calculated loss of value of a building or other real estate improvements (other than land), resulting from physical wear and economic obsolescence. Depreciation is a non-cash expense that is deducted annually from net income to arrive at taxable income.

Development loan: A short-term loan, advanced before a construction loan, used by developers to acquire land and install basic improvements such as utilities, roads, sewers, and water supply systems.

Development process: The process through which development projects are conceived, initiated, analyzed, financed, designed, built, and managed.

Discount: The sale of a note for less than its face value.

Discount points: The amount that is payable to the lender by the borrower or seller to increase the lender's effective yield. One point is equal to one percent of the loan. See *Points*.

Down payment: The amount of cash a buyer is required or willing to put up in order to purchase a property. It is equal to the purchase price, less the amount of any mortgage loans used to finance the purchase.

Draw: A request from a borrower to obtain a partial payment from the lender as provided in the loan agreement. Typically, the lender will request that a percentage of construction work be completed before the payment is made to the borrower (or contractor).

Due-on-sale clause: A clause in a loan or mortgage stating that if the borrower sells, transfers, or in any way encumbers the property, the lender has a right to make the balance of the loan due.

Encumbrance: Mortgages, loans, or other restrictions that alter or restrain full title of ownership.

Endorsement: The acceptance of a mortgage instrument by HUD for insurance.

Entitlement: Money allocated by a federal agency to a specific city or local government; distinguished from non-entitlement.

Equity capital: Money invested by owners or others who share in profits; distinguished from debt capital.

Escrow: A deposit of good faith money, which is entrusted to a third party until certain conditions of a contract or agreement are fulfilled.

Execute: To perform or complete.

Fair market rent: An amount determined by HUD to be the cost of modest, non-luxury rental units in a specific market area. With certain exceptions, it is the highest rent chargeable for that market under Section 8.

Fair market value: The price at which a property is sold by buyer to seller when both have good information and are under no compulsion to buy or sell.

Farmers Home Administration (FmHA): A federal government agency that administers programs for non-urban communities.

Feasibility study: A detailed investigation and analysis conducted to determine the financial, economic, technical, or other advisability of a proposed project.

Federal Home Loan Mortgage Corporation (FHLMC): A quasi-government agency that purchases mortgages in the secondary mortgage market from insured depository institutions and HUD-approved mortgage bankers.

Federal Housing Administration (FHA): A federal agency designed to encourage private housing financing through the insurance of mortgages made by financial institutions.

Federal National Mortgage Association (FNMA): Also known as Fannie Mae. Federally chartered private corporation providing a secondary market for residential mortgages.

Final closing: The date when a permanent mortgage lender funds a mortgage loan.

Foreclosure: A legal procedure in which a property used as security for a mortgage or note is sold to pay the defaulting buyer's debt.

Government National Mortgage Association (GNMA): Also known as Ginnie Mae. A government corporation that provides a secondary market for housing mortgages and special assistance to housing mortgages financed under special HUD mortgage insurance programs.

Gross income: Total project income before any expenses are deducted.

Ground lease or rent: A lease of land alone, as distinguished from a lease of land with improvements on it, usually on a very long-term basis.

Guaranty: An agreement where one party pledges to perform a service or repay an obligation.

Housing assistance plan: A part of the CDBG plan that describes local housing conditions and sets quantitative goals for providing decent and affordable housing to low- and moderate-income persons.

Housing finance agency (HFA): State agency responsible for the financing of housing and the administration of subsidized housing programs.

Income approach to value: A method of estimating income property value by capitalizing income.

Income limits: Family income limits established by law for admission into low- and moderate-income housing projects. Used to qualify for rent supplement assistance or to qualify for special government loans. Based on family size and geographic location.

Inspection certificate: A certificate that a property is as described. The inspection is usually performed by a designated agent and may be accepted in place of a survey.

Institutional lender: A mortgage lender that invests its own funds in mortgages and carries a majority of such loans in its own portfolio, e.g. life insurance companies, banks, and savings and loan associations.

Interest reduction programs: HUD programs like Section 235 and 236, which subsidize the market interest rate on mortgage loans for low- and moderate-income housing, thus lowering the consumer's housing costs.

Interim financing: Loan for land and construction costs, current real estate taxes, and other incidental expenses attributable to a construction period. Also called a *construction loan*.

Joint tenancy: Joint ownership by two or more persons, giving each tenant equal interest and equal rights in the property, including the right of survivorship.

Joint venture: A partnership formed for a limited specific purpose by investors in a development project. The joint venture agreement establishes the partners' duties in the development process and specifies how the ownership and profits are to be divided.

Judgment: Final determination by a court of the rights and claims of the parties to an action.

Junior mortgage: A mortgage that is subordinated to the claims of a prior lien or mortgage.

Letter of credit: A document that approves the credit of an individual or corporation and enables it to borrow or get bank funds.

Leverage: A technique that utilizes borrowed money to reduce the actual equity cash invested in a property and increase the investment's profit-to-investor-equity ratio.

Lien: A lender's claim on assets that are pledged for a loan. Typical liens are for mortgages, taxes, and unpaid repair or construction bills.

Limited dividend entity: Profit-motivated housing development sponsor. Eligible for HUD/FHA insured mortgage loans of as much as 90 percent of the total development costs; can earn up to 6 percent cash flow annually on its equity investment.

Limited partnership: A partnership that limits the limited partner liability to the amount of the investment. At least one partner (the general partner) is fully liable for the obligations of the partnership and its operations. The limited partners participate as investors only and may not participate in the management or operations of the project.

Liquidity: The dollar value of assets that can be readily converted into cash.

Loan fee: The charge made for negotiating a loan in addition to interest; sometimes used in reference to an additional fee paid directly to a lender either for commitment or at the time the loan money is advanced.

Loan-to-value ratio: The relationship of a mortgage to the appraised value of a security. This ratio is expressed to a potential purchaser of property in terms of the percentage a lending institution is willing to finance.

Manufactured home: Any of a number of different categories of factory-built or prefabricated housing, including mobile homes.

Market approach to value: Using the marketplace as a yardstick to measure the value of property.

MFH: Multifamily homes. HUD/FHA designation for properties with five or more units.

Minimum property standards: HUD/FHA criteria that dictate the lowest acceptable technical standards for insurable mortgage loans.

Moderate income: Term used by HUD to describe those persons with income above Section 8 limits and no more than 130 percent of the median income for the area. Moderate incomes will vary from one city to another. The FmHA sets maximum levels by state.

Moderate Rehabilitation: A part of the Section 8 program that involves rehabilitation of at least $1,000 per unit to upgrade a dwelling to comply with HUD housing quality standards.

Moratorium: Legally delaying of the payments on a note or mortgage until a later agreed-upon date.

Mortgage: A formal document executed by an owner of a property, pledging that property as security for payment of a debt or performance of some other obligation. The mortgage is the security instrument for the loan on the property.

Mortgage banker: A lender who originates loans and then sells them to investors. The mortgage banker generally continues to service the loans. Not to be confused with *mortgage broker*.

Mortgage broker: A person who arranges financing through other lenders. He does not finance the loan, but brings together the borrower and the lender and receives a fee for his services.

Mortgage insurance premium: The amount paid by a borrower to insure a mortgage loan.

Mortgage note: A promissory note secured by a mortgage on a specific real estate property.

Multi-family development: Development of more than two dwellings as part of a single development. Generally associated with garden apartments, townhouses, and highrise apartment complexes.

Negative amortization: A loan payment schedule in which the outstanding principal balance increases rather than decreases, because the payments are not enough to cover the full amount of the interest due. The unpaid interest is added to the principal balance. Negative amortization occurs in some variable rate and graduated payment mortgages.

Negative cash flow: Occurs when the expenses necessary to maintain an investment exceed the income that the investment generates.

Non-profit sponsor: A group organized to undertake a housing project for reasons other than making a profit. Units can be rented on a non-profit basis or the sponsor can create individual, cooperative, or condominium ownership.

Notice of funding availability: A notice issued by HUD area offices to inform potential project sponsors that contract authority is available under Section 8.

Option agreement: Right acquired, for a consideration, to buy or sell property at a fixed price within a specified time.

Ordinary income: Income subject to tax at full or ordinary rates rather than favorable capital gains rates.

Partnership: An association of persons joined by contract in order to combine resources and to participate in the sharing of profits and losses in a proportionate manner. The profits and losses are passed through the partnership to the partners, who report them on their individual tax returns. The partnership itself pays no taxes.

Performance bond: A bond to guarantee performance of certain specified acts, such as the completion of construction of a property or off-site improvements.

Permanent financing: Mortgage loan covering development costs, interim loans, construction loans, finance charges, and marketing, administrative, and other costs. This loan differs from a construction loan in that a permanent loan goes with the property after all construction or rehabilitation work is done. It is a long-term loan.

PITI: A loan payment that includes *principal, interest, taxes* and *insurance*.

Points: The fees a lender charges for arranging a loan. On a $1,000 loan where the borrower is required to pay two points, the borrower would receive $980 (one point equals 1 percent of the loan amount).

Prime rate: The interest rate banks charge to their most preferred customers.

It tends to be a yardstick for general interest rate trends.

Principal: The amount of debt, exclusive of accrued interest, that remains on a loan.

Private mortgage insurance (PMI): A form of mortgage insurance without governmental participation that protects the mortgage lender against loss in the event of default on a mortgage.

Pro forma: A projection of anticipated income, expense, and cash flow from an investment.

Public housing authority (PHA): State or local agency that finances or operates low-income housing.

Purchase agreement: A written offer to buy a property that becomes binding upon the acceptance of the seller.

Purchase money mortgage: A mortgage that a seller receives as all or part of the purchase price in exchange for the property sold. A non-cash loan that the seller makes to the buyer in lieu of cash.

Recapture: A taxable gain from the sale of a property which, though otherwise qualified for favorable capital gains treatment, is taxed at ordinary income tax rates in order to "recapture" the tax benefits or certain depreciation deductions taken prior to the sale of the property.

Refinance: To pay off an existing loan with the proceeds of a new loan.

Rehabilitation: Property improvement. According to HUD, a rehabilitated housing unit is a unit where more than 20 percent of the total mortgage proceeds or development costs are spent on improvement, as opposed to property acquisition. Rehabilitation takes many forms, from repainting and modernizing a building to bring it up to building code standards, to the complete gutting of the interiors of a property and replacement of the mechanical systems and roof.

Replacement cost: The cost of replacing a structure with one of equal value and function. HUD calculates replacement by determining current cost of improvements to the land and the cost of structures, including builder and architect fees. It also includes financing costs, carrying charges, and legal and organizational expenses. Replacement cost figures are used in determining a HUD mortgage amount.

Second mortgage: A mortgage that is junior to a first mortgage. This means that in the event of a foreclosure, any proceeds from the foreclosure sale would go first to the holder of the first mortgage and any remaining proceeds would go to the second mortgage holder.

Secondary financing: A loan secured by a second mortgage or trust deed on a property.

Secondary mortgage market: Opportunity for lenders and investors to buy existing mortgages as long-term investments. The secondary mortgage market provides a greater availability of funds for mortgage loans by banks, mortgage bankers, and savings and loan associations. The Federal Home

Loan Mortgage Corporation (FHLMC), Federal National Mortgage Association (FNMA), and Government National Mortgage Association (GNMA) are typical agencies involved in buying mortgages as investments.

SFH: Single-family home. HUD/FHA designation for properties with one to four units.

Site Appraisal and marketing analysis letter: Issued by HUD/FHA to a multi-family housing sponsor, providing preliminary authority to begin submission of an application for a conditional commitment for mortgage insurance.

Small Business Administration (SBA): A federal agency that provides grants, loans, and loan guarantees to small businesses experiencing difficulty in obtaining financial assistance through private lenders.

Small city: Pertaining to the CDBG program, any city with a population of less than 50,000 and not a central city of an SMSA (Standard Metropolitan Statistical Area).

Spot loan: A loan on a property made by a lender who was not involved in the original financing of the subdivision or project.

Spot zoning: Zoning that is in no specific or prescribed pattern.

Standard Metropolitan Statistical Area (SMSA): A term describing a central city area and its surrounding suburbs and other smaller jurisdictions.

Straight Line Depreciation: A depreciation method that permits the owner of a building to take a constant annual deduction to recover the cost of the building over its useful life.

Subchapter S: A provision in the Internal Revenue Code that allows certain qualifying business corporations to elect to eliminate the corporate income tax by taxing income directly to the shareholders.

Subsidy: A government grant to a sponsor to reduce the cost of one or more housing components (land, labor, material, financing) in order to lower the cost to the occupant.

Substantial rehabilitation: Improvement of a property from substandard to safe and sanitary conditions. It can vary from gutting and reconstruction to repairing deferred maintenance. It may also include the conversion of non-residential property into residential property.

Sweat equity: Equity created through the work and services an owner gives to a property.

Syndication: The sale of equity interest or shares in real estate projects to investors other than the original owners (developers).

Take-out commitment: A commitment whereby a permanent lender agrees to buy a construction mortgage from a construction lender or to issue a new permanent mortgage upon the completion of construction. Such a commitment is usually a prerequisite to the making of a construction loan by a construction lender.

Tandem plan: A GNMA program where a permanent HUD/FHA-insured multi-family mortgage is purchased at a below-market rate. See *Government National Mortgage Association (GNMA)*.

Tax-exempt bond: A bond on which the interest income is not subject to taxation. Commonly sold by state housing finance agencies to raise money for the first-time home buyer program.

Tax write-off or shelter: Any tax reduction that lessens an individual's tax liability. Common shelters or write-offs include real estate taxes, mortgage interest payments, depreciation, finance charges, and operational losses.

Tenants in common: Joint ownership by two or more persons holding individual but not necessarily equal interests in a property. There is no right of survivorship among persons who own property as tenants in common.

Total development costs: The sum of all HUD-approved costs. Include planning, site acquisition, demolition, construction, and equipment costs; interest and carrying charges; costs of on-site improvements and non-dwelling facilities; a contingency allowance; insurance premiums; costs of off-site facilities; any initial operation loss; relocation costs; administration costs; and all other costs necessary to develop the project.

Urban Development Action Grant (UDAG): Competitive grant awards given by HUD to help distressed communities leverage private investment for the purpose of increasing local economic, employment, and tax bases. Local communities are awarded Urban Development Action Grants based on absolute necessity to their economy.

Vacancy factor: The percent of a building that is not occupied.

Variable interest rate: An interest rate that a lender is allowed to adjust during the life of a loan to reflect changes in the prime rate. Interest rate changes are usually within a predetermined range and with advance notice.

Wraparound mortgage: A refinancing technique involving the creating of a subordinate mortgage that includes the balance due on the existing mortgage plus a new secondary loan.

Zoning: Regulations provided by a governmental entity for the purpose of establishing which land or building uses may be put in specific areas, and the types of architectural, structural, and/or spatial elements the land or buildings may have.

ANSWERS TO TWENTY OF THE MOST OFTEN ASKED GOVERNMENT LOAN QUESTIONS

Now that you are ready to get involved with government loans and the fantastic benefits they have to offer, you probably have a few questions. Below are twenty of the questions most often asked by our seminar graduates. For a more detailed update of what's going on with government loans, return the coupon on the inside back jacket of this book for a free copy of my "Government Loans Newsletter."

1. *Can you really buy rental property with fifty-year 1 percent mortgages?*

Yes, thanks to the FmHA. In rural communities throughout the nation, there are apartments with fifty-year 1 percent loans. These properties can be bought and the 1 percent loans assumed. Many times the properties will have subsidized rents, too.

2. *Can I get an FmHA loan in my area?*

New FmHA loans are available to persons living in cities with less than 20,000 people or counties with populations smaller than 200,000. Of course, you can always buy a property with an existing FmHA loan on it and receive all the benefits of the loan when you assume it.

3. *What's going to happen to housing programs with all the government cutbacks?*

Although the Gramm-Rudman deficit reduction act was passed in 1986, our Congress still allocated over $15,000,000,000 for housing programs. This means that low interest rate loans are still available, rent guarantees are still alive and well, and rehab programs are still funded. Instead of providing as many low interest loans for new construction, the government is funneling the money into the rehabilitation of older rental properties. This is because it takes three dollars of new construction money to get the same results as from one dollar of rehab money. That suits me fine, because it's those low interest rehab loans that I like.

4. *Where can I get a list of VA and HUD repos?*

Property lists are available in three places, depending upon where you live. First, the lists are available through VA- and HUD-approved brokers. The local VA or HUD office will provide you with a list of these brokers. Second, repos are often advertised in major newspapers in your area. To find out how often the lists are publicized, either call the newspapers or visit your local VA and HUD offices. Third, lists are sometimes available to individuals from the local HUD and VA offices on a one-time basis. Visit these offices to see if they will provide you with a list.

Keep in mind that the VA repos are sold through Veterans Administration offices and the HUD repos are sold through Housing and Urban Development offices.

5. *How do I buy a VA or HUD repo?*

A VA or HUD repo is sold only through government-approved real estate brokers. A broker will submit a bid on your behalf and fill out the necessary forms. For these services he is paid a commission by the VA or HUD.

6. *What other government agencies sell repossessed properties?*

You can buy government property from all three levels of government. The General Services Administration, the IRS, state surplus sales divisions, county property tax offices, and local government housing and community development offices sell property at prices well below market value.

7. *What can the gold mine loan be used for?*

The gold mine or Title I loan can be used to make improvements to the property for which the money was borrowed. If any money is left over from the proceeds of the loan after you make your repairs, I suggest you save it for improvements that you may plan to make in the future. You can get a gold mine loan from most FHA-approved lenders. The FHA insures the loan, and lenders such as banks, savings and loans, and credit unions actually loan you the money.

8. *Where can I get money directly from the government to buy a house?*

Loans at as low as 1 percent are available from the Farmers Home Administration. Most of the time the federal government does not lend money directly. It only insures loans that are funded through lenders such as banks or savings and loans. The FHA division of HUD is the primary source of this loan insurance.

9. *Is there a government loan to buy a condo or co-op house?*

Yes. The government has four loan insurance programs to help you buy individual units in condominium projects, cooperative housing, or condominium conversion projects. There are three FHA loans, Section 234(c), Section 234(d), and Section 213; and one VA loan; Title 1819.

10. *Does the federal government make any direct loans to individuals?*

Yes. Through a variety of federal loan programs, the government makes direct rehab loans and grants to individuals and corporations. Also, the Farmers Home Administration (FmHA) will lend money directly to individuals wishing to rehab their homes and rentals.

11. *Are more low interest rate loans available for rehabilitation or for purchase?*

Most low interest rate loans are for the rehabilitation of properties. However, many cities do have low interest rate loan programs that you can use to buy property. Detroit, for example, has a 7 percent home purchase loan program. Almost every state and many cities have first-time home buyer programs that provide low interest rate loans to help you finance the purchase of a home.

12. *I own a house now. Can I still qualify for the first-time home buyer loans in my state?*

Yes. If you buy a property in certain areas of your state or city, the typical first-time homeowner requirements are waived. Income restrictions are also often waived for home purchases in these target areas.

13. *Are Section 8 rent subsidy tenants undesirable?*

Absolutely not. Contrary to the popular misconception that Section

8 tenants are "welfare bums," Section 8 tenants can be elderly, hand-icapped, laid off from a job, or single parents. I prefer to rent to Section 8 tenants because I get my rent checks mailed to me each month without hassle.

14. *Where do 3 percent loans come from?*

Congress allocates money to HUD. HUD then gives the money to state and local agencies through Community Development Block Grants. These agencies take this "free" money and lend it out at very low interest rates to encourage development and redevelopment in specified areas of the community. HUD *does not* make 3 percent loans directly.

15. *Do I have to own property or have a property in mind to get a government loan?*

No. As a buyer you can use an option to purchase agreement to tie the property up (take it off the market) until you solidify the government financing. I have used options to buy real estate worth over $2 million.

16. *Why is housing for the elderly the wave of the future?*

We are a population that is getting older. Housing that caters to elderly individuals is preferred by older people over conventional housing. Another important point to remember is that many elderly persons qualify for rent subsidies. This means that:

- Rent is guaranteed by the government.
- Checks are mailed directly to you.
- Rents are typically higher than you might be able to receive otherwise.
- The government will reimburse you for tenant damages.
- Tenants are treated like any other tenants and are subject to the same landlord–tenant laws applicable in your city.

17. *How do I qualify for a zero percent deferred payment loan (forgiveness loan)?*

To qualify for a forgiveness loan, you only need to own a house or rental property that is in need of repairs. Some cities require that the rental property be rented to Section 8 tenants after the repairs are made. Not all cities have this program, and the requirements do vary. Contact your local community development agency for more information.

18. *Why does the government give so much money away?*

- To provide decent and affordable housing
- To encourage development within a community
- To increase the local tax base
- To provide jobs
- To provide better services to local communities
- To improve local economies

In general, for every dollar local governments lend out for rehab loans, several dollars are returned to the community in the form of goods and services created by the rehabilitation project.

19. *I called the HUD office and a government official told me that I can't get a 3 percent rehab loan. What gives?*

The first thing you did wrong was to call the HUD office. Remember, don't call these government offices. Visit the agencies in person and talk with the government officials, face-to-face. Also, I never said that HUD makes 3 percent loans. In fact, HUD does *not* make 3 percent loans. The local community development agencies make low interest rate rehab loans. Don't give up. Go to your community development agency and speak with the department head.

20. *How do I find out more about programs in my area?*

You can do the legwork I did when I first started out. Visit each local agency and ask questions to find out what is offered in your area. Or, you can call my toll-free hotline at 1–800–446–8400 to find out when the next Wayne Phillips "Creating Wealth with Government Loans" seminar will be held in your area to learn the details about government programs available.

Government Program Reference Chart

GOVERNMENT HOUSING LOANS AND MORTGAGE INSURANCE PROGRAMS

HOMEOWNERS AND WOULD-BE HOMEOWNERS

AGENCY	PROGRAM	GOAL
HUD	Homeownership assistance for low- and moderate-income families (Section 235)	To enable purchase of new homes
HUD	Homeownership assistance for low- and moderate-income families (Section 221 (d)(2))	To increase homownership opportunities
HUD	Home mortgage coinsurance (Section 244)	To facilitate homeownership financing
HUD	Purchase of manufactured homes (Title I)	To help provide alternative low-cost housing
VA	Guaranteed home loans	To help veterans finance purchase of home
FmHA	Housing loans	To aid low- to moderate-income families purchase homes

INVESTORS OR HOMEOWNERS

AGENCY	PROGRAM	GOAL
HUD	One- to four-family home mortgage insurance (Section 203 (b)(i))	To facilitate homeownership and construction of housing
HUD	Home improvement loan insurance (Title I class a)	To facilitate financing home improvements
HUD	Rehabilitation mortgage insurance (Section 203 (k))	To facilitate rehabilitation
HUD	Housing in declining neighborhoods (Section 223e)	To aid purchase or rehabilitation in certain areas
HUD	Condominium housing (Section 234)	To facilitate ownership of individual units
HUD	Cooperative housing (Section 213)	To finance housing projects

DESIGNED FOR	FINANCING	COMMENTS
Low-income families in certain areas	Mortgage insurance and interest subsidy	Now applicable only in statutorily exempt areas
Low- or moderate-income families; those displaced by urban renewal	Mortgage insurance for purchase, construction, rehabilitation	One- to four-family units Ceilings on loans
Home buyers	Federal government and private lender jointly insure mortgage	Expedites processing one to four-family units
Any one able to make investment and payments	Home loan insurance	
Veterans	VA guarantees loan made by private lender	May have no down payment
Families in rural areas who can't get ordinary loans	Loans from FmHA	

DESIGNED FOR	FINANCING	COMMENTS
Anyone able to make investment and payments	Mortgage insurance	
	Loan insurance	
One- to four-family units	Mortgage insurance	Can be used for refinancing or purchase
Property otherwise ineligible for FHA mortgage insurance	Mortgage insurance	Property must be "acceptable risk"
Sponsor or individual	Mortgage insurance	Project must contain at least four units
Construction, rehabilitation, acquisition	Mortgage insurance	Sponsors must intend to sell the project to non-profit group

INVESTORS

AGENCY	PROGRAM	GOAL
HUD	Multifamily rental housing (Section 207)	To encourage broad cross section of rental housing
HUD	Existing multifamily rental housing (Section 223f)	To facilitate purchase or refinancing
HUD	Multifamily rental housing for moderate-income families (Section 221(d)(3) and (4))	To facilitate rental housing for the income group
HUD	Lower-income rental assistance (Section 8)/Housing voucher	To help low-income families with rent
HUD	Direct loans for housing for the elderly or handicapped (Section 202)	To provide housing and related facilities
HUD	Flexible subsidy	To aid financially troubled projects

STATES, LOCAL COMMUNITIES, PUBLIC BODIES (AND COOPERATING INVESTORS AND LENDERS)

AGENCY	PROGRAM	GOAL
HUD	Community Development Block Grants	To promote sound community development
HUD	Urban Development Action Grants	To help stimulate economic development activity
Community Development	Rental rehabilitation	To encourage rental housing rehabilitation
Community Development	Urban homesteading	To transfer federally owned property to cities
State Housing Finance	First-time home buyer	To facilitate home ownership.

DESIGNED FOR	FINANCING	COMMENTS
Investors, developers, builders	Mortgage insurance	Area must be approved by HUD
Investors, developers, builders	Mortgage insurance	At least five units and at least three years old
Private or nonprofit agencies	Mortgage insurance	
Rental housing	Rent subsidies	Important assurance of positive cash flow
Nonprofit sponsors	Direct loans	
Projects in which HUD has financial interest	Cash subsidies	Project owner must provide management satisfactory to HUD

DESIGNED FOR	FINANCING	COMMENTS
Metropolitan cities, urban counties, states, some small cities	Grants from federal government	
Distressed cities and urban counties	Grants on a sharing basis	
Cities and states	Grants from federal government	
State or local government bodies		Property awarded to homeowners for rehabilitation
First-time homebuyers, investors.	Low interest rate home purchase loans.	Investors can participate in target areas.

ACKNOWLEDGMENTS

Where do you start when you have so much to be thankful for and so many people to thank?

First my wife, Cathie, whose help and steadfast faith in me made it all possible. My Mom and Dad (though he passed away years ago), for the positive attitude they helped instill in me. Aunt Polly and Kitty, for their love. My brother and partner, Richard, for going along with my crazy wheelings and dealings, and for instructing our all-day seminar. Bob and Linda, for helping me get started in real estate. All of the sellers who have helped us on our way, and all of those people who didn't help us. They made me help myself. Charlie, for not giving me the raise when I asked for it. My office staff and work crews. And of course, Mr. Brad Huss, who runs Wayne Phillips Seminars, Inc. And a very special thanks to Debbie Long, who patiently took the thoughts from my head and the right words from my mouth, then put them together in this book for you. Last but not least, my editor at Simon and Schuster, Fred Hills. Yes Fred, the postcards did work, didn't they?

INDEX

ABOUT THE AUTHOR

Wayne Phillips is America's leading expert in obtaining low-interest-rate government loans to build a profitable real estate portfolio. His first book, *How to Get Government Loans*, was a smashing best seller and started a whole new investment trend in real estate. A few years ago Mr. Phillips was voted the seventh best jazz drummer in the United States. Since leaving the music industry, Mr. Phillips has amassed a fortune utilizing government loans from various federal, state, and local governments at interest rates as low as three or even zero percent interest. His career is an example of how public and private sectors can work together to achieve community improvements.

Mr. Phillips was the very first person to write, teach, and lecture about the opportunities government programs provide and how they can help each one of us achieve what we want in life. In addition to his personal real estate holdings in the United States, Mr. Phillips oversees his other business investments including those in the area of entertainment, restaurants, insurance, and Arabian horses. He is the chief executive officer of Wayne Phillips Seminars, Inc. which airs nationally televised investment programs as well as investment education seminars.

Mr. Phillips resides in Scottsdale, Arizona with his wife, Cathie, and daughter Nicole. He is a world traveler and pilots his own private plane.